POLICING THE PLANET

Jordan T. Camp is a Postdoctoral Fellow in the Center for the Study of Race and Ethnicity in America and the Watson Institute for International and Public Affairs at Brown University.

Christina Heatherton is an Assistant Professor of American Studies at Trinity College.

POLICING THE PLANET

Why the Policing Crisis Led to Black Lives Matter

Edited by
Jordan T. Camp
and
Christina Heatherton

VERSO
London • New York

Verso
UK: 6 Meard Street, London W1F 0EG
US: 20 Jay Street, Suite 1010, Brooklyn, NY 11201
versobooks.com

Verso is the imprint of New Left Books

ISBN-13: 978-1-78478-316-7
ISBN-13: 978-1-78478-317-4 (US EBK)
ISBN-13: 978-1-78478-318-1 (UK EBK)

British Library Cataloguing in Publication Data
A catalogue record for this book is available from the British Library

Library of Congress Cataloging-in-Publication Data

Names: Camp, Jordan T., 1979- editor. | Heatherton, Christina, editor.
Title: Policing the planet : why the policing crisis led to black lives
  matter / edited by Jordan T. Camp, Christina Heatherton.
Description: New York : Verso, 2016.
Identifiers: LCCN 2016007516 | ISBN 9781784783167 (paperback)
Subjects: LCSH: Police brutality—United States. | Discrimination in law
  enforcement—United States. | Police—Complaints against—United States. |
  Police-community relations—United States. | BISAC: SOCIAL SCIENCE /
  Sociology / Urban. | LAW / Civil Rights. | POLITICAL SCIENCE / Political
  Freedom & Security / Civil Rights.
Classification: LCC HV8141 .P5977 2016 | DDC 363.2/30973—dc23
LC record available at http://lccn.loc.gov/2016007516

Typeset in Garamond Prop by MJ & N Gavan, Truro, Cornwall, UK
Printed in the US by Maple Press

Contents

III. THE CRISIS OF BROKEN WINDOWS COMMON SENSE

How We Could Have Lived or Died This Way

Not songs of loyalty alone are these,
But songs of insurrection also,
For I am the sworn poet of every dauntless
rebel the world over.

—Walt Whitman

I see the dark-skinned bodies falling in the street as their ancestors fell
before the whip and steel, the last blood pooling, the last breath spitting.
I see the immigrant street vendor flashing his wallet to the cops,
shot so many times there are bullet holes in the soles of his feet.
I see the deaf woodcarver and his pocketknife, crossing the street
in front of a cop who yells, then fires. I see the drug raid, the wrong
door kicked in, the minister's heart seizing up. I see the man hawking
a fistful of cigarettes, the cop's chokehold that makes his wheezing
lungs stop wheezing forever. I am in the crowd, at the window,
kneeling beside the body left on the asphalt for hours, covered in a sheet.

I see the suicides: the conga player handcuffed for drumming on the subway,
hanged in the jail cell with his hands cuffed behind him; the suspect leaking
blood from his chest in the backseat of the squad car; the 300-pound boy
said to stampede bare-handed into the bullets drilling his forehead.

I see the coroner nodding, the words he types in his report burrowing
into the skin like more bullets. I see the government investigations stacking,
words buzzing on the page, then suffocated as bees suffocate in a jar. I see
the next Black man, fleeing as the fugitive slave once fled the slave-catcher,
shot in the back for a broken tail light. I see the cop handcuff the corpse.

I see the rebels marching, hands upraised before the riot squads,
faces in bandannas against the tear gas, and I walk beside them unseen.
I see the poets, who will write the songs of insurrection generations unborn
will read or hear a century from now, words that make them wonder
how we could have lived or died this way, how the descendants of slaves
still fled and the descendants of slave-catchers still shot them, how we awoke
every morning without the blood of the dead sweating from every pore.

Martín Espada

INTRODUCTION: POLICING THE PLANET

Jordan T. Camp and Christina Heatherton

I

Eric Garner lived on the brink of uncertainty. His death at the hands of New York City police officers in 2014 followed years of incessant harassment for small-scale infractions, including the sale of untaxed loose cigarettes. Garner was regularly stopped and searched, and—as his 2007 civil rights lawsuit detailed—humiliated and sexually violated by police in public. Before he was slain on a Staten Island sidewalk, he pleaded with approaching officers, "Every time you see me you arrest me. I'm tired of it. It stops today." Garner's murder, filmed on a phone by his friend Ramsey Orta, was viewed millions of times by people around the world. Garner's final desperate words to the officers choking him, "I can't breathe," became a rallying cry for organizers and activists fighting to end police violence and impunity. Similarly, his plea, "This stops today" was transformed into a demand to end the prosaic surveillance, arbitrary harassment, and intimate violations—the daily life of policing—that led to Garner's fatal assault. Protesters not only questioned how Eric Garner died; they also challenged the conditions under which he was forced to live.[1]

Eric Garner's name has joined a morbidly expanding roll call of the racialized poor killed by police and vigilante violence. Demonstrators have refused to let these premature deaths be explained away as mere excess or accident. They instead cast this violence as routinized and

---

1   For more information, see #thisStopsToday, thisstopstoday.org.

widespread.[2] In so doing, they have called attention to the underlying material conditions that have preceded and ultimately enabled these killings. Rather than asking *how the police can kill less*, they have forced a broader set of questions: Why have the police been endowed with the arbitrary capacity to regulate the lives of the racialized poor in US cities? Why do they have expanding and unfettered access to the bodies of poor people in general and poor people of color routinely? How and why are poor people criminalized for occupying public space? Can the problem of police violence actually be solved with the addition of more police (even better trained, more diverse, or better monitored) as many police departments and federal proposals suggest? How have these issues been addressed in other global contexts? And finally, what alternate definitions of security might we imagine?

This book, *Policing the Planet*, is a collaborative effort between social movement organizers, scholar-activists, journalists, and artists to address these questions. Following the lead of social movements, it reassesses the policing philosophy known as "broken windows theory." Praised as a comprehensive model of "community policing," this doctrine has vastly broadened the capacities of police both nationally and globally. Through essays and interviews, the book explores the rise and spread of broken windows policing. In analyzing vengeful policing campaigns waged against the racialized poor, Native people, immigrant workers, Black and Brown youth, LGBTQI and gender-nonconforming people, the homeless, sex workers, and others, it demonstrates that broken windows policing emerged as an ideological and political project. In examining its spread throughout the United States and around the world, it explores how broken windows policing has become the political expression of neoliberalism at the urban scale. Racism, it argues, has sustained and naturalized these processes as inexorable and inevitable. The book therefore considers the struggle against racism, militarism, and capital—the policing of the planet—as a central political challenge of our times.[3]

---

2 Anthony Bogues's comments at the "Ferguson Teach-In," at Brown University, September 9, 2014, available at youtube.com; Keeanga-Yamahtta Taylor, *From #BlackLivesMatter to Black Liberation* (Chicago: Haymarket, 2016).

3 Neil Smith, "Global Social Cleansing: Postliberal Revanchism and the Export

The underlying concept of broken windows policing is deceptively simple: to stop major crimes from occurring, police must first prevent small signs of "disorder" from proliferating, such as graffiti, litter, panhandling, public urination, the sale of untaxed cigarettes, and so forth. It proposes that the best way to prevent major crimes is for people to take responsibility for their neighborhoods and for the police to facilitate that process.[4] The metaphor goes that if a window in a neighborhood stays broken, it signals neglect and encourages small crimes, which then lead to larger ones. Disorder in the form of minor violations is presumed to breed larger disorder. Instead of addressing "individual crimes," broken windows theory has given police new authorization to control and moderate behavior. While analysts note that such invasive policing is by no means unique to the present moment, given the broad transformations in police policy, training, and funding, there is a general consensus that broken windows policing has constituted a fundamental expansion and redefinition of state capacities at the urban scale both across the country and worldwide.

In the current crisis of mass incarceration, broken windows is often presented as the milder, more community-minded alternative to more aggressive forms of policing. As Bernard E. Harcourt notes, this false presentation of broken windows as a substitute to mass incarceration belies its function as a robust supplement to it. Such supplements have only enhanced the collective punishments of communities already under siege. As deindustrialized cities have become veritable landscapes of broken windows—replete with abandoned homes, job sites, and factories—policy makers and police departments have utilized the logic of broken windows to locate disorder within individuals, off-loading liability onto the bodies of the blamed.[5]

---

of Zero Tolerance," *Social Justice* 28, no. 3 (2001): 73; Ruth Wilson Gilmore, *Golden Gulag: Prisons, Surplus, Crisis, and Opposition in Globalizing California* (Berkeley: University of California Press, 2007).

4   James Q. Wilson and George Kelling, "Broken Windows Theory," *Atlantic* (March 1982), theatlantic.com; William J. Bratton, "This Works: Crime Prevention and the Future of Broken Windows Policing," *Manhattan Institute Civic Bulletin*, no. 36 (May 2004), available at manhattan-institute.org.

5   Bernard E. Harcourt, *Illusion of Order: The False Promise of Broken Windows Policing* (Cambridge: Harvard University Press, 2001), 5–6.

Broadly speaking, broken windows policing has normalized a shift in state capacities away from the production of social goods and towards "security" concerns produced in their absence. Under this arrangement, the police can effectively function in an array of roles, such as mental health facilitators, school disciplinarians, public housing managers, and guards against park trespassing. In some municipalities, the police also aggressively function as surrogate tax collectors or "revenue generators" as the Department of Justice investigation into the Ferguson Police Department recently concluded.[6] In less-well-studied examples, such as Los Angeles, $87 million of the $100 million city budget devoted to homelessness has been allocated to policing. Lest we forget, Akai Gurley was assassinated by officers patrolling public housing projects; twelve-year-old Tamir Rice was killed by police charged with securing a public park; and Eric Garner was strangled by police regulating a public street for the sale of untaxed cigarettes. Broken windows policing produces such fatal encounters wherein one overfunded segment of the state dominates, assaults, and helps to reinforce the eradication of another.[7]

The recent protests suggest that this arrangement will not go unchallenged. Uprisings against police violence from New York, Ferguson, Baltimore, and beyond indicate a crisis of authority and legitimacy for US policing.[8] As tens of thousands of demonstrators took to the streets following Garner's death, New York City police commissioner William Bratton assessed the situation:

> Let's face it, we're in a crisis at this time, in this country, on issues of race, around effectiveness of policing, around police tactics, probably the most significant I've seen since I joined policing in 1970.[9]

6   United States Department of Justice, *Investigation of the Ferguson Police Department* (Washington, D.C.: United States Government, March 4, 2015); Walter Johnson, "Ferguson's Fortune 500 Company," *Atlantic* (April 26, 2015), theatlantic.com.

7   Angela Y. Davis, *Are Prisons Obsolete?* (New York: Seven Stories Press, 2003), 85, 112; Don Mitchell, *Right to the City: Social Justice and the Fight for Public Space* (New York: Guilford, 2003), 175.

8   Stuart Hall, *The Hard Road to Renewal: Thatcherism and the Crisis of the Left* (New York: Verso, 1988), 96.

9   William Bratton quoted in Kevin Fasick and Lorena Mongelli, "Bratton Says

Given his formative role in the popularization of this model, the commissioner's insights were unwittingly poignant. Bratton has the dubious distinction of being twice appointed as New York City police commissioner, first in 1993 and twenty years later in 2013. In the intervening twenty years, Bratton's broken-windows style policing has been successfully exported around the planet. From New York to Baltimore, Los Angeles, London, San Juan, San Salvador, and beyond, Bratton's model has become a neoliberal urban strategy practiced and adapted worldwide.[10]

Broken windows took shape as a political response to the urban crises of the 1960s and 1970s. It became the hegemonic strategy of community policing alongside the consolidation of the carceral state and neoliberal transformation of cities in the late twentieth century. Bratton oversaw its implementation as part of his dedication to "reclaiming the public spaces of New York" during the 1990s. In the logic of broken windows policing, "aggressive panhandling, squeegee cleaners, street prostitution, 'boombox cars,' public drunkenness, reckless bicycles, and graffiti" constituted the source of economic and even existential insecurity. Bratton, alongside Mayor Rudolph Giuliani and intellectual architects from the neoliberal think tank Manhattan Institute, proposed "zero tolerance" measures as the solution to these problem "behaviors."[11] The purported success in New York (its "turnaround," as the Manhattan Institute and Bratton like to tout) provided a transportable model for cities facing social and economic crises. This volume argues that the "success" of broken windows policing has functioned as an urban strategy enabling the gentrification of cities—a class project that has displaced the urban multiracial working class worldwide.[12]

Policing 'in a Crisis' at Tribute to Slain NYPD Cop," *New York Post*, May 6, 2015, nypost.com.

10   Neil Smith, "Giuliani Time: The Revanchist 1990s," *Social Text* 56 (1998): 1–20; Smith, "Global Social Cleansing," 69.

11   William Bratton, et al., *Police Strategy No. 5: Reclaiming the Public Spaces of New York* (New York: NYPD, 1994); Smith, "Giuliani Time," 2–5.

12   William Bratton and Peter Knobler, *The Turnaround: How America's Top Cop Reversed the Crime Epidemic* (New York: Random House, 2009); Neil Brenner and Nik Theodore, "Preface: From the 'New Localism' to the Spaces of Neoliberalism," in *Spaces of Neoliberalism: Urban Restructuring in North America and Western Europe*

Most perniciously, broken windows policing has been presented as a race-neutral response to criminality. Its disproportionate deployment against poor communities of color has been justified as mere statistical inevitability. Consider, for example, Bratton's recent assertion that the mass arrest of African Americans and Latinos stems from "intractable racial disparities in who commits—and more importantly, *who suffers from*—crime and disorder." In turn, he purports that African Americans and Latinos are not targeted in broken windows policing campaigns but rather are subject to mass arrest because, he claims, they have a greater propensity for crime just as they are greater victims of it.[13] Broad consent to policing and prisons has been legitimated through such circular racial logic. Just as mass incarceration has depended on a selective suturing of racial categories to criminality, so too has broken windows policing conflated the racialized poor with spatialized disorder. By doing so, racism eludes discussions of policing at the same moment that it animates its practice. The essays and interviews gathered here suggest ways in which we might confront the policy of broken windows while overcoming the racist common sense underpinning it.

Policing the Planet traces the exportation of the broken windows model as Bratton himself became a highly sought-after security consultant for urban governments worldwide. In turn, it highlights how this new urban security regime has given rise to dramatic and increasingly internationalized social movements confronting racist and uneven capitalist developments worldwide. Accordingly, this book situates the protests in Ferguson, New York, Baltimore, Chicago, and beyond in 2014 and 2015 in the context of global struggles against policing and prisons in the early twenty-first century.[14] Through interviews with and essays from prominent writers and activists, *Policing the Planet* foregrounds the visions that have emerged from antiracist social movements. This volume explores how the demand to abolish broken windows policing

---

(Malden, MA: Blackwell Publishing, 2002), x; Neil Smith, "New Globalism, New Urbanism: Gentrification as Global Urban Strategy," *Antipode* 34.3 (2002): 433.

13   William J. Bratton, *Broken Windows and Quality-of-Life Policing in New York City* (New York: New York Police Department, 2015), 6.

14   Gillian Hart, *Rethinking the South African Crisis: Nationalism, Populism, and Hegemony* (Athens: University of Georgia Press, 2013), 47–48.

and mass incarceration might contribute to popular democratic struggles against neoliberal racial regimes and for social and economic justice across the United States and the world.[15]

II

The essays and interviews in this volume seek to intervene in urgent public debates about structural racism, policing, and urban uprisings in the neoliberal present. The first section considers the crisis of US policing and situates it in a global context. As Robin D. G. Kelley shows in the first chapter, "Thug Nation: On State Violence and Disposability," protests around high-profile police killings of civilians in the US during 2014 and 2015 are domestic instances of a global struggle. He describes how organizers from Ferguson to Baltimore to Gaza have been engaged in a dynamic social movement against global neoliberal racial regimes, settler colonialism, and permanent war. In the interview "BlackLivesMatter and Global Visions of Abolition," #BlackLivesMatter co-founder Patrisse Cullors reflects on the movement's struggle against the US police state. Cullors asserts that reformist solutions to the policing crisis are insufficient, and she argues for abolitionist alternatives including access to jobs, healthy food, and shelter.

Since its inception, broken windows policing has regulated space appropriate for capital, targeting the poor, people of color, queers, trans and gender-nonconforming people, immigrants, the homeless, and youth when their existence is not conducive to the accumulation process. In "Broken Windows at Blue's: A Queer History of Gentrification and Policing," Christina B. Hanhardt explores how radical queer activists in places like Times Square and Greenwich Village have long resisted Bratton's use of broken windows policing as a tool of gentrification. Hanhardt concludes that this success, led by organizations such as the Audre Lorde Project and Fabulous Independent Educated Radicals for Community Empowerment (FIERCE), has been premised on

---

15   Jordan T. Camp, *Incarcerating the Crisis: Freedom Struggles and the Rise of the Neoliberal State* (Oakland: University of California Press, 2016); Barbara Ransby, "The Class Politics of Black Lives Matter," *Dissent*, Fall 2015, dissentmagazine.org.

grassroots visions of large-scale social and economic transformation, a principle organizers like Joo-Hyun Kang understand well. In "Ending Broken Windows Policing in New York City," Kang, the former director of the Audre Lorde Project, longtime community organizer, and current director of Communities United for Police Reform (CPR), describes the ongoing work of New York coalitions to mobilize in the current moment. She delineates how CPR, a coalition of over sixty organizations from every borough in the city, has built on this long history of activism.

In "The Baltimore Uprising," journalist Anjali Kamat describes the spontaneous rebellion sparked by the murder of twenty-five-year-old Freddie Gray as the logical outcome of residential segregation, mass criminalization, austerity policies, and the aggressive application of broken windows–style or zero tolerance policing. Until the mass criminalization of the Black working class stops and a fundamental transformation of the political economy occurs, Kamat concludes, "perhaps it will soon be time for another uprising." The quality of state vengeance is no mere metaphor, as counterterrorism analyst Arun Kundnani explains in his interview "Total Policing and the Global Surveillance Empire Today." According to Kundnani, such policing models must be traced to the history of counterinsurgency campaigns, technologies, and practices that have long crossed the planet in imperial exchanges of information.

In "*Mano Dura Contra El Crimen* and Premature Death in Puerto Rico," Marisol LeBrón shows how the Puerto Rican elite have sought to manage social and economic crisis through the aggressive policing policy of *mano dura*. As LeBrón makes clear, this punitive and authoritarian strategy "is an essential component of a racist, neocolonial, and capitalist system," a sentiment echoed by members of Albuquerque's the Red Nation. In "Policing the Crisis of Indigenous Lives," an interview with the Native-led council Red Nation, members Melanie Yazzie, Nick Estes, Sam Gardipe, Paige Murphy, and Chris Banks suggest how the criminalization of Native people, particularly the poor and homeless, represents a colonial strategy of crisis management that has been legitimated by an "anti-Indian common sense." In turn, they elaborate the Indigenous Left's strategy for building a broad-based alliance with the poor and working people of color in order to overcome colonialism and capitalism.

The second section of the volume considers broken windows policing as a neoliberal urban strategy, one that depicts the racialized poor as the source of disorder. In "Policing Place and Taxing Time on Skid Row," George Lipsitz explores how the Los Angeles Community Action Network (LA CAN) has organized itself to confront the criminalization of poverty. While describing these specific LA struggles, he also shows how such campaigns could be the basis for a new "social warrant," a new counterhegemonic alliance, and thus new ways of confronting the policies that affect the lives of the racialized poor, homeless, and dispossessed in Los Angeles and beyond. In "Asset Stripping and Broken Windows Policing on LA's Skid Row," LA CAN co-executive directors Becky Dennison and Pete White reflect on the meaning of the decade-long struggle against the Safer Cities Initiative (SCI) in Los Angeles, a joint broken windows effort by the mayor's office and the LAPD led by then Police Chief William Bratton and his associates. Dennison and White argue that SCI, in reality, has served as a tool favored by elites to enable gentrification, displacement, and the stripping of assets from the poor and communities of color in Skid Row, Los Angeles, the area with the highest rates of homelessness and poverty in the country. The conditions produced in Los Angeles have had global implications for cities worldwide, as lead organizer for the Stop LAPD Spying Coalition Hamid Khan explains in "Broken Windows, Surveillance, and the New Urban Counterinsurgency." Khan elaborates how Skid Row serves as a testing ground for policing practices and policies that are in turn exported around the world.

The multiple high-profile killings of people like Eric Garner as well as Akai Gurley, Ramarley Graham, Kimani Grey, and many others continue to make cities like New York ongoing and central sites of struggle. Alex S. Vitale and Brian Jordan Jefferson examine the roots and intensification of this struggle in their essay, "The Emergence of Command and Control Policing in Neoliberal New York." Here Vitale and Jefferson describe how this form of policing has transformed segregated places into "quasi-correctional complexes, an extension of the carceral state." In thinking through this neoliberal turn, Ruth Wilson Gilmore and

Craig Gilmore consider how the present struggle is to be understood and fought out. In "Beyond Bratton," they argue that the expansion of the #BlackLivesMatter movement in the wake of the Ferguson uprising has brought "some aspects of US policing to the brink of a legitimacy crisis." Tracing this legitimation crisis and its long historical and geographical roots in Southern California, they consider how activists can continue to exploit the contradictions of the current moment.

The interview with the executive director of Los Angeles–based Homies Unidos Alex Sanchez by scholar-activist Steven Osuna, "They're Not Solving the Problem, They're Displacing It," explores the transnational circulation of criminalization strategies between the United States and El Salvador. Alternative methods to finding actual security will undoubtedly be complex and expensive, "but as it is," Sanchez concludes, "we've been wasting billions of dollars on mass incarceration." Such wasteful and expansive spending also encompasses immigration control. In "Resisting State Violence in the Era of Mass Deportation," immigrant rights activist and photojournalist Mizue Aizeki describes the relationship between broken windows policing and immigrant detention. Aizeki also suggests the political possibilities for forging alliances in the struggle against broken windows policing and mass deportation.

The third and final section of the book considers how broken windows policing is falsely presented as a community-minded alternative to more aggressive forms of social control. In his essay "Community Policing Reconsidered," law professor and activist Justin Hansford reflects on his experience testifying before President Obama's Task Force on 21st Century Policing in the wake of the Ferguson uprising. Hansford explains why community policing is not the solution, despite its traction among policy makers. Naomi Murakawa expands on these insights in the interview "How Liberals Legitimate Broken Windows." She describes how efforts to enhance "procedural justice" and produce "racial reconciliation" are effectively public relations strategies to legitimate the carceral state's expansion. In turn, she elaborates ways to move away from reformist solutions to the policing crisis and towards more fundamental social change.

In their essay "'Broken Windows Is Not the Panacea': Common Sense, Good Sense, and Police Accountability in American Cities," geographers Don Mitchell, Kafui Attoh, and Lynn A. Staeheli characterize the current moment as perhaps the greatest crisis of legitimacy for US policing since the urban insurrections of the 1960s. In turn, they interrogate how the "common sense" motivating broken windows has entered into crisis. Such a moment of crisis has provoked internationalist linkages as Breanna Champion, Page May, and Asha Rosa Ransby-Sporn detail in their interview "We Charge Genocide." These activists from the Chicago-based group We Charge Genocide reflect on their trip to Geneva, Switzerland, to submit a report to the United Nations Committee Against Torture, which documented the systemic racist violence perpetuated by the Chicago Police Department.

The neoliberal state's reactions to the policing crisis has been tangled in its own seemingly inescapable logic. In "The Magical Life of Broken Windows," writer and organizer Rachel Herzing offers some thoughts towards breaking its spell. Warning against "magic solutions and quick fixes" such as body cameras, more cops, racial profiling bills, and related reforms, Herzing instead argues that the current moment of crisis "presents new challenges and new opportunities for us to act on our dreams." Hence we begin and nearly end this book with the insights of the poet Martín Espada, who uniquely describes "Poetry and the Political Imagination," which is also the title of the interview. He explains how poetry can articulate the visions of social movements, as well as help them move from "imagination to reality." By way of conclusion, Vijay Prashad provides a theory for understanding the political economy of racism in his essay "This Ends Badly: Race and Capitalism." The task, he argues, is to develop a "framework of an alternative" including universal access, economic power, and the social wage. This framework, Prashad concludes, should be taken seriously by all or else the "common sense of our times will lead us to a bad end."

We submit this book as part of the struggle for an alternative common sense to realize a different future emerging in the present.

I. THE PLANETARY CRISIS OF POLICING

1. THUG NATION: ON STATE VIOLENCE AND DISPOSABILITY

Robin D. G. Kelley

The tradition of the oppressed teaches us that the "state of emergency" in which we live is not the exception but the rule.
—Walter Benjamin, "Theses on the Philosophy of History"

Racism is based on an ontological affirmation. It is the notion that the very being of a people is inferior. And the ultimate logic of racism is genocide ... The first thing that must be on the agenda of our nation is to get rid of racism.
—Martin Luther King, Jr., March 14, 1968.

Policing the Crisis

On May 15, 2010, as sixteen-year-old Kalief Browder and a friend headed home from a party in the Bronx, a small fleet of police cruisers surrounded them. A man had just been robbed of his backpack, an officer told them, and they were suspects. Browder and his friend maintained their innocence and willingly consented to a search. When no contraband was found, the officer retreated to confer with the alleged victim, a Mexican immigrant named Robert Bautista, who was sitting in a squad car. A few minutes later, the officer returned with a different story: the alleged robbery had occurred two weeks earlier and Bautista had just identified Browder and his friend as the culprits. They were then arrested and charged with robbery, grand larceny, and assault. After seventeen hours behind bars, the judge released Browder's friend pending trial but held Browder on bail—Browder was on probation for watching his friends bang up a delivery truck they had stolen as a prank. Browder's family could not afford the bail, so eventually, Browder was sent to Rikers Island—all for a crime he had not committed.[1]

Browder's story up to this point is not exceptional. He was assigned a public defender whose main objective was to convince his client to cop a plea in order to reduce the charges or mitigate the sentence and avoid trial—a standard strategy for defendants both innocent and guilty. But Browder refused, choosing to maintain his innocence and wait for a trial. He waited three years, during which he was beaten by guards and inmates, was deprived of food, endured seventeen months in solitary confinement, suffered several psychiatric breakdowns and suicide attempts, braved deeply unhygienic environments, and was denied decent protection and his constitutional right to a speedy trial. There were no eyewitnesses to the crime and no physical or forensic evidence—only Bautista's testimony. Eventually, Bautista returned to Mexico, leaving the prosecution with no material witness. Every time a judge tried to get Browder to plead guilty, even for a lesser crime, he refused. The state had no choice but to drop the charges. He was released in June 2013.[2]

On Saturday, June 6, 2015, a little over five years from the day his ordeal began, Kalief Browder hanged himself.[3] He had just turned twenty-two.

Browder ended his own life, but the state bears responsibility for his death. He was caged as a sixteen-year-old child, mostly in solitary con-finement, and freed at the age of twenty. He lost weight. He lost part of his childhood. He lost part of his mind. But he did not lose his dignity

---

1   Jennifer Gonnerman, "Before the Law," *New Yorker*, October 6, 2014.

2   Ibid.

3   Jennifer Gonnerman, "Kalief Browder, 1993–2015," *New Yorker*, June 7, 2015.

or his sense of justice, which were all he had left. "Before I went to jail," he told journalist Jennifer Gonnerman, "I didn't know about a lot of stuff, and, now that I'm aware, I'm paranoid … I feel like I was robbed of my happiness."[4]

His ordeal was not merely the result of an administrative glitch, "bad" policing, poor legal defense, or an unanticipated backlog of cases. Mass arrests, obscene numbers of young Black and Brown people corralled into jails and prisons, habeas corpus suspended through plea bargains, and the maintenance of a racial political economy that keeps the poor in a precarious state are all tactics to which the current system is well suited. "Zero tolerance" policing turns select neighborhoods into open-air prisons and strips vulnerable residents of habeas corpus, freedom of movement, and even protection from torture. The police are trained to observe, contain, constrain, and arrest bodies they deem suspicious or engaged in acts of law-breaking. Constitutional guarantees of "equal protection" notwithstanding, Black and Brown bodies carry from birth the mark of "suspicion."

Even if he had stolen Bautista's backpack, would Browder's punishment, under accusations of grand larceny, have fit the crime, a reported loss of $700, an iPod Touch, and a digital camera? Is this the value of Browder's life? According to the logic of broken windows theory, which insists that infractions of any scale be punished swiftly and mercilessly, the loot's monetary value is irrelevant. Browder was a Black kid with a "criminal" record walking freely in a high crime neighborhood. The cops and the prosecution likely assumed that he was guilty of something even if he'd had no part in the Bautista crime, thereby justifying Browder's arrest on such flimsy evidence, his detention for so long without a trial, and the ferocious physical abuse of his still-developing teenaged body. Much like the Obama administration's policy of signature strikes— lethal drone attacks on young men who *might* be terrorists or *may* one day commit acts of terrorism—the presumption of guilt based on racial profiling is an essential component of broken windows policing.[5]

---

4   Gonnerman, "Before the Law."

5   Jeremy Scahill, *Dirty Wars: The World Is a Battlefield* (New York: Nation Books, 2013); Danya Greenfield, "The Case Against Drone Strikes on People Who Only 'Act' Like Terrorists," *Atlantic*, August 19, 2013.

So what is Kalief's life worth? Apparently nothing. The state has long treated Black life as disposable, as is clear in our expanding prison population and the shockingly high rate of Black casualties caused by police, private security guards, and vigilantes. The list of unarmed Black people killed by police in just the four months after eighteen-year-old Michael Brown was gunned down in Ferguson, Missouri by officer Darren Wilson reveals that Black people are not only devalued in the United States but treated as enemy combatants.[6] It is not simply that our lives don't matter. We are a threat, an enemy, which largely explains why the police employ lethal force as a *first* resort. None of the victims during these four months were engaged in violent crimes at the time they were killed, and most had committed no crime at all. Michael Brown and his friend Dorian Johnson were stopped for walking in the middle of the street, a violation commonly overlooked or in rare instances minimally fined. As is taught in Broken Windows 101: disrespect for authority and non-compliance by the criminal element can lead to the breakdown of civilization. Wilson regarded Brown's non-compliance as a challenge to his authority, a dynamic that escalated into a verbal and physical confrontation between the armed officer and the unarmed teenager. We'll never know exactly what transpired, but we do know that Brown had his hands up in a gesture of surrender when he died.

Looking back one year later, neither the killing nor the protests have let up. In what some activists have dubbed "Black Spring" of 2015, the people of Baltimore rose up to protest the death of twenty-five-year-old Freddie Gray, who was arrested on April 12, 2015, merely for making eye contact with a police officer and running away. He was apprehended, shackled, tossed on to the floor of a police van without a safety belt, and likely beaten. By the time the van arrived at central booking, Gray was unresponsive, his spine 80 percent severed at the neck, and his voice box crushed.[7]

---

6   The list includes Ezell Ford, Dante Parker, Roshad McIntosh, Darrien Hunt, Aura Rain Rosser, Tanisha Anderson, Tamir Rice, Eric Harris, Walter Scott, Tony Robinson, Kajieme Powell, Vonderitt D. Meyers, Jr., John Crawford, III, and Margaret LaVerne Mitchell, to name but a few.

7   Peter Hermann and John Woodrow Cox, "A Freddie Gray Primer: Who Was He, How Did He Die, Why Is There So Much Anger?," *Washington Post*, April 28, 2015.

None of this brutality is new. In my fifty-three years on this planet, I've witnessed not a wave but a continuous stream of police violence that has never let up. I came of age when Eleanor Bumpurs, Michael Stewart, Eula Mae Love, and Arthur McDuffie were the war's iconic victims, to be followed by Amadou Diallo, Oscar Grant, Patrick Dorismond, Malice Green, Tyisha Miller, and Sean Bell. And I'm only speaking of the dead —not the harassed, the beaten, the humiliated, the stopped and frisked.

Our parents, grandparents, and great-grandparents experienced "no tolerance" policing long before that term was in vogue. My late father-in-law lost his hearing in one ear after a cop in Bessemer, Alabama, took a nightstick to his head for being insufficiently deferential. Many African Americans were arrested for not yielding the sidewalk to whites, for lacking a job (vagrancy), using profanity in public, spitting, loitering, violating segregation ordinances, "reckless eyeballing," and other absurdities intended to turn human beings into the caricatures with which white people were familiar through coon shows, soapbox sermons, darky films, and mass advertising.

The law never protected Black women from sexual violence, treating all sexual encounters between them and white men as not only consensual but initiated by the women. Criminalized as presumptive sex workers, all Black women were vigilantly policed while remaining vulnerable to the sexual predations of those wearing the badge. We can trace the all-too-common brutalization and criminalization of Black women's bodies to slavery, during which routine violence—flogging, torture, slaps and punches, assaults with household and agricultural tools, and, of course, rape—was their most common cause of flight. Masters, overseers, and drivers were not the only source of violence; Black women were vulnerable to partner violence, especially around harvest time when both white and Black men consumed large amounts of alcohol. As the late historian Stephanie Camp revealed, enslaved women experienced violence more frequently than men resulting from their presence in the big house completing secondary work, their perceived vulnerability as women, and perceptions of them as sexual property and as objects of sexual jealousy.[8]

8   See Stephanie M. H. Camp, *Closer to Freedom: Enslaved Women and Everyday Resistance in the Plantation South* (Chapel Hill: University of North Carolina Press, 2004).

In the Jim Crow era, law enforcement officials operated on the presumption that every unescorted Black woman was a sex worker soliciting employment. The New York race riot of 1900 began when a Black man came to the defense of a Black woman falsely arrested for solicitation, who had been merely waiting for her husband. In Atlanta, the police enforced a so-called sundown law under which any Black woman seen alone at a restaurant or club was vulnerable to arrest.[9]

A century later, the surveillance, criminalization, and presumed disposability of Black women continues. Broken windows policing has done nothing to ensure Black women's safety or reduce the alarming incidents of femicide that plague Black communities. Instead, Black women—especially poor women—continue to be monitored, harassed, and subject to reproductive control on the pretext that they possess illicit or diseased bodies. Their presumptive criminality allows murders and disappearances to go undetected and uninvestigated. A string of unsolved murders of Black women in the Boston area, in fact, led to the formation of the renowned Combahee River Collective, known for drafting one of the most radical and visionary manifestos of the twentieth century. Less known, however, is their searing critique of sexual violence and the inaction—if not complicity—of the state in ensuring that these murder cases went unsolved.[10] It addressed the incidents of Black femicide since the late 1970s that had engulfed cities such as Detroit, Charlotte, Peoria, Chicago, and Los Angeles, and that had been met in nearly every case with complete indifference from the police. Many of the victims were labeled sex workers or described as homeless, thus rendered doubly invisible and doubly disposable.

Is Bratton-era broken windows policing so different from the long and persistent tradition of "broken bodies" policing originating with slave patrols and military campaigns intended to "pacify" indigenous people? One difference, ironically, is the triumph of racial liberalism.

---

9   Clifford M. Kuhn, Harlon E. Joye, and E. Bernard West, *Living Atlanta: An Oral History of the City, 1914–1948* (Athens: University of Georgia Press, 1990), 190; Robin D. G. Kelley, *Race Rebels: Culture, Politics, and the Black Working Class* (New York: New Press, 1994), 49.

10   See "Why Did They Die? A Document of Black Feminism," *Radical America* 13, no. 6 (1979): 41–51.

Although the rise of mass incarceration and the deepening criminalization of urban space after World War II is generally assumed to be the
product of a sharp right-wing turn, we know from the work of Naomi
Murakawa, Heather Ann Thompson, Jordan T. Camp, and Elizabeth
Hinton that liberals also backed an expanding criminal justice system—
ostensibly to protect African Americans from mob violence, to quell
urban rebellions, and to address what were perceived as rising crime
rates following the triumph of desegregation.[11] How the unintended
consequences of such policies ultimately bequeathed to the nation a
criminal justice architecture that fueled mass incarceration has been
addressed by other scholars and activists. What I'd like to address here,
however, is the shifting political landscape created by triumphalism on
the part of racial liberalism—that is to say, the birth of the "post–Civil
Rights" era and the myth of color blindness.

Color-Blind Violence

The legitimacy of broken windows policing as a "race neutral" practice
rests on the common fiction that we are now living in the "post–Civil
Rights" era—a time "after" the victory of the Civil Rights Movement,
whose achievements, such as the Civil Rights Act of 1964, the Voting
Rights Act of 1965, and the Fair Housing Act of 1968, are tangible
and indisputable. Most proponents of color blindness do not claim that
racism has been completely eradicated, but rather that racist incidents
are isolated and rare, resulting from anachronistic behaviors by "bad"
actors. In this post–Civil Rights age of color blindness, we are told the
story of an active federal government—its conscience pricked by the
war against fascism abroad and the principled struggle for inclusion by

---

11   Naomi Murakawa, *The First Civil Right: How Liberals Built Prison America*
(New York: Oxford University Press, 2014); Heather Ann Thompson, "Why Mass
Incarceration Matters: Rethinking Crisis, Decline, and Transformation in Postwar
American History," *Journal of American History* 97, no. 3 (December 2010): 703–34;
Jordan T. Camp, *Incarcerating the Crisis: Freedom Struggles and the Rise of the Neoliberal
State* (Oakland: University of California Press, 2016); Elizabeth Kai Hinton, *From
the War on Poverty to the War on Crime: The Making of Mass Incarceration in America*
(Cambridge: Harvard University Press, 2016).

Black activists at home—that took bold steps to eliminate legal segregation completely and promote equal opportunity. (Even this formulation has undergone revision, with the movement playing a smaller and smaller role, and politicians increasingly elevated as the real heroes in the struggle.)

What this sanitized national narrative occludes are the chief issues that gave rise to the Civil Rights Movement in the first place: the violent subjugation of Black people by the state and its vigilante allies; taxation without representation and the denial of the franchise through terror and administrative means; and a government-dominated racial economy that suppressed Black wages, dispossessed Black people of land and property, excluded them from equal public accommodations, and subsidized white privilege by way of taxation. Violence held this precarious system together, and violence proved a stronger catalyst for Black activism than abstract desires for integration, with the murder of fourteen-year-old Emmett Till a particularly galvanizing event for the Civil Rights generation. But even before Till's brutal lynching in 1955, police brutality was a major issue for Black communities across the country. During World War II, confrontations between Black residents and white policemen sparked full-scale riots in almost a dozen cities.[12]

As civil rights protests escalated throughout the South and across the country, however, the problem of police violence worsened. A study conducted by the Department of Justice found that in the eighteen-month period between January 1958 and June 1960, 34 percent of all reported victims of police brutality were Black.[13] Within four years, relations between Black people and the police had escalated to a state of war. Between 1964 and 1972, incidents of police violence ignited rebellions in some 300 cities. Altogether, the urban uprisings involved close to half

---

12   James A. Burran, "Urban Racial Violence in the South during World War II: A Comparative Overview," in *From the Old South to the New: Essays on the Transitional South*, ed. Walter J. Fraser, Jr., and Winfred B. Moore, Jr. (Westport, CT: Greenwood Publishers, 1981), 167–77; Dominic J. Capeci, Jr., *Race Relations in Wartime Detroit: The Sojourner Truth Housing Controversy of 1942* (Philadelphia: Temple University Press, 1984).

13   Mary Frances Berry and John W. Blassingame, *Long Memory: The Black Experience in America* (New York: Oxford University Press, 1982), 242.

a million African Americans, resulted in millions of dollars in property damage, and left 250 people dead, 10,000 seriously injured, and countless without a home. The casualties were overwhelmingly Black. Police and the National Guard turned Black neighborhoods into war zones, arresting at least 60,000 people and employing tanks, machine guns, and tear gas to pacify the community.[14]

Faced with urban insurrections and the proliferation of community-based militant organizations, most urban police departments responded militarily, employing methods of surveillance and anti-guerrilla tactics developed in Vietnam.[15] Even liberal politicians, social scientists, and policy analysts who disavowed the deployment of military force in Black communities sought to understand why African Americans rioted, as American military advisors in Southeast Asia had questioned why so many North Vietnamese supported the Communists. To the surprise of several research teams, those who rioted tended to be better educated and more politically aware than those who did not. One survey of Detroit Black residents after the 1967 riot revealed that 86 percent of the respondents identified discrimination and deprivation as the main reasons behind the uprising, with police brutality topping the list.[16]

During the wave of ghetto insurrections, many urban police departments tried to combine community outreach, minority-hiring initiatives, and racial sensitivity training with increased militarization and repression. In Baltimore, just weeks before that city blew up in

---

14   James Baldwin, *Nobody Knows My Name: More Notes of a Native Son* (New York: Dial Press, 1961), 192; Herbert J. Gans, "The Ghetto Rebellions and Urban Class Conflict," in *Urban Riots: Violence and Social Change*, ed. Robert H. Connery (New York: Vintage, 1969), 45–54; Manning Marable, *Race, Reform and Rebellion: The Second Reconstruction in Black America, 1945–1990*, 2nd ed. (Jackson, MS.: University Press of Mississippi, 1991), 92–3.

15   Tracy Tullis, "A Vietnam at Home: Policing the Ghetto in the Era of Counterinsurgency" (PhD diss. New York University, 1998); Harlan Hahn, "Ghetto Sentiments on Violence," *Science and Society* 33 (Spring 1969): 197–208; Gerald Horne, *The Fire This Time: The Watts Uprising and the 1960s* (Charlottesville: University Press of Virginia, 1995).

16   Hahn, "Ghetto Sentiments on Violence"; U.S. National Advisory Commission on Civil Disorders, *Report of the National Advisory Commission on Civil Disorders* (New York: Bantam Books, 1968).

April 1968, the *Baltimore Sun* ran a lengthy article about the city's extraordinary ability to stay riot-free. Recently appointed police commissioner Donald Pomerleau boasted of his department's commitment to "service" rather than force. Pomerleau had increased the number of African Americans on the community relations board and even established a "Negro history course" to prepare his officers to engage the community with more sensitivity.[17] But he regarded Black militants as enemy combatants, and despite his best reform efforts, reports of police misconduct continued to strain relations with the community. As one independent investigator put it, "Police are thought to employ brutality frequently, and the backroom of the precinct house is known as a dangerous place for a black man."[18]

The Maryland Crime Commission issued a report siding unequivocally with the police while acknowledging that "the new type of rioting is likely to be set off by an incident involving the police in the ghetto ... where some actual violation of accepted police practice has taken place."[19] The report concluded, however, that aggressive policing rather than the jobs and social investment of liberal bromides could bring an end to civil unrest. It recommended expanding the force to include more Black officers, improving intelligence, and training officers in crowd control, and directed police to attack "any lawlessness ... quickly and aggressively."[20] The authors made a distinction between food riots driven by starvation and desperation and the new "commodity riots" which they regarded as "political violence or political terror," terms that turned Black youth into enemy combatants.[21] Strikingly, the report proposed "organizing and arming a semi-military force to fight a war in the streets" but only under intelligent leadership willing to "employ force wisely."[22]

---

17   Floyd Miller, "How Baltimore Fends Off Riots," *Reader's Digest*, March 1968, 109.

18   Quoted in Jane Motz, *Report on Baltimore Civil Disorders, April 1968* (Middle Atlantic Region, American Friends Service Committee, 1968), 7.

19   Baltimore Committee on the Administration of Justice under Emergency Conditions, *A Report on the Baltimore Civil Disturbance of April 6 to April 11, 1968* (Maryland Crime Investigating Commission, 1968), 12.

20   Ibid., 2.

21   Ibid., 14.

22   Ibid., 10.

One year later, the department announced that it had invested heavily in military hardware, including tear gas grenades, gas masks, and "pepper foggers."[23]

Donald Pomerleau's liberal dreams of police "serving" America's ghettoes found few takers after 1968. Fearing that ghetto rebellions would spill into white suburbs and that their taxes were being used to support lazy colored people on welfare, white Americans increasingly embraced the belief that "minorities," particularly African Americans, needed to stop complaining. Black people, they rationalized, no longer had any excuses, given that the Civil Rights Movement had succeeded in abolishing racism once and for all.[24]

It was in this context that the seeds of late-twentieth-century color-blind discourse began to take root, preparing the way for broken windows theory. First elaborated in a 1982 essay by George L. Kelling and James Q. Wilson, "broken windows" placed the blame for urban decay on the social values and behaviors of poor, primarily Black people. It argued that criminals flourished in deteriorating, disorderly neighborhoods, and that disrespect for one's community led to disrespect for authority and the law. As long as ghetto residents lacked concern for the condition of their neighborhoods, crime would run rampant; small infractions would become gateways to violent crime. Ignoring the structural factors that suppressed home values, perpetuated health and environmental catastrophes, and divested neighborhoods of essential services, jobs, government programs, and legal protections, broken windows theory blamed culture and immorality for crime and, in turn, poverty.[25]

This theory-turned-policy was based on some very old and familiar ideas about race and class. Kelling and Wilson built on urban theorist Edward Banfield's premise that cultural differences, not structural

23   "Better Prepared to Handle Riots, Police and National Guard Claim," *Baltimore Sun*, April 3, 1969.

24   George Lipsitz, *The Possessive Investment in Whiteness: How White People Profit from Identity Politics* (Philadelphia: Temple University Press, 1998), see especially 1–46; Michael Goldfield, *The Color of Politics: Race and the Mainsprings of American Politics* (New York: New Press, 1997), 310–14; Jill Quandango, *The Color of Welfare: How Racism Undermined the War on Poverty* (New York: Oxford University Press, 1994).

25   George L. Kelling and James Q. Wilson, "Broken Windows: The Police and Neighborhood Safety," *Atlantic*, March 1982.

racism, were the primary sources of ghetto poverty and inequality in the post–Civil Rights era. Banfield, in fact, did acknowledge historical prejudice but declared, in his widely cited *The Unheavenly City Revisited* (1974), that racism had become so insignificant as to lose its explanatory power. A relic of the past, racism now existed as a figment in the minds and rhetoric of dishonest Black leaders whose raison d'être was blaming "Whitey" for Black misery. "Negro leaders cannot be expected to explain that prejudice is no longer *the* obstacle," he wrote. "Those of them who understand that it is not are bound to pretend otherwise."[26] Beneath Banfield's dizzying tables and statistics is a "liberal" gloss on arguments made almost a century earlier by sociologist Herbert Spencer, who vulgarized Darwin in order to claim that the poor lacked character, frugality, thrift, and a work ethic because of their place on the evolutionary ladder. Like Banfield, Spencer considered this behavior to be the result of social and cultural values (not genetically ingrained behaviors) that could be eliminated over time—so long as the poor were not crippled by government aid, irresponsible charity, or trade unions. Yale University professor William Graham Sumner echoed Spencer's assertions in his 1883 book *What Social Classes Owe to Each Other*, which argued that aid to the poor provided by the rich or the government would disrupt the natural order of things. The only legitimate role of government was to protect "the property of [white] men and the honor of [white] women."[27]

To put it crudely, Sumner's vision of the state—as a mechanism to protect capital and control the passions of the Negroes and the poor—anticipated the neoliberal state and its attendant racial regime. In the era of capital flight, privatization, deregulation, free trade policies, the dismantling of the welfare state, the weakening of antidiscrimination laws, and the expansion of the carceral and security state in the form of domestic policing, surveillance, the militarization of the US/Mexico border, the war on drugs, and the exponential growth of prisons, Black and Brown people became both disposable and rendered as enemy combatants.

---

26 Edward C. Banfield, *The Unheavenly City Revisited* (Boston: Little, Brown, 1974), 97.

27 William Graham Sumner, *What Social Classes Owe to Each Other* (1883; New Haven: Yale University Press, 1925).

Permanent War

The protests in the wake of Michael Brown's murder displaced Israel's war on Gaza in the twenty-four-hour news cycle. It wasn't Brown's death that was deemed newsworthy but the "riots" that followed. And it wasn't the mere existence of protesters that made Ferguson an international story; it was the fact that the people who took to the streets faced down police with riot gear, rubber bullets, armored personnel carriers, semi-automatic weapons, and a dehumanizing policy designed to contain and silence. To the world at large, Ferguson looked like a war zone because the police looked like the military. For Black residents of Ferguson and St. Louis proper, as well as ghetto communities across the country, it was already a war zone—hence Mike Brown's and Dorian Johnson's initial trepidation in the face of police officers. Suddenly critics and pundits who had little to say about the killing of Black and Brown people by the police were indignant about the *hardware*, the AR-15s, the armored personnel carriers, the helmets and flak jackets.

Activists wasted no time in drawing the obvious connections between Israeli state violence in the name of security and US state violence, from drone strikes abroad to domestic police killings. They exposed the role that Israeli companies and security forces have played in arming and training US police departments and issued solidarity statements, including advice on how best to deal with tear gas, regarding the protesters in Ferguson and in New York City following the NYPD killing of Eric Garner.[28] By recognizing the US and Israeli security states not as exceptional but as part of a global, neoliberal racial regime firmly rooted in the history of settler colonialism, we see some revealing parallels and relationships. Like Operation Ghetto Storm, or Brazil's Pacifying Police Units waging war on poor Black favela residents, the consequences for

---

28   Jaime Omar Yassin, "The Shortest Distance between Ferguson and Palestine," *Counterpunch*, August 15–17, 2014; Dean Obeidallah, "Michael Brown, Gaza, and Muslim Americans," *Daily Beast*, August 20, 2014; Sydney Levy, "Jewish Voice for Peace Stands in Solidarity with the Community of Ferguson, Missouri," August 20, 2014; David Gilbert, "Michael Brown Shooting: Gaza Strip Tweets Ferguson About How to Deal with Tear Gas," *International Business Times*, August 14, 2014; Mark LeVine, "Ferguson Is Not Gaza … Yet," *Al Jazeera America*, August 18, 2014.

the ruled ought not to be measured merely by the destructive force of American-made F-15s, cluster bombs, and white phosphorous, but also by the everyday routine of occupation: unemployment, poverty, insecurity, precarity, illegal settlements, state-sanctioned theft of water and land, destruction of local economies and agriculture, a racially defined security regime, the effects of permanent refugee existence.

Our militarized culture places cops and soldiers on pedestals and frames their actions as "security" or as acts of self-defense. Police are in the streets to protect "citizens" from out-of-control (Black and Brown) criminals. This is why in virtually every case involving an unarmed person shot by police, the victim is depicted as an assailant. Living under occupation means enduring a permanent war in which virtually all civilians are deemed combatants and collective punishment is the fabric of everyday life. In Mike Brown's hometown, this takes the form of routine stops and fines for noise ordinance violations (e.g., playing loud music), fare-hopping on St. Louis's light rail system, uncut grass or unkempt property, trespassing, wearing "saggy pants," an expired driver's license or registration, "disturbing the peace," or merely walking in the middle of the street. Unpaid fines or tickets often result in jail time, having to pay inordinate sums to bail bondsmen, losing one's car or other pieces of property, and losing one's children to social services.

The point here is not just to punish Black communities but to mark them, to create a record of "criminal behavior," to transform them from citizens to thugs.[29] As soon as protesters gathered on Florissant Avenue in Ferguson, Missouri, to demand answers, reactionary bloggers, police officers, and even mainstream media were quick to label Michael Brown a "thug." When the Ferguson Police Department decided to release footage of Brown wrestling a store clerk over a pack of cigarillos, it only confirmed his criminality.

Criminalization is to be subjected to regulation, containment, surveillance, and punishment, but deemed unworthy of protection.[30] Those targeted by the state are not rights-bearing individuals to be protected

---

29   See Shana L. Redmond and Damien Sojoyner, "Keywords in Black Protest: A(n Anti) Vocabulary," *Truthout*, May 29, 2015.

30   Lisa Marie Cacho, *Social Death: Racialized Rightlessness and the Criminalization of the Unprotected* (New York: New York University Press, 2012), 4.

but criminals poised to violate the law who thus require vigilant watch—not unlike prisoners. In lieu of habeas corpus, terms like "thug" and "hoodlum" are used to differentiate the criminal element from the good Negroes, thus closing off the possibility of empathy with those who may have broken the law. Decriminalizing Blackness, in other words, occurs not in the court of law but in the court of public opinion. It requires proving that one is *not* a thug—that is, by portraying the Mike Browns and Trayvon Martins of the world as the *undeserving* dead, rendering them good kids, college-bound, honor students, sweet, as if their character is the only possible evidence that exists of their innocence.

"Thug" works to both criminalize and dehumanize the dispossessed while masking the violent operations of the state and capital: criminal neglect by landlords and city officials; rampant fraud (from mortgage brokers and loan companies to insurance firms and bail bondsmen); unwarranted price hikes for commodities, rent, and services; and the daily violation of human rights—in short, the actual source of thuggery. President Obama dismissed the uprising in Baltimore following Freddie Gray's death as the handiwork of "thugs and criminals."[31] Of course, in times of civil unrest, distinguishing thugs from the "community" is an old tactic that serves to delegitimize grievances expressed by those whom Dr. Martin Luther King, Jr., called "the unheard." Once expressions of anger, pain, even euphoria, become criminal acts, the citizen becomes the perpetrator. And the perpetrator's intentions are always self-evident. Following the April 1968 riots in Baltimore, the Maryland Crime Investigation Committee report observed, "Many hoodlums, who neither knew nor cared about Dr. Martin Luther King, or have interest in the fate of an opposed minority, concealed their criminal acts during the holocaust under the guise of protest against injustices."[32]

Black people are also made to pay for the very system that renders them non-persons. As we learned long before the Justice Department issued its report on Ferguson, summons and warrants are used as a kind of racial tax, a direct extraction of surplus by the state that produces nothing but discipline and terror and the reproduction of the state—in

31   Payton Guion, "The Baltimore Riots: President Obama Calls Rioters 'Criminals and Thugs,'" *Independent*, April 28, 2015.

32   Baltimore Committee on the Administration of Justice, *Report*, 4.

other words, *revenue by primitive accumulation.* In 2013, Ferguson's municipal court issued nearly 33,000 arrest warrants to a population of just over 21,000, generating about $2.6 million dollars in income for the municipality. That same year, the St. Louis county and city municipal courts acquired more than $61 million in fines and fees, accounting for almost half of all fines and fees collected by the municipal courts throughout the state. The top twenty-one "collectors" were municipalities that generated at least one-third of their revenue from court fines and fees, where, on average, 62 percent of the residents were Black and 22 percent lived below the poverty line.[33]

Yet talk of "Black-on-Black" homicides, sagging pants, and teen pregnancies almost always dislodges the focus from state violence. This classic bait and switch forecloses a deeper interrogation of the ways that state violence manifests in neoliberal policies (for example, in the erosion of the public safety net and the privatization of necessary services such as health care and transportation—that is to say, policies rendered logical under a racist security regime and that produce scarcity, environmental and health hazards, poverty, and alternative economies rooted in violence and subjugation). The prime target of neoliberal violence has been our youth, our children. Let's not forget that Kalief Browder, Mike Brown, Tamir Rice, Ayana Stanley-Jones, and others were children when the bullet, the jail, or the prison took their lives.

We see the consequences of neoliberalism in the laws that make it easier to prosecute juveniles as adults, in the deluge of zero-tolerance policies that mandate unconditional expulsion of students for possession of any weapons or drugs or other violations on or around school grounds, in the startling rise of expulsions and suspensions. Problems that were once handled by teachers, principals, and parents are now remanded to juvenile and criminal courts and the police. Crisis, moral panics, neoliberal policies, and racism fuel an expansive system of human management based on incarceration, surveillance, containment, pacification, lethal occupation, and gross misrepresentation. The toxic mix of privatization, free-market ideology, and a "punitive state" come

---

33   Erika Hellerstein, "'It's Racist as Hell': Inside St. Louis County's Predatory Night Court," *Thinkprogress.org*, April 10, 2015; Better Together, "Public Safety—Municipal Courts," October 2014, bettertogetherstl.com.

together in our schools.[34] Those who survive the school of "discipline and punish" and high-stakes testing are faced with increasingly narrow opportunities for higher learning and social advancement. Mike Brown is a perfect example. He was, after all, "college-bound," a fact cited as evidence that his death was unwarranted and that he was a victim of misrecognition. But what did "college-bound" mean for Brown?

He graduated from a high school in the Normandy school district, one of the poorest, most racially segregated districts in the state that had ranked last in overall academic performance and had just lost its accreditation. He planned to attend Vatterott College, a chain of for-profit trade schools that have come under investigation for charging exorbitant tuitions, saddling students with debt, and failing to deliver the promised skills that could ensure secure employment. A congressional report documented numerous student complaints at the Missouri campus, ranging from poor teaching and ill-equipped labs to an exceedingly high instructor turnover rate. In 2009, Vatterott's profits exceeded $26 million, while a year earlier over 26 percent of the students had defaulted on their loans.[35]

The proliferation of for-profit "colleges" and the dismantling and shrinking of public community colleges is a consequence of the neoliberal state's expansion. What appears as a "free market" solution to replace a bloated state is actually a partnership: the federal government underwrites these privatized, virtually unregulated institutions, which in turn buttresses US militarism. In 2010, 88.1 percent of Vatterott's total revenue came from the federal government: 86.9 percent from Title IV federal financial aid and the rest from Department of Defense Tuition Assistance and post-9/11 GI Bill funds. While educating veterans is an important and noble goal, Vatterott's website boasts that the school is "military friendly" and "ranks nationally in the top 15% of

---

34   Annette Fuentes, "Arresting Development: Zero Tolerance and the Criminalization of Children," *Rethinking Schools* 26, no. 2 (Winter 2011–2012): 18–23.

35   Nikole Hannah-Jones, "School Segregation, the Continuing Tragedy of Ferguson," *ProPublica*, December 19, 2014; U.S. Senate Committee on Health, Education, Labor and Pensions, *For Profit Higher Education: The Failure to Safeguard the Federal Investment and Ensure Student Success*, Vol. 1 (Washington DC: US Government printing Office, 2012), 761–770.

all schools providing military educational services."[36] In other words, Vatterott targets veterans, redirects their meager benefits into its own coffers, and promotes US militarism in the process.

Yet veterans are not their main targets. Vatterott recruiters are instructed to pursue students like Mike Brown—Black and Brown, poor and vulnerable. According to internal documents, recruiters are told that promising enrollees are convicted felons, people in drug rehab, "Welfare Mom w/ Kids … [and] Pregnant Ladies," people whose "decision to start, stay in school or quit school is based more on emotion than logic … Pain is the greater motivator in the short run." Brown's life was cut short, but had he lived he would have faced the prospect of a slow death, of bearing enormous debt without the prospect of a fulfilling livelihood while continuing to navigate a world of constant surveillance and harassment.

"Pain is the greater motivator in the short run" is the perfect mantra for neoliberal logic. That is to say, pain and profit. Pain, or bearing witness to pain, is also a motivator "in the short run" for ending the thuggery of the state. For every young person we bury, there are ten more driven to act against state violence, criminalization, and immiseration. We see them in Ferguson and St. Louis, Missouri, in organizations such as Hands Up United, Lost Voices, Organization for Black Struggle, Don't Shoot Coalition, and Millennial Activists United; we see them erupt phoenix-like in Florida with the Dream Defenders, in Chicago with We Charge Genocide and the Black Youth Project 100, in Los Angeles with the Community Rights Campaign, all over the country behind the banner #BlackLivesMatter.

We see them in the form of Dreamers and 67 Suenos (the 67 percent of undocumented youth who are not college-bound and thus excluded from the Dream Act's provisions), taking new "freedom rides" on the Undocubus under a banner reading "No Papers, No Fear," fighting SB 1070 in Arizona and defending ethnic studies, taking on NYPD "stop and frisk" practices and the exportation of broken windows theory around the country, and everywhere backing people around the world

---

36   US Senate Committee on Health, Education Labor, and Pensions, *For Profit Higher Education* (2012), 758, gpo.gov/fdsys/pkg/CPRT-112SPRT74931/pdf/CPRT-112SPRT74931.pdf; quotations from Vatterott website, vatterott.edu.

who remain subject to US warfare and violence unleashed by late imperial policies, to water privatization and enclosure, to occupation and ongoing settler colonialism, to the poverty, low wages, and modes of neoliberal governance that have stripped most of the planet of any semblance of democracy.

These activists and revolutionaries are our children. They are on the front lines resisting their own criminalization, fighting to demilitarize schools and streets, and taking on the state directly. Pain may be the motivator in the short run, but love is their long-term motivation. They are trying not only to stop state thuggery, but also to create a new community dedicated to a post-racist, post-sexist, post-homophobic, and post-colonial world.

~

Robin D. G. Kelley is the Gary B. Nash Endowed Chair of US History at the University of California, Los Angeles. His books include *Thelonious Monk: The Life and Times of an American Original* (Free Press, 2009) and most recently *Africa Speaks, America Answers: Modern Jazz in Revolutionary Times* (Harvard University Press, 2012).

2. #BLACKLIVESMATTER AND GLOBAL VISIONS OF ABOLITION: AN INTERVIEW WITH PATRISSE CULLORS

Christina Heatherton

Patrisse Cullors is the co-founder and co-visionary, along with Alicia Garza and Opal Tometi, of the #BlackLivesMatter movement. Together these three queer Black women, veterans of labor, immigrants' rights, and other social justice organizing, have created the "infrastructure" for a movement that has spread internationally. Cullors is also the founder of Dignity and Power Now!—a Los Angeles–based organization that fights for the rights of incarcerated people and their communities—and is currently the director of the Truth and Reinvestment Campaign for the Ella Baker Center for Human Rights.

Heatherton: How is the principle of abolition central to your organizing work?

Cullors: Oftentimes, in our anti–state violence work or anti–police brutality work, we don't actually have a conversation about abolition. In the current #BlackLivesMatter movement, we are seeing some of the most vibrant, creative responses to state violence. We're also hearing some of the oldest arguments, like the call for special prosecutors or indictments. All of these things actually reify the state rather than insisting that the state should not be a part of this process. There's a much larger conversation to be had, which is ultimately about abolishing the police. Therein lies the necessary intervention. I'm not sure #BlackLivesMatter has made that intervention successfully. We need a discourse that gives our communities clear alternatives and new visions, new imaginings of our public safety.

Heatherton: Why do you think that the current discourse is divorced from abolition? Why do you think this is a difficult barrier to overcome?

Cullors: A number of reasons. We live in a police state, in which the police have become judge, juror, and executioner. They've become the social worker. They've become the mental health clinician. They've become anything and everything that has to do with the everyday life of mostly Black and Brown poor people. They've become the through line. They've become the expectation. Instead of a mass movement saying "No, we don't want them," the mass movement is saying, "How do we reform them? How do we hold a couple of them accountable?" The conversation should be: "Why are they even here?"

There are obviously many of us who have had that conversation, but it hasn't been the popular dialogue. Why do the police even exist? What are their origins? Many of us understand that their original task was to patrol slaves. Many of us understand that the first sheriff's departments patrolled the US-Mexico border. That's not the public discourse. This has everything to do with the position that they've played in the last thirty years. It's also deeply rooted in anti-Black racism. The idea of not having police scares people. People say, "What are we going do with criminals?" by which they mean "What are we going to do with Black people?"

Heatherton: How do you answer those questions?

Cullors: I believe we should abolish the police. I think they are extremely dangerous and will continue to be. That doesn't mean I don't believe in police reform. There's an amazing campaign happening in New York that is calling on our movement to reclaim the idea of public safety as access to jobs, healthy food, and shelter—in other words, having a framework that is about the community's response to social ills instead of a police response to social ills.

Heatherton: How do you envision a movement against police violence also acting as a movement for jobs, housing, and healthy food?

Cullors: Let's look at where our money has been invested over the last thirty years, where we've seen the rise of policing, incarceration, and surveillance—what Angela Davis called the "prison industrial complex," an idea popularized by Critical Resistance.[1] I think we need to have a movement around divestment—to divest from police and prisons and surveillance and to use that money to reinvest in the communities that are most directly impacted by poverty and the violence of poverty.

Heatherton: What does it mean to organize in a police state, as you described it?

Cullors: When our political activism isn't rooted in a theory about transforming the world, it becomes narrow; when it is focused only on individual actors instead of larger systemic problems, it becomes short-sighted. We do have to deal with the current crisis in the short term. That's important. We have to have solutions for people's real-life problems, and we have to allow people to decide what those solutions are. We also have to create a vision that's much bigger than the one we have right now.

I was talking to one of the organizers in Ferguson. I said to her, this work is bigger than us. It's bigger than Black people. It's bigger than humans. This is a planetary crisis. If we don't solve it or at least set up a system that can help solve it, I don't think we'll survive. It's very primal. Sure, we want to change conditions and make people's lives better. But also, in 200 years, I want to know that humans survived and are living in much healthier and more holistic ways.

Heatherton: The mass media has depicted #BlackLivesMatter as a "leader-less" movement. You have called the movement "leader-full." Can you explain?

---

1   Critical Resistance is a national organization dedicated to opposing the expansion of the prison industrial complex.

Cullors: Our organizing is decentralized, with many leaders. It's an organizing that is rooted in healing justice and in principles of abolition. It's an organizing that rejects respectability politics and reinforces the fight for all Black lives. It's an organizing that is deeply rooted in what our long-term vision can be as Black people and their allies.

Heatherton: You now work for the Ella Baker Center for Human Rights. In her famous article "More than a Hamburger," Baker reflected on the Student Nonviolent Coordinating Committee, writing, "This feeling that they have a destined date with freedom was not limited to a drive for personal freedom ... The movement was concerned with the moral implications of racial discrimination for the 'world.'" You've seen #BlackLivesMatter spread internationally. Can you comment on the international implications of anti-racist struggle here in the United States?

Cullors: Anti-Black racism has global consequences. It is completely and absolutely necessary that, as Black people in the United States, we do not center the struggle around a domestic fight for our "civil rights." Rather, this is a broader fight for the Black diaspora, both on the continent and across the globe. It's essential that we center this conversation and also our practice in an international frame. If we don't have those critical dialogues, if we don't have that praxis around internationalism, we won't have a movement that is about all Black lives. The reality is that there are Black undocumented folks, Black migrants, here in the States. The conversation about their Black lives is crucial to this broader conversation about forming an international perspective and practice.

I don't actually think we're fully integrated around this. The focus on the US is so intense and hyper-vigilant. It doesn't allow for Black Americans to see ourselves as part of a global movement. We have a #BlackLivesMatter chapter in Toronto. They see themselves as part of the movement in ways that I don't think we see them as part of the movement. I think we need a shift. We need to have a much more integrated theory but also practice around all Black lives globally.

Heatherton: How does #BlackLivesMatter Toronto's vision of the movement differ?

Cullors: I'm talking to my #BlackLivesMatter Toronto chapter, witnessing their rallies, and I'm like, "Wow, y'all ride hard for us." They have signs for the Black folks who have died here, yet we have no idea what Black folks have died in Toronto from state violence. Why? Why are we so focused on only *our* Black lives? Why aren't we thinking of the Black lives across the globe? We know that our folks are suffering. I think that has to do with the US being so US-centered. We're going to have to work actively to push ourselves out of that narrative. That work has been done historically. The [Black] Panther Party did amazing work internationally. I think we're in that place right now.

Heatherton: Earlier this year you joined the Dream Defenders on a delegation to Palestine. How did #BlackLivesMatter resonate there? How did the trip shape your organizing here?

Cullors: It was probably the most profound trip of my life. It was really intense, walking through the streets of East Jerusalem, Ramallah, and throughout the West Bank. I remember walking with a Palestinian woman who asked me, "How are you feeling?" I said to her, essentially, "I've only felt this way when I visited a prison." I think it was important for us to let Palestinian people know, just like Malcolm did, and like the Panthers did, that we are in solidarity with their struggle against occupation and also that the #BlackLivesMatter movement is most definitely not going to align itself with the state of Israel. It was important to show that.

It's also extremely important that we build Black communities in deep solidarity with Indigenous people, given how much Black people have been displaced and given that we end up occupying other people's land. Conversations about Palestine have been very binary, about Palestinians and Israelis. We haven't actually had a conversation about all the Black people that are there, and the plight that Black folks face, and the potential coalition that could be built between Black folks and Palestinians to fight against occupation.

Heatherton: In a movement led by queer Black women, how are queer, gender-nonconforming, and trans people placed at the center of the movement? How do these processes help people reimagine freedom?

Cullors: When those who are most marginal are centered in practice and theory, we gain the ability to save all Black lives. When the poorest are cared for, so is everybody else. We are dispelling the myth that women have never been involved in the movement. In fact, women have been architects of the movement; they've just been erased. We've decided, collectively, that that's not what's going down this generation. We aren't going to give up parts of our community in an effort to save some of our community. It's either all of us, or it's none of us. That's been the reason, coming specifically from #BlackLivesMatter and its co-founders, for why we ride and fight so hard for Black trans women. Over and over again they have been iced out of our communities. It is our duty to ensure that we understand, as cis people in particular, that our liberation is only going to happen if Black trans women, and Black trans people in particular, are liberated.

Heatherton: Your vision adheres very closely to Angela Y. Davis's definition of abolition democracy, which draws on W. E. B. Du Bois in arguing that no one can be free in a society premised on exclusion. What does an abolitionist society look like to you?

Cullors: An abolitionist society is not based on capital. I don't think that you can have a capitalist system and also have an abolitionist system. I think an abolitionist society is rooted in the needs of the community first. It's rooted in providing for and supporting the self-determination of communities. It's a society that has no borders, literally. It's a society that's based on interdependence and the connection of all living beings. It's a society that is determined to facilitate a life that is full of respect, a life that is full of honoring and praising those most impacted by oppression. I think an abolitionist society is deeply spiritual.

3. BROKEN WINDOWS AT BLUE'S: A QUEER HISTORY OF GENTRIFICATION AND POLICING

Christina B. Hanhardt

On September 29, 1982, over thirty New York City police officers raided Blue's, a bar in Manhattan's Times Square. The following year, activist James Credle testified at congressional hearings on police misconduct, describing the brutal beatings of the Black and Latino gay men, and trans people who made up the bar's main clientele.[1] The event galvanized lesbian, gay, bisexual, and transgender (LGBT) activists for whom police violence was a primary concern. Although one mention of a rally made it into the *New York Times*, Credle noted in his testimony that the incident itself had been ignored by major media outlets, an insult certainly made worse by the fact that the bar sat across the street from the *Times*'s own headquarters.[2]

Gay activist and journalist Arthur Bell wrote a front-page story about the raid for the alternative weekly the *Village Voice*. In it, he quoted Inspector John J. Martin, commanding officer of the Midtown South Precinct, who described Blue's as "a very troublesome bar" with "a lot

---

1 James Credle, "November 28, 1983: Police Brutality: The Continual Erosion of Our Most Basic Rights," in *Speaking for Our Lives: Historical Speeches and Rhetoric for Gay and Lesbian Rights*, ed. Robert Ridinger (Binghamton, NY: Harrington Press, 2004).

2 "Marchers Protest Raid on 43rd Street Bar," *New York Times*, October 16, 1982. Eric Lerner also noted the lack of major media coverage for the raid in "Militant Blues Rally Draws 1,100," *New York Native*, November 8–21, 1982, as did Sarah Schulman and Peg Byron in "Who Wants to Drive Blues Out of Business?" *WomaNews*, November 1982, reprinted in Sarah Schulman, *My American History: Lesbian and Gay Life During the Reagan Years* (New York: Routledge, 1994), 54–6.

of undesirables" and "a place that transvestites are drawn to ... probably for narcotics use." Bell also noted the striking contrast between the raid and another press-worthy event held that same night: a black tie dinner, $150 a plate, sponsored by the Human Rights Campaign Fund (HRCF), a gay and lesbian political action committee, at the Waldorf Astoria Hotel with a keynote by former vice president Walter Mondale.[3]

Years earlier, Bell had written about a much more famous police raid and response, which had taken place at the Stonewall Inn bar on June 28, 1969. At the time, police raids of gay bars were common, and bar owners often sought protection through payoffs to the police. On June 28, however, the Stonewall patrons and others socializing outside the bar responded to the unexpected raid with a three-day rebellion that is now credited with spurring a more militant and visible LGBT movement.

In the decade following the Stonewall uprising, police abuse remained a problem for many LGBT people, but it was joined by growing concerns about general street safety. In response, many activists attempted to convince the public that gay life was far from "undesirable" and could even be seen as a valuable asset in a city in which the discourses of crime and economic crises had become tightly intertwined. In September 1977, for example, the gay magazine *Christopher Street* featured a cover story titled "Can Gays Save New York City?" that included a picture of two men embracing a miniaturized image of Lower Manhattan and asked, "How many neighborhoods in Manhattan would be slums by now, had gay singles and couples not moved in and helped maintain and upgrade them?"[4] The magazine often addressed itself to the question of how gay men were reshaping the landscape of New York, regularly featuring *New Yorker*–style cartoons that poked fun at gay men who were developing niche businesses or at the supposed value of gayness to new forms of industry.[5] In another issue, the editors celebrated urban

---

3   Arthur Bell, "Black Tie and Blood," *Village Voice*, October 12, 1982, 1.

4   David Rothenberg, "Can Gays Save New York City?" *Christopher Street*, September 1977, 9.

5   Cartoons include one in which the sign for a toy store has been renamed "Toys 'R' S&M," with the caption "A major firm seeks a market with a higher discretionary income." In another, two men in T-shirts reading "Le Hunk" chat on the street next to a car labeled "Le Car" and a sign that reads "Le Gay Ghetto." In a third, two men

scholarship highlighting the leadership of gay men in "revitalization" efforts, describing their creativity, adaptability, ego, and openness to risk-taking as key features for achieving success in a speculation-based economy.[6]

For many commentators, new gay investment in the central city was understood to be part of a broader process of middle-class reinvestment in urban areas—what became known as the "back-to-the-city" movement. Often called "gay gentrification," the phenomenon of new, concentrated gay investment was debated not only by gay journalists but also by city boosters and developers, scholars, and activists, many of whom linked the rise of gay social movements with the growth of gay neighborhoods. These gay neighborhoods, they argued, provided a kind of protection for those escaping the presumed anti-gay sentiments of non-urban areas. Cast in such general terms, though, these arguments primarily described a professional class of white gay men, assumed, unlike LGBT people in general, to be free of the obligations of family, territorial, and suited to the so-called *new* service economy.[7]

But as the raid on Blue's attests, there were many other people—including many white gay men—pursuing same-sex intimacy, non-normative kinship arrangements, and gender expressions that did not conform to mainstream expectations who did not profit from restructuring real estate markets. Liberal and conservative policy makers alike condemned what they saw to be the erosion of traditional family values and gender roles as a sexual zeitgeist gone too far and among the key causes of the "social disorder" that threatened urban cores. They invoked still-popular "culture of poverty" arguments that blamed Black low-income mothers and praised new zoning restrictions that targeted public spaces and businesses in these areas. *Disorder* as a category would be crafted through

---

tell a professionally dressed woman, "We divide all of the work. I do the dishes and he gentrifies."

6   "Out & Around: Brownstoning," *Christopher Street*, August 1976, 3.

7   This argument was most famously elaborated by geographer Manuel Castells, "City and Culture: The San Francisco Experience," in *The City and the Grassroots: A Cross-Cultural Theory of Urban Society Movements* (Berkeley: University of California Press, 1983), 97–172.

the very strategies used to contain and curtail it, in policing philosophy as well as models of municipal governance, and in attacks on not only social uprisings but also the daily lives of those increasingly cast as a "permanent underclass."

In fact, at the same time that gay people's affirmative role in real estate was being praised by the mainstream and alternative press, journalists and social scientists were also publicizing theories about the need for police practice to target disorder and the "discovery" of an often amorphously defined sector of the supposedly intractable poor. In 1982, the year of the Blue's raid, criminologists George L. Kelling and James Q. Wilson introduced the ethos of "broken windows" policing to the broader public via the *Atlantic* magazine, and journalist Ken Auletta published *The Underclass* based on a series of articles from the *New Yorker*. Broken windows theory emphasizes the problem of disorderliness on residents' sense of safety and in particular the effect of destabilizing, unfamiliar elements, including "loiterers," "rowdy teenagers," "drunks," "prostitutes," and the "mentally disturbed."[8] Similarly, Auletta explained that the contemporary underclass consisted of the "hard-core unemployed," which he summarized in the pages of the *New Yorker* as "criminals, drug addicts, or pushers, alcoholics, [and] welfare mothers."[9]

The HRCF's event committee for its fundraiser at the Waldorf Astoria included senators Daniel Patrick Moynihan and Edward Kennedy (who did not, however, appear in person). Unlike the politically conservative architects of broken windows theory, Moynihan and Kennedy were liberals. Yet their respective ideas about a culture of poverty and a permanent underclass were easy fits with broken windows theory, insofar as all three revolved around diagnosing cultural pathology and regulating the social norms of the poor.[10] In these shared contexts, then, disorder

8   George L. Kelling and James Q. Wilson, "Broken Windows: The Police and Neighborhood Safety," *Atlantic*, March 1982.

9   Ken Auletta, "The Underclass—I," *New Yorker*, November 16, 1981, 63. See also Auletta, *The Streets Were Paved with Gold* (New York: Random House, 1979) and *The Underclass* (New York: Random House, 1982).

10   When he was the assistant secretary of labor, Moynihan authored the 1965 report "The Negro Family: The Case for National Action," which explained African American poverty as due to cultural practices passed down though matriarchal families. The term "permanent underclass" was used by Kennedy in 1978 at an NAACP

functioned as a catchall for poverty in general as well as for specific forms of unregulated street life. It was also a convenient description for those seen as obstructions to the urban improvements promised by a new middle class.

Since then, gentrification has proven to be ongoing and global, and policing approaches based on broken windows theory—also known as "order maintenance" policing—have been central to the cycles of devalorization and revalorization that have reshaped New York City and cities around the world.[11] In 1993, William J. Bratton was appointed New York City's police commissioner for the first time. Empowered by a decade of broken windows policing in New York's transit system (including under his own leadership), Bratton quickly crafted a city-wide police strategy of "zero tolerance" for "quality of life" infractions, escalating the enforcement and punishment of misdemeanor crimes, particularly in public spaces.

Bratton's approach was first tested in Greenwich Village, home to the famed Stonewall riots and one of the world's best-known gay enclaves.[12] Among its key targets were nonresident LGBT people of color who enjoyed the neighborhood's abundance of LGBT-oriented services and reputation as a safe haven for LGBT people. As the strategy expanded across the city, it was governed by the logic of its different spatial contexts: taking aim at homeless people and workers in the informal economy in tourist zones (such as Times Square); at unregulated street life in newly gentrified areas; and, in the form of "stop and frisk," at Black and Latino men, especially in parts of the city devalued long enough to become new hot spots for speculative investment.

In this way, it is clear how *queerness*—both as an umbrella term for lesbian, gay, bisexual, and transgender identities and as a lens for

---

dinner in Detroit to describe persistent poverty and was reported by Ken Auletta in "The Underclass—I" and *The Underclass.*

11   See Neil Smith, *The New Urban Frontier: Gentrification and the Revanchist City* (London: Routledge, 1996).

12   Clifford Krauss, "Efforts on Quality of Life in Village a Success, the Police Say," *New York Times*, June 24, 1994. Also see Tanya Erzen and Andrea McArdle, eds., *Zero Tolerance: Quality of Life and the New Police Brutality in New York City* (New York: New York University Press, 2001).

examining the operation of power via normalization, stigma, and kinship regulation—offers a helpful analytic for understanding the intersection of gentrification and order maintenance policing. The celebration of gay investment alongside attacks like the one at Blue's demonstrates the often bifurcated function of marginalized identity and social non-normativity in postwar urban development policy. Here certain lesbian and gay claims of vulnerability and calls for safety, especially those paired with or perceived as amenable to redevelopment, are celebrated at the same time that those who stand outside of white, middle-class heterosexuality (including many lesbians and gay men) continue to be targeted by police strategies that pave the way for that selective reinvestment. This framework also allows for a more complex play of identity in urban political economy more generally, refusing to substitute individual choice in the marketplace for a structural critique of capitalism or dismiss the functions of race, gender, or sexuality in ordering the city. Most important, it is an argument that has been developed by a variety of activists, then and now.

Times Square, 1982

The raid on Blue's was violent and destructive. Bell, Credle, and other observers described the scene they encountered the next morning: blood pooled on the floor and streaked across the wall; furniture, liquor bottles, glasses, pinball machines, and mirrors smashed to fragments; and spent bullets scattered on the floor. Those present reported being beaten with nightsticks and called anti-gay and racist epithets as officers threatened to kill them and stole their money and identification. In turn, the police claimed that the raid was a response to a fight that got out of hand. Yet Bell noted in his coverage that, although the police reported that some officers had been injured, they had arrested none of the bar-goers.

Activists and journalists—mostly in the gay and leftist press—suggested that the raid had been part of an ongoing effort to "clean up" Times Square. This effort would have included Operation Crossroads, initiated by Mayor Edward Koch in 1978, which had tripled the police presence in the neighborhood and focused on "hustlers," "prostitutes," "drifters," and "drug sellers." That year, the city also passed a new zoning regulation restricting "adult physical culture" (primarily massage parlors).[13] People familiar with the bar also pointed fingers at *New York Times* reporters, whom they suspected had called in complaints about patrons of Blue's hanging out on the street.[14]

Activist James Credle's observation (described at this chapter's beginning)—that the mainstream press had ignored the raid—can thus be understood as part of a broad indictment; it pointed not only to the paper's failure to recognize the police violence experienced by the gay and trans people of color next door, but also to its literal investment in policing strategies like Operation Crossroads. Writers such as Sarah Schulman and Peg Byron explicitly named gentrification in their coverage of the incident.[15] In fact, police efforts to "clean up" Times Square promised to raise the value not only of the *Times* headquarters but also, more importantly, of its biggest advertisers and, ultimately, to fuel the city growth machine. As John Logan and Harvey Molotch have shown, major city newspapers often serve as growth boosters across urban regions, advocating for development that will increase subscribers and, in turn, advertiser revenue. The *New York Times* has long applied this strategy.[16]

True to form, in 1981, the paper had celebrated Times Square as undergoing a "revival," in which the area was at last to be saved from "sin and decay" with the assistance of private funds, following an (albeit failed) Ford Foundation initiative (whose own offices were further east on 42nd Street).[17] By the time of the Blue's raid, the transformation of Times Square had reached a fevered pitch; no fewer than five theaters were destroyed in 1982 alone to clear the way for luxury hotel

13   Selwyn Raab, "Koch Gets Plan for Cleanup of Times Sq. by 1980," *New York Times*, July 3, 1978; Selwyn Raab, "Police Manpower Tripled in the Times Square Area," *New York Times*, June 13, 1978.

14   "Midtown Cops Go Berserk in Gay Bar," *New York Native*, October 11–24, 1982, 1; Bell, "Black Tie and Blood."

15   Sarah Schulman and Peg Byron, "Who Wants to Drive Blues Out of Business?"

16   John Logan and Harvey Molotch, *Urban Fortunes: The Political Economy of Place* (Berkeley: University of California Press, 1987), 70–3.

17   Ralph Blumenthal, "A Times Square Revival?" *New York Times*, December 27, 1981.

development.[18] These projects were facilitated by popular claims about supposed new forms of disruptive, self-chosen poverty. Drawing on a colorful vocabulary and detailed descriptions, journalists and other writers generated categories of people ("bag ladies," for example) and named them as the most difficult denizens of the broader Times Square area: "In the notorious section of midtown surrounding the Port Authority bus terminal, amid throngs of workers, transients, and tourists, lives a compact society of outsiders," feminist Alix Kates Shulman wrote. "Hustlers, hookers, three-card monte players, con men, drug dealers, jackrollers (thieves who specialize in robbing the poor of their welfare funds) work over their marks between Times Square and the Stroll, that strip of Eighth Avenue serviced by prostitutes and pimps."[19]

It is thus no surprise that a policing theory targeting signs of so-called disorder would gain approval in the press, which, in turn, would help build popular consensus in support of it. While broken windows certainly had precedent in other forms of anti-poverty doctrine, racial segregation, and status-based policing, the theory would appeal to a broader political swath than the conservative criminologists who coined it.[20] Developed out of local studies of police foot patrols, based particularly in nearby Newark, New Jersey, during the 1970s, the theory focused less on the immediate reduction of crime per se than on the perception of safety, under the assumption that certain environments

---

18   John Corry, "Broadway Stages a Drama to Save 2 Theaters," *New York Times*, March 5, 1982.

19   Alix Kates Shulman, "Bag Ladies," *New York Times*, September 29, 1981. It is worth noting that in her essay Shulman critiques the language of pathology and blame. Samuel R. Delany has written eloquently of life in Times Square during this period, confirming the existence of a cross-class community forged through sexual exchange while noting the often exploitative aspects of the drug economy. He also notes the devastating impact of redevelopment, arguing that it destroyed supportive social networks and replaced the intimacy of "contact" with the depersonalizing structures of profit motives. Samuel R. Delany, *Times Square Red, Times Square Blue* (New York: NYU Press, 1999).

20   For earlier models of policing, see Khalil Gibran Muhammad, *The Condemnation of Blackness: Race, Crime, and the Making of Modern America* (Cambridge: Harvard University Press, 2011) and David Garland, *The Culture of Control: Crime and Social Order in Contemporary Society* (Chicago: University of Chicago Press, 2002).

cultivated future criminal opportunity. As Kelling and Wilson argued, cops working their beats, in collaboration with local residents, were best equipped to identify who belonged and who did not and to quell signs of disorder lest they lead to escalating crime.

Kelling and Wilson drew on the research of Philip Zimbardo to explain this causal relationship. In Zimbardo's famous social psychology experiment, a run-down and seemingly abandoned car led anonymous bystanders to cause it even greater damage. Yet Kelling and Wilson interpreted abuse of the built environment narrowly: quality-of-life policing should target graffiti, per their theory, but not surrounding buildings dilapidated due to landlord neglect. The majority of the theory's examples of disorder, moreover, are not physical but manifest instead in the status and practices of marginalized *individuals*, who are then considered eligible for arrest.

The emphasis on the primacy of an individual's sense of safety or fear, the proposed solution of citizen-police collaboration, and the idea that signs of disorder might lead to bigger threats were, at the time, not only tenets of conservatism but consistent as well with the approach to inequality adopted by postwar liberal politics. The influence of social psychology and faith in the power of rational choice as well as the idea that liberal politics could coexist easily with greater police power bolstered rather than loosened the relationship between the police and the new middle-class communities moving into central city regions abandoned by capital years before.[21] In the case of the new lesbian and gay movement, the social liberalism that celebrated sexual freedom would be understood by some to support place-based land claims, an argument that required separating the terms of sexual/kinship non-normativity from lesbian and gay identity formation. Moreover, gay and lesbian activists held a newly formed belief that individualized, violent threat might be made manifest and promised by the representational signs of the city.

---

21   See Christopher Lowen Agee, *The Streets of San Francisco: Policing and the Creation of a Cosmopolitan Liberal Politics, 1950–1972* (Chicago: University of Chicago Press, 2014).

Safe in the City

Prior to the late 1960s and early 1970s, the idea of a gay neighborhood as it is commonly held today did not exist, and LGBT people were most associated with areas that housed a range of other social outsiders—such as artists and bohemians, drug users, sex workers, and those made itinerant due to poverty, often in areas considered to be vice districts or skid rows.[22] The risk of street violence was rarely understood as shared by all gay people; instead, police abuse stood at the fore, and activists—in some cases associated with War on Poverty programs—tied the problem of policing to street cleanups intended to facilitate new development.

They also fought criminalization and stigma, drawing, as historian Christopher Agee has shown, on the concept of the "harm principle" (arguing that acts that hurt no one should not be considered crimes) and fighting status-based anti-vagrancy laws, both of which disproportionately targeted homosexuals.[23] And, like many participants in the Great Society, they drew on liberal psychology to emphasize the healthiness of prideful identification and increasingly framed "gay" as an affirmative identity rather than simply a stigmatized practice. But in the process of distinguishing homosexuality from categories of harm—those labeled as criminal, sick, or causing psychic damage—the racial and economic associations of those other stigmatized practices were left intact.

By the start of the 1970s, popular acceptance of homosexuality had grown, and realtors began marketing gay people as the ideal *tenants* of changing neighborhoods, focusing especially on middle-class white gay men as high-earning, risk-taking, and family-free. But, in an important distinction, the celebration of renters and owners did not include those whose displays of *queerness* primarily took the form of public intimacy,

---

22   The middle sections of this essay draw significantly on research from my book *Safe Space: Gay Neighborhood History and the Politics of Violence* (Durham, NC: Duke University Press, 2013), which provides a longer and more detailed history of LGBT activism and neighborhood politics.

23   For an excellent discussion of the function of the harm principle in gay urban organizing, see Agee, *The Streets of San Francisco*; on gay challenges to vagrancy laws, see Nan Alamilla Boyd, *Wide Open Town: A History of Queer San Francisco to 1965* (Berkeley: University of California Press, 2005).

gender non-conformity, or participation in street-based economies. As one journalist explained in late 1969, vice districts that were associated with public and commercial sex, such as Times Square, were not considered to be gay neighborhoods since their "gay legions are transient rather than permanent."[24]

Gay neighborhoods emerged alongside a growing movement that had inherited from earlier activism commitments to fighting police abuse and arguing that homosexuality be designated as neither a crime nor an illness. But as the decade continued, vulnerability to violence as a general category was increasingly cast as a unifying gay experience writ large. In turn, on the streets, activism manifested increasingly in campaigns for self-protection (such as safe-streets patrols) that blurred the terms of gay community cohesion and crime control. In other words, in arguing that they were *not* criminals or safe from harm, many gay men and lesbians—in particular those who benefited from the protection of whiteness or class status—aligned themselves with dominant narratives about those who *were*. These assumptions shaped their sense of who did and did not belong in gay neighborhoods: the same determination at the core of Kelling and Wilson's own solution.

And with time, these suppositions achieved the status of common knowledge. Aligned with the popular uptake of urban research—including public familiarity with theories of, for example, the culture of poverty, Black rage, and rational choice criminology—white gay activists turned to cooperative *and* crime of opportunity policing rather than anti-poverty solutions, deeming the latter impossible to realize. Even the very concept of *homophobia* would be ascribed to a uniform culture of racialized poverty. Moynihan's use of the culture of poverty thesis described a Black propensity for violence and attributed it to inequality and emasculation resulting from female-headed households. At the same time, definitions of homophobia outlined a vulnerable masculinity that might take expression in violent behavior. Considered together, Black poverty—rather than the structural constraints upholding the ideals of the normative nuclear family or procreative sex—was seen as a risk to gay identity, which thus functioned, by default, as white, male,

---

24 Hector Simms, "New York Gay Ghettos," *Gay*, December 15, 1969, 4–5.

and middle-class, even as activists sought to expand the category of gay identity beyond these lines. As a result, the fight against crime was often expressed as a fight against homophobia, itself increasingly understood as the expression of *disorder* associated with those most targeted by police policy dedicated to normalization and control. And, borrowing from the feminist anti-rape movement, activists often found danger in the signs of *potential* threat—whether in the embodiment of those who seemed to be outsiders or in line with the race and class terms of a "homophobic" diagnosis—which aligned with a broken windows–style fixation on the outsider rather than the violent act itself.[25]

By the end of the 1970s, gay activists were leaders in community-partnership policing models. While some were certainly influenced by the broad law-and-order politics set into motion by Richard Nixon and other conservative politicians of the era, mainstream lesbian and gay ideas of urban crime, safety, and the role of the police continued to borrow from liberal visions.[26] These included the ongoing influence of racialized ideas of psychological injury and the values of self-help from the War on Poverty and other liberal programs of the period, but also from new municipal police policies. The growth of national gay anti-violence politics was anchored in anti-crime models based in New York and San Francisco. As Agee has shown, the emergence of a cosmopolitan liberalism in San Francisco merged the ethos of inclusiveness with a hard-nosed fight against crime. This followed the development of empirically oriented managerial growth politics: the eventual strategies adopted would privilege the localist visions of a professional class that supported stronger police discretion as part of community-based policing—the cornerstone of broken windows theory's participatory, collaborative solutions.[27]

---

25 I discuss this dynamic in more detail in *Safe Space*, as well as in Christina B. Hanhardt, "Butterflies, Whistles, and Fists: Gay Safe Streets Patrols and the New Gay Ghetto, 1976–1981," *Radical History Review* 100 (2008): 61–85.

26 For a detailed study of the influence of liberals on postwar prison expansion, see Naomi Murakawa, *The First Civil Right: How Liberals Built Prison America* (New York: Oxford University Press, 2014). Also see Ruth Wilson Gilmore, *Golden Gulag: Prisons, Surplus, Crisis, and Opposition in Globalizing California* (Berkeley: University of California Press, 2007).

27 Agee, *The Streets of San Francisco.*

As gay safety activism moved onto a national stage, activists sought partnership with other national—and even international—efforts dedicated to fighting crime. The crime victims' rights movement, for example, had gained prominence in the early 1980s and, along with the Anti-Defamation League (ADL) of B'nai B'rith, become leaders in the fight for hate crime statutes (which further penalize crimes found to be motivated by bias). LGBT activists found common ground with the ADL's fight against religious persecution, arguing that lesbians and gay men shared the experience of non-visible marginalized identities and that threats to both groups often manifested in attacks on the built environment or within neighborhoods that *represented* those targeted.

It is also worth noting that among the ADL's leading projects during this period were campaigns combating US student activism against Zionism and supporting US–Israeli police training exchanges. The latter efforts were facilitated by the ADL's affiliated William and Naomi Gorowitz Institute on Terrorism and Extremism. In 2010 the Gorowitz Institute honored William Bratton, noting the connection between his early training in hate crime policy in Boston and his later implementation of broken windows policing in New York.[28] As mentioned above, broken windows theory first formalized in New York quality-of-life policing in the gay enclave of the West Village. Both gay and straight residents collaborated with one of the policy's biggest advocates—the Guardian Angels, a controversial anti-crime vigilante group supported by then New York mayor Rudolph Giuliani—as they targeted loitering, noise, drugs, sex work, and gangs, and took aim at LGBT youth and trans women of color.

"Gay, Straight, Black, White, All United to Fight the Right!"

The activists who mobilized on behalf of Blue's represented a broad range of organizations.[29] This included members of Black and

---

28 "Top Cop William Bratton Honored by ADL for His Vision and Service," Anti-Defamation League press release, October 11, 2010, adl.org.

29 The most detailed academic treatment of the political response to the raid on Blue's can be found in Abram J. Lewis, "'Within the Ashes of Our Survival': Lesbian and Gay Antiracist Organizing in New York City, 1980–1984," Thinking Gender

White Men Together (BWMT), Dykes Against Racism Everywhere (DARE), the Coalition against Racism, Anti-Semitism, Sexism, and Heterosexism (CRASH), Salsa Soul Sisters, All-People's Congress, Harlem Metropolitan Community Church, Third World Lesbian and Gay Alliance, El Comité Homosexual Latinamericano, Lavender Left, and the New York Prostitutes Collective (which was associated with both Black Women for Wages for Housework and Wages Due Lesbians), among others. Many of these groups also joined the newly founded Coalition Against Police Repression.[30] The raid in late September 1982 was followed by another police raid in early October, considered by activists to be retaliation by the police for the attention they had garnered. With momentum continuing to build, over 1,100 people turned out to the organizers' biggest protest, on October 15, 1982. The issue was covered by the gay press nationwide, and San Francisco activists even held a solidarity rally.[31]

The focus of the protests was twofold: most immediately, activists sought to link the attack on Blue's to other challenges to gay and lesbian bars in the city as well as to new patterns of gentrification and policing. They highlighted, for example, how lesbian bars had been targeted for removal by the city's administrative strategies; both the Duchess and Déjà Vu, the latter of which had a large lesbian of color clientele, had been denied liquor licenses despite a lack of official complaints. Activists also protested police sweeps that profiled trans women of color for suspected prostitution in Greenwich Village, especially near the piers at the end of historic Christopher Street and up the West Side to the meatpacking district.[32] They connected the attacks on gay bars and trans

---

Papers, University of California, Los Angeles, available at escholarship.org.

30   "1000 Lesbians, Gays, Supporters March to Hit Cop Attacks on Black Gay Bar," *Workers World*, October 22, 1982, 6; New York Prostitute's Collective, Press Release, October 12, 1982. Both of these can be found in the International Gay Information Collection at the New York Public Library (hereafter IGIC) under Ephemera—Bars, Blue's Bar. See also Coalition Against Police Repression, "Fightback! Stop the Police," flyer, n/d, IGIC (under Ephemera—Organizations, Coalition Against Police Repression).

31   Ibid; "Bay Area Action Condemns Raid on NYC Black Gay Bar," *Workers World*, November 5, 1982, 9, IGIC (under Ephemera—Bars, Blue's Bar File).

32   Coalition Against Police Repression, "Stop the Arrests!" Flyer, IGIC (under

women with the denial of public housing to nontraditional family units, the enforcement of rigid anti-immigration laws, and the criminalization of prostitution, all of which were understood to be part and parcel of the gentrification of the city more generally.[33]

Activists' second focus was to tie these issues to the risks of an ascendant Right on a local and national scale. They named the threat of Ronald Reagan's proposed Family Protection Act, arguing that the ideal of the normative family was linked to efforts to "clean up" places like Times Square. And many activists, especially those associated with Left/socialist political parties, put the blame for the attack on Blue's squarely on newly elected mayor Edward Koch. Although a Democrat, Koch won the election with promises to use law-and-order and austerity tactics to facilitate the transformation of places such as Times Square. Like Reagan, his supposedly charismatic charm and populist appeal was part of the rise of neoliberal centrist coalitions in the early 1980s. In 1981, Koch praised Reagan at a press conference at the Waldorf Astoria, aligning himself against Jimmy Carter with his position on Israel and calling Reagan a "man of character." In exchange, the White House approvingly acknowledged Koch's lack of a strong opposition to massive federal cuts to city services.[34]

In later years, Koch would occupy a contradictory place in the political estimations of the gay community: he was unforgivably slow to respond to AIDS but was also an active public supporter of anti-discrimination legislation. In this context, the attack on Blue's and the political

---

Ephemera—Organizations, Coalition Against Police Repression); Dykes Against Racism Everywhere, Open Letter/Undated Statement (circa 1983), Lesbian Herstory Archives (hereafter LHA) (under DARE). Consistent with the dominant language of the time, trans women—as an expansive category—were referred to as "transvestites" and "transsexuals." This solidarity with trans women is a striking feature of these campaigns within the history of queer Left and lesbian-feminist organizing.

33   See, for example, Dykes Against Racism Everywhere, "How Do We Work?" n.d., LHA (under DARE); Dykes Against Racism Everywhere, public letter on behalf of the Anti-Police Abuse Coalition, 1984, LHA (under DARE).

34   Steven Weisman, "The Reagan–Koch Alliance," *New York Times*, March 17, 1981. For a personality comparison of Reagan and Koch that also notes their shared status as former liberals, see Norman Podhoretz, "Why Reagan and Koch Are the Most Popular Politicians in America," *New York Magazine*, April 6, 1981, 30–2.

response to it presented an opportunity to mobilize those lesbians and gay men who had become complacent about the issues affecting the most marginalized LGBT people, their distance from these issues well represented by the Mondale-headlined fundraiser. Activists emphasized that the attack on Blue's was more violent than the Stonewall raid had been, and that the targets of gentrification and policing who were not always LGBT-identified—such as sex workers, homeless people, and drug users—should also be included in LGBT political coalitions. Their approach contrasted with that of more mainstream gay organizations, who responded to the rise of the Right with solutions to reported heightening of street violence based in self-protection and "crime awareness."[35]

In the early 1980s, activists across the country adopted and refuted the merged terms of gay protection and gentrification. In San Francisco, Lesbians Against Police Violence (LAPV) staged a skit about the interaction of lesbian vulnerability, policing, and neighborhood transformation. Titled "Count the Contradictions," it was organized as a sequence of scenes in a gentrifying neighborhood in which the realization of opportunity for some foreclosed it for others: white lesbians calling for police protection from random street harassment that increased violence against working-class Latino men; multiple-adult lesbian households outpricing single mothers; gay men's desires for an affirmative, visible identity manifesting in private property; and gay developers' claims of group identity excluding gay men without the ability to afford the rent. LAPV members performed on street corners and hosted discussions and reading groups that explored changing policing strategies in the context of capitalist development, locating the vexed terms of safety as the key ground for debate.

Years later, the formalization of quality-of-life policing in New York and its application in laws such as "sit/lie" ordinances (which prohibit sitting or lying down in public spaces) in San Francisco and other California cities would also meet creative responses from social movements. In Greenwich Village, for example, where Bratton's new policy affected LGBT youth of color most directly, activists from groups

---

35 For example, see Gay People's Self-Protection Program, Sponsored by Chelsea Gay Association and Safety and Fitness Exchange, "New York Can Be a *Safe* Place!" IGIC (under Ephemera—Organizations, Chelsea Gay Association).

such as Fabulous Independent Educated Radicals for Community Empowerment (FIERCE) fought quality-of-life policing in an attempt to stall the hyper-development of a long-gentrified area. Among their most innovative tactics were protests in which demonstrators simply enacted prohibited acts: eating or playing cards while seated on street corners, drawing graffiti (on disposable objects), listening to music and having fun. Activists also participated in community meetings, despite official regulations stipulating that only those with residential—as opposed to use—claims on the neighborhood could participate.

Conclusion

For decades, those who have engaged in critical debate about gentrification instead of celebrating the process as a natural achievement of the market have been divided into two main camps: those who emphasize the significance of individual consumer choice and those who highlight the global dynamics of uneven economic development. Examining the role of gay men as motors of gentrification has been a key way to explore moral imperatives within a consumer landscape; this has also been the case in discussions of artists and others seen as occupying ambiguous class positions in the urban context. But as Neil Smith once argued, it was capital moving "back to the city" rather than the origins or preferences of individual new residents that most determined people's claims to place.[36]

In this way, LGBT populations should not be understood as the vanguard of gentrification or as uniquely vulnerable to the violence of policing. Such arguments restrict themselves to the framework of consumer choice and distill police violence as motivated by individual responses to singular categories of alterity. These assumptions are central to liberal critiques of gentrification and policing that maintain both as open to remediation. Rather, the correlation between gay identity and gentrification is most secured by those who capitalize on what they claim

36 Neil Smith, "Toward a Theory of Gentrification: A Back to the City Movement by Capital, Not People," *Journal of the American Planning Association* 45, no. 4 (1979), 538–48.

to be essential characteristics or conditions that are celebrated by the market. To repeat, mainstream gay political claims in the city emerged by expanding the distance—conceptual *and* spatial—between affirmative gay identity and the broad matrix of so-called deviances often associated with racialized poverty. This was facilitated by the claim that policing should focus on behavior (such as loitering) rather than status (such as homosexual). But that strategy did little to assist those who remained locked within the stronghold of criminalization's categorizations, releasing some without challenging one of their greater purposes—namely, to prime the city for private investment.

Here gay identity functions in opposition to *disorder*; the people marked for dispossession in the new economy may be targeted in the name of "gay safety." This is the material of quality-of-life policing: Kelling and Wilson's treatise is in many ways a rejection of the separation of status from behavior. As Allen Feldman writes, "Arrest is the political art of individualizing disorder."[37] These ideas are also in line with social science research and policy that treats poverty as a pathology that harms not only the individual but neighborhoods as well, justifying "cleanups" that provide profits to owners rather than resources to residents. Such research and policies underscore the central role liberal psychology has played in neoliberal policing that individualizes ideas of harm and protection. Today the idea of "safe space" so common in classroom and social service contexts can sometimes be, like broken windows theory, more about the perception of safety than anything else.

This analysis of the relationship between policing and gentrification has also been elaborated by activists such as James Credle, with whom I opened this essay and who was a member of Black and White Men Together (BWMT; later, Men of All Colors Together) in the 1980s. In general, radical anti-gentrification groups such as BWMT, DARE, LAPV, and CRASH fought gay participation in gentrification less by targeting individual consumer choice—DARE, for example, recognized the benefits of pooled resources among lesbians while warning against

---

37   Allen Feldman, *Formations of Violence: The Narrative of the Body and Political Terror in Northern Ireland* (Chicago: University of Chicago Press), 109. I am grateful to Ruth Wilson Gilmore, who first introduced me to this quotation in *Golden Gulag* (p. 235).

those who would capitalize on that shared identity for profit—and more by dedicating themselves to organizing around issues like policing (such as the raid on Blue's) that facilitated gentrification on the ground.

This multi-issue and multi-scale tactic currently characterizes a new generation of activism against order maintenance policing as it has taken form in policies across the United States and the world: whether in heightened ticketing in Ferguson, Missouri; stop and frisk in New York and Baltimore; or police–community partnerships in Chicago and Milwaukee. Political scientist Cathy Cohen recently described some of this activism—notably led by Black youth, and that she groups as part of a broad "black lives movement"—as among the most interesting examples of radical queer politics today. Her contention is based not only on the significant proportion of LGBT and queer-identified people in the movement's leadership, but also on the focus of these campaigns on how such policies seek to normalize and discipline kinship, gender, and everyday pleasures in ways inclusive of but not reducible to LGBT identity alone.[38]

In many of these campaigns in recent years, activists have shown how the regulation of behavior deemed to be non-normative can be tightly entwined with real estate interests. For example, in Milwaukee, Dontre Hamilton was shot to death by a police officer who had responded to a call from Starbucks workers who had supposedly followed company protocol and reported Hamilton's behavior as making them feel uncomfortable.[39] Hamilton had been sleeping in Red Arrow Park, and the placement of the café there is an example of the kind of public–private partnerships that Wisconsin governor Scott Walker had so prized when he was Milwaukee County executive.[40] In New York City, police killed

38   Cathy Cohen, "#DoBlackLivesMatter? From Michael Brown to CeCe McDonald on Black Death and LGBTQ Politics," Kessler Lecture, Center for Lesbian and Gay Studies, City University of New York, December 12, 2014. Also see Cathy J. Cohen and Sarah J. Jackson, "Ask a Feminist: A Conversation with Cathy Cohen on Black Lives Matter, Feminism, and Contemporary Activism," forthcoming in the summer 2016 issue of *Signs*.

39   This claim is based on the testimony of one of the Starbucks workers reported by the organization Occupy Riverwest and repeated by the local press. Her full testimony is available at occupyriverwest.com.

40   Harold A. Perkins, "The Production of Urban Vulnerability through

Akai Gurley in a stairwell of the Louis H. Pink Houses in East New York, one of Brooklyn's poorest neighborhoods and currently the site of rampant real estate speculation. The police cited the dangerous reputation of the complex, but little if any responsibility was assumed by the New York City Housing Authority, which failed to provide sufficient lighting in its stairwells.[41] And Eric Garner was killed by police in New York after suspicion of selling "loosies" (single cigarettes)—exactly the type of minor violation targeted by quality-of-life laws.[42]

In all of these cases, radical LGBT and queer activists were among those who organized in response, and they countered the claims of mainstream LGBT organizations that prioritize inclusion in the status quo over broad social and economic transformation. In the words of Cara Page of the Audre Lorde Project and Krystal Portalatin of FIERCE, the real threats are not those individuals whose lives are considered to be at a distance from dominant "norms," but rather:

> when banks are allowed to engage in predatory practices that target communities of color and force groups to remain in poverty; when Detroit can declare bankruptcy on a city of mostly black communities and then take away basic rights such as water; when corporations are allowed to abuse other countries and depress US economies; when the US military continues to back and support Israel's oppression of Palestinian people and land.[43]

Market-Based Parks Governance," *Cities, Nature, and Development: The Politics and Production of Urban Vulnerabilities*, eds. Sarah Dooling and Gregory Simon (Surrey, England: Ashgate Publishing, 2012).

41   Michael Wilson, "Officer's Errant Shot Kills Unarmed Brooklyn Man," *New York Times*, November 21, 2014.

42   For a discussion of the NYPD's targeting of the sale of single cigarettes as a way to combat "disorder" and of its role in the arrest of Eric Garner, see Al Baker, J. David Goodman, and Benjamin Mueller, "Beyond the Chokehold: The Path to Eric Garner's Death," *New York Times*, June 13, 2015.

43   See "Wake Up, Rise Up!" press release written by Cara Page, executive director of the Audre Lorde Project, and Krystal Portalatin, co-director of FIERCE, and cosigned by the Griot Circle, New York City Anti-Violence Project, Streetwise and Safe, and the Sylvia Rivera Law Project, December 3, 2014, available at fiercenyc.org.

In this way, activists continue to draw the connections between local and global acts of policing and dispossession, while tracing how the construction of social norms—and how they are made legible through the interplay of, in particular, race, gender, and sexuality—are central to this process. And, finally, they show how the promises of solidarity offer much more than those of safety, and provide a collective alternative to solutions defined within rather than against the market.

~

Christina B. Hanhardt is an associate professor in the Department of American Studies at the University of Maryland, College Park. She is the author of the book *Safe Space: Gay Neighborhood History and the Politics of Violence* (Duke, 2013).

4. ENDING BROKEN WINDOWS POLICING IN NEW YORK CITY: AN INTERVIEW WITH JOO-HYUN KANG

Jordan T. Camp and Christina Heatherton

Joo-Hyun Kang is the director of Communities United for Police Reform (CPR), a campaign to end discriminatory policing practices in New York, which comprises over sixty organizational members from all five boroughs. Members include the Audre Lorde Project, Brooklyn Movement Center, Bronx Defenders, Center for Constitutional Rights, CAAAV Organizing Asian Communities, DRUM South Asian Organizing Center, FIERCE, Justice Committee, Legal Aid Society, Make the Road NY, Malcolm X Grassroots Movement, New York Civil Liberties Union, Picture the Homeless, Streetwise and Safe, VOCAL-NY, and many others. Kang is a longtime organizer in New York City; she was a program director at Astraea Lesbian Foundation for Justice and the first staff member and director of the Audre Lorde Project, an organizing center for LGBTST (lesbian, gay, bisexual, two-spirit, and transgender) and gender-nonconforming communities of color.

Camp: Since 2012 CPR has led mass mobilizations in response to several high-profile police killings, such as the murders of Ramarley Graham and Eric Garner. Your demands include justice for the families of those slain by police and an end to broken windows policing. Why is ending broken windows policing key to your organizing response to police violence?

Kang: Many of us who are active now were influenced or mentored by the late Richie Perez. Richie was a former Young Lord and co-founder of the National Congress for Puerto Rican Rights' Justice Committee (now known as the Justice Committee). Richie used to say that police killings are just the tip of the iceberg. They are tragedies and must be organized around, but they are ultimately enabled by the daily abuses, disrespect, and human rights violations faced by our communities at the hands of NYPD officers that go unaddressed. When we don't deal with these daily abuses, it's no wonder that there's a lack of accountability in high-profile killings. Particular communities are targeted for disproportionate and discriminatory policing. The huge abuses of stop and frisk resulted from racial profiling, gender and sexual orientation profiling, profiling of people who are homeless and young, and anti-immigrant profiling. Back in 2011 there were close to 700,000 reported stops.

By targeting particular communities and going after minor offenses and minor infractions in those communities, police resources are dedicated to the mistaken theory that broken windows policing heads off violence. Hyper-aggressive enforcement of minor nonviolent infractions that targets communities of color doesn't make any of our communities safer. In reality, as community members and New Yorkers know, violence prevention has to be undertaken by all parts of the community. It's not only the police who are engaged in violence prevention. We believe it is more effective to build up community infrastructure to maintain safe communities than it is to rely solely on police.

Heatherton: The current CPR campaign against broken windows policing is being led by people of color, queer, transgender, gender-nonconforming, two-spirit, immigrant, homeless, and youth-led groups in the city. This is not the first time such an alliance has emerged against William Bratton–style policies. How were people confronting broken windows policing when it was first implemented in the 1990s, when Bratton was police commissioner?

Kang: At that time in the mid-1990s, when broken windows theory was formally introduced and branded "broken windows policing," there was a big public push to go after "quality of life" offenses. Grassroots organizations rooted in communities of color in New York came together to ask, "Whose quality of life are we focusing on?" It didn't seem like the quality of life of all New Yorkers was being uplifted. If that were the case we wouldn't have seen budget cuts around education. We wouldn't have seen budget cuts around health and human services. What we would have seen is a reinvestment in community infrastructure in all the different ways that contribute to safety. That includes housing, health care, education, and employment.

Back in the mid-1990s there was a grassroots coalition called the Coalition Against Police Brutality that included the Malcolm X Grassroots Movement, the National Congress for Puerto Rican Rights, CAAAV Organizing Asian Communities, and Audre Lorde Project. At different times there were also other organizations that made up the core, including Sista II Sista, Youth Force, and Forever in Struggle Together. Much of the work in that period was supporting families of those killed by the NYPD, educating our communities, mobilizing around racial violence, as well as organizing around specific cases of police brutality like the brutal beating of JaLea Lamot, a trans women, and her family by NYCHA (New York City Housing Authority) officers. We were also trying to promote this idea that in order for New Yorkers to have safety and quality of life, we needed to respect the dignity of all New Yorkers. After the rape and torture of Abner Louima by NYPD officers and the killing of Amadou Diallo in a hail of forty-one police bullets, those organizations pulled together a broader coalition, which at that point was called People Justice 2000—knowing that both cases would have trials in 2000 and that those moments would offer an opportunity to organize to expose the systemic racism and lack of police accountability that enabled both tragedies. Separate from those two cases, there was a multi-strategy campaign that included direct action as well as a courtroom strategy. Richie Perez, along with members of the Malcolm X Grassroots Movement and others in the Coalition Against Police Brutality, went to the Center for Constitutional Rights to ask that they file a lawsuit against the NYPD's stop-and-frisk practices and racial profiling that resulted in the killing of Amadou Diallo. We specifically targeted the Street Crimes Unit (SCU) on the legal side as well as in the street organizing because at that point SCU was the unit responsible for the most stops in New York. We knew that the people primarily being targeted were young people of color, the homeless, and others who are seen as marginalized, and that the reasons for the stops weren't legal. The stops were part of the broken windows strategy that targeted particular communities. The work that folks did in the late 1990s into the early 2000s was really trying to push back on that.

Heatherton: How has this long history of intersectional organizing in New York City impacted the most recent rounds of struggle? How, specifically, have questions of race, class, gender, and sexuality informed CPR's critique of police violence and state violence?

Kang: Whenever we're looking at a new rollout of NYPD policies —whether it's the version of broken windows being rebranded as "neighborhood policing" or ongoing stop-and-frisk abuses—what's important to us is being clear about and uplifting the experiences and perspectives of communities that are directly affected. We're trying to bring clarity across communities that young people of color who identify as LGBT or are gender-nonconforming are experiencing something very specific in particular parts of the city, such as the West Village. Trans Latinas in Jackson Heights are experiencing policing in a particular way. People who are homeless have different experiences in different parts of the city and yet the abuses that individuals face are very similar. Bringing that all together for us is what helps us understand the broader picture. It informs our strategy of ending discriminatory and abusive policing.

Since discriminatory and abusive policing is systemic, our strategy needs to be multi-pronged. For us that means we have to coordinate among different tactics, and we need to be creative in the tactics we use. We can't only rely on policy advocacy. Policy advocacy, as far as we're concerned, is a tool. It's a very important tool, but that's what it is. It's a tool that, if integrated as part of a community organizing strategy, can help strengthen organizations, build the power of communities, increase movement building, create broader awareness of the problem and potential solutions, and get more New Yorkers engaged. Our broader strategy includes training people to document and observe police misconduct, also known as "copwatch." There are copwatch teams that our groups—particularly the Malcolm X Grassroots Movement and the

Justice Committee—coordinate across the city. Our member groups do "Know Your Rights" trainings throughout the city with a framework that looks at what we call "the three Rs." We look at not only what people's *rights* are and what laws govern police interactions, but also what *reality* people of color experience regardless of their rights, and what our *responsibilities* are individually and collectively to address that. This is also why we incorporate civic engagement work, research, litigation, legal support and communications work into the broader strategy.

We know that the deep crisis of police violence and lack of police accountability doesn't exist only in New York. It's national. What we've seen in the past year is a growing awareness of this crisis, but it's not a new crisis. We know that it will be a very long, protracted struggle to truly transform conditions so that all New Yorkers can be safe and be treated with dignity and respect.

Camp: Mayor Bill de Blasio successfully appealed to New Yorkers' frustration with the NYPD's racist policing. In fact, he was one of several candidates who campaigned to end stop-and-frisk abuses. Yet, early on in his administration, he rehired police commissioner William Bratton, who had held the position twenty years before under Rudolph Guiliani. Bratton has continued broken windows policing while asserting that it is entirely distinct from the policy of stop and frisk. How has CPR responded to Bratton's return, and what do you make of Bratton's attempt to distinguish between broken windows policing and stop and frisk?

Kang: The commissioner's attempt to make a distinction between stop and frisk and broken windows policing is pretty ludicrous. Discriminatory stop-and-frisk abuses come directly out of the framework of broken windows theory that the NYPD has employed for the past two decades. It didn't fall from the sky. It's part and parcel of a broader strategy that relies on discriminatory and abusive targeting of particular communities. When we look at the specifics of how broken windows is carried out, it's basically the selective police enforcement of regulations against minor offenses—nonviolent offenses—that disproportionately impacts particular communities. One example is riding your bike on the sidewalk. If you're riding your bike on the sidewalk in Bedford-Stuyvesant you're more likely to get a ticket, maybe even get arrested, than if you are riding your bike on the sidewalk just a few miles down in Park Slope in Brooklyn.[1] It's the same thing with open container violations—having alcohol in open containers in public. People have been ticketed on their own stoops of brownstones in Brooklyn, for example, for having a can of beer in front of their own homes. In Central Park, you're generally not going to see folks being ticketed or hassled by the NYPD for having a picnic with glasses of champagne. Part of our job is to point out what this kind of discriminatory and abusive treatment is, why it doesn't contribute to the safety of New Yorkers, and to end these practices.

Camp: Recently, CPR has been campaigning against the city's budget proposal to add 1,300 new police officers; you've pointed out that the NYPD already constitutes the largest police force in the country. Why has CPR been opposing this proposal? How else could the city use its resources to improve the safety and security of the poor and people of color?

Kang: Unfortunately, this was not a victory for us since they did decide to increase the NYPD head count by 1,300. They also civilianized 400 additional positions, so additional desk duty cops will be moved to the streets. Even so, what we are still trying to achieve in New York City is an improvement to safety. This is a multi-pronged and long-term effort.

We can't really talk about improving safety without addressing material conditions. This is what we did when the plan to hire 1,000 new NYPD officers was first unveiled. We identified other places in the city budget that needed to be increased that could contribute to safety in a better way. We included things like fully funding summer youth employment, which the current budget does not do. We also advocated for increasing the amount of truly affordable housing, not "affordable housing"

---

1   Bedford-Stuyvesant is a historically Black working-class neighborhood in New York City; Park Slope is a neighborhood with a much higher proportion of white and wealthy people.

based on abstract numbers that don't actually relate to what most New Yorkers make and how much it costs to live in the city. We included full employment, not only for young people but also for adults. Finally, we included guidance counselors, arts and sports programs, fully funding transformative justice and other kinds of programs in all the schools. All of this, we think, would contribute to a healthy and safe New York more than increasing the head count of the NYPD.

Part of the challenge now is that there is a lack of oversight over the increased head count and also over the 400 civilianized positions. New Yorkers know that officers are often placed on desk duty for specific reasons—some of them, for example, have abusive histories and misconduct claims filed against them. Desk duty is where people are often assigned after civilian complaints have been lodged. We're very concerned that there is no public record of which officers are being moved from desk to street.

Heatherton: I'd like to invite you to reflect on CPR's biggest struggles as well as the biggest victories that you've encountered when organizing against police violence. What can organizers across the country learn from your experience in New York?

Kang: Those of us in New York are learning all the time from organizers around the country. I definitely want to be clear that we don't think we're the only game in the country on this. It's really important for us to maintain regular communication with other campaigns in the US because we all have a lot to learn from each other and share with each other. We also really need to move some national-level strategy. Lack of police accountability is a national problem, and communities are impacted similarly across the country.

We're a pretty new campaign. We launched in the early part of 2012, so we're about three and a half years old. So far we've been able to help to build a cohesive coordinated campaign across sectors throughout New York City. Before 2012, fights against police abuse in New York City were largely in different silos. The legal organizations might have been communicating with each other, and the policy advocates did some work together, and some of the grassroots organizations worked together, but there was very little crossover across sector in terms of trying to develop a coordinated strategy. We've not only developed a coordinated strategy, we also center and prioritize the perspectives and leadership of directly affected communities. That's something that's central to the way we do our work.

The types of solutions we're trying to uplift, whether we're talking about copwatch and Know Your Rights or about defining community safety so that we're accounting for the core conditions that make our communities less safe or about policy solutions, are coming from grass-roots activists and directly affected community members from across the city. The legislative and policy initiatives that we support are coming from directly affected people saying, "This is a problem that needs to be fixed"—and then framing what the policy fix should be.

There are a few victories I'd like to reflect on. One of the specific changes we've helped to achieve is that reported stops have decreased dramatically. This is a direct result of New Yorkers basically saying "Enough! The NYPD's stop-and-frisk program is the largest racial pro-filing program in the country. This is clearly discriminatory and abusive and it needs to stop."

We believe the huge reduction in reported stops was a result of some of the tactics and strategies we were able to coordinate. The city council's passage of the Community Safety Act (which was two laws that established an NYPD oversight framework and which became law after a big campaign to override the veto of then-mayor Michael Bloomberg) was a huge accomplishment because it was very grassroots-driven. There really hadn't been much legislation related to the NYPD in the past several decades by the city council so the fact that grassroots organizations like Picture the Homeless, Make the Road New York, Streetwise and Safe, copwatch teams, and others helped make this victory real is really significant.

The court victory that Center for Constitutional Rights and the plaintiffs were able to achieve in *Floyd et al. v. City of New York*—the big federal class action stop-and-frisk lawsuit—was very connected to the attorneys' work in the courtroom but also the huge community involvement. Community members from across New York City packed the courts every day for nine weeks and held actions in neighborhoods and in front of the courthouse pretty consistently. In fact, a number of the key plaintiffs and witnesses were members of different organizations, including the lead plaintiff David Floyd, who is a member of the Malcolm X Grassroots Movement. In fact, members of MXGM were also lead plaintiffs in the prior Daniels lawsuit.

More recently, thanks to the leadership and tireless work over the past several months of families of New Yorkers who were killed by police and our members and partners who stood by them, Governor Cuomo was pushed to sign an executive order authorizing the New York State Attorney General's office to act as special prosecutor in cases of police killings. This recent victory is something we reflect on as being decades in the making. It was a core demand of families whose loved ones were killed by the NYPD in the 1990s, including Iris Baez, the mother of Anthony Baez, and Margarita Rosario, the mother of Anthony Rosario and aunt of Hilton Vega—co-founders of Parents Against Police Brutality. Iris and Margarita, along with the families of Eric Garner, Ramarley Graham, Shantel Davis, Kimani Gray, Mohamed Bah, Sean Bell, Jayson Tirado, Alberta Spruill, and others came together in the past several months, organizing with the Justice Committee, one of our leadership organizations, to be part of and help to lead a tightly coordinated campaign to secure a special prosecutor in New York State.

There's much more work to be done, and no one is under the illusion that any of these victories are a final solution. What they represent are steps to changing conditions in our neighborhoods, building our collective skills and power to create the city we want to live in, where everyone is treated with dignity and respect.

Across the board, we've been able to implement strategies in different ways by centering the work, experiences, perspective, and leadership of directly affected people and grassroots community-based organizations. In the long term, our theory of change relies on the idea that we've got to build strong, fighting community infrastructure—not only in terms of core services needed in different communities, but really an engaged and politically developed core of folks in different organizations throughout New York City in different neighborhoods who are going to be able to maintain and sustain a campaign and work against police violence regardless of what other citywide organizational forms exist.

5. THE BALTIMORE UPRISING

Anjali Kamat

On May 1, 2015, a small tense crowd standing across from Baltimore's city hall erupted in hoots and cheers, quickly followed by tears and warm embraces. Marilyn Mosby, the newly elected state's attorney, had just announced criminal charges against all six police officers involved in the death of twenty-five-year-old Freddie Gray. In a city rife with unsolved murders, it wasn't his death that was novel. But the possibility that his alleged killers—the police—might be brought to justice was remarkably unusual. Between 2010 and 2014, 109 people died in police custody in Maryland, and criminal charges were brought against police officers in only two of the cases.[1] In a city governed with impunity, Mosby's announcement was a significant victory.

Raw emotions spilled onto the streets. For the rest of the weekend, the run-down West Baltimore intersection of Pennsylvania and North Avenues, the site of tense clashes with heavily armed riot police just days before, turned into the epicenter of spontaneous citywide celebrations. A system that had betrayed the hopes of generations of African Americans seemed, at long last, to be responding to the demands of a popular movement: "To the people of Baltimore and demonstrators across America, I heard your call: No justice, no peace!" Mosby declared.[2] Of course, everyone knew the charges might be dropped and

---

1   "ACLU Briefing Paper on Deaths in Police Encounters in Maryland, 2010–2014," ACLU of Maryland, March 2015, available at aclu-md.org.

2   Transcript of Baltimore state's attorney Marilyn J. Mosby's statement on Freddie Gray, May 1, 2015 available at time.com.

that the powerful police union could still win their case, but for one brief moment, the customary cynicism and pain were set aside. The mere prospect of justice felt like a benediction. And that Sunday, longtime community activist Reverend Heber Brown, III, titled his electrifying sermon at Pleasant Hope Baptist Church "This Can't Be Real!"

Gray was a well-loved young man who grew up in the dilapidated Gilmore Homes projects in Baltimore's poorest Black neighborhood, Sandtown-Winchester. Life here is precarious by design; decade upon decade of residential segregation, criminalization, and neoliberal economic policies have entrenched inequality and elevated every social indicator to levels far above the national average. With 20 percent unemployment and 31 percent poverty, one in four juveniles has experienced arrest, one in four buildings is abandoned, lead paint violations are four times higher than the citywide rate, and the rates of domestic violence, shootings, and homicides are among the highest in the city. Deindustrialization, compounded by disinvestment, the crack epidemic, displacement through urban renewal programs, and the subprime mortgage crisis decimated the wealth and well-being of communities like this. While the city poured hundreds of millions of dollars into redeveloping its harbor district and building new sports stadiums to attract tourists, neighborhoods like Sandtown-Winchester were left to rot.[3] Since 1991, funding for programs supporting young people in Baltimore—recreation centers, parks, libraries, summer jobs, and after-school programs—has been either frozen or slashed. In the same period, by contrast, the budget of the Baltimore Police Department tripled, and tax subsidies to corporations have increased.[4] One glaring exception to the disinvestment in poor communities is incarceration: Maryland allocates $17 million a year just to incarcerate people from Sandtown-Winchester in state prisons.[5]

---

3   Lawrence Brown, "Down to the Wire: Displacement and Disinvestment in Baltimore City (the 2015 State of Black Baltimore)," unpublished paper. Brown is an assistant professor of public health at Morgan State University.

4   Lester Spence, "Corporate Welfare Is Draining Baltimore," *Boston Review*, May 14, 2015.

5   Justice Policy Institute and Prison Policy Initiative, "The Right Investment? Corrections Spending in Baltimore City," 2015.

Indeed, for residents of Sandtown-Winchester, there was no shortage of reasons to be enraged by a system that showed them little respect. But it was Gray's arrest—moments of which were captured on a cellphone camera and went viral—and his subsequent death a week later that sparked a spontaneous rebellion that would come to be known as the Baltimore uprising.

When Gray died on April 19 from a spinal cord injury sustained in police custody, all the anger and sadness that had built up for years in this deeply divided city exploded. Gray's friends rushed to the local police station demanding answers, and in the days that followed, hundreds and then thousands of people—seasoned community organizers and first-time protesters alike—took to the streets in response to yet another Black man dead after an encounter with the police. The city's initial response appeared tone-deaf: the officers involved in Gray's arrest were placed on paid leave, and, as the protests swelled, the police focused on safeguarding Baltimore's symbols of wealth and power—Inner Harbor, Camden Yards, and City Hall.

The breaking point came on April 27, hours after Gray was laid to rest. Just as the school day was ending, riot police appeared in full force near the working-class Mondawmin Mall, citing rumors on social media about a gang truce and an alleged plot to attack the police. Dominique Stevenson, an activist with the American Friends Service Committee who lives across the street from the mall, described the police presence to me as a "clear provocation."[6] When the police shut down the public transportation system near the mall, effectively preventing students from getting home, the tinderbox exploded.

By that evening, Sandtown, as it is known locally, was on fire, with police cars, a drug store, and various storefronts set ablaze. Politicians denounced the violence as a riot that needed to be controlled immediately: the governor called in the National Guard, the mayor declared a curfew, and the media largely focused on the looting of liquor and drug stores and the cost of the property damage. But for people who lived and worked in the community, many of whom—elders, church leaders, activists, and gang members alike—instantly came together to try and contain the violence, it was an understandable, if regrettable, outburst

6   Author interview with Dominique Stevenson, April 28, 2015.

by a generation brought up on despair and systemic neglect. "It was the community saying we've had enough," Brown told me, as we sat in a small garden outside his church. The protesters were not, he emphasized, "thugs" or "criminals," as the mayor and President Obama had initially described them. "We've been down in Annapolis, we've been at the city council, trying to get reforms. We've pursued every one of the avenues we're told to pursue in order to see changes come about. And we've gotten nothing significant. It's unfortunate that only after buildings were burned and cars were smashed, only then did people start listening," he said.[7]

On May 6, 2015, Baltimore mayor Stephanie Rawlings-Blake announced that she had requested the Department of Justice to initiate a civil rights investigation into the "patterns and practices" of the Baltimore Police Department, citing the "fractured relationship" between the police and the community and the need to restore trust in the police. The mayor's announcement was welcomed, but many wondered why it had taken so long. After all, the breakdown in trust between the police and Baltimore's African American community hadn't begun with Gray's death.

In Sandtown, unsurprisingly, opinions of the police have been overwhelmingly negative for as long as people can remember. Gray's friends, some of whom starting having run-ins with the police as early as middle school, laughed bitterly when I asked if they trusted the police. "Their job isn't to protect us; it's to come here and arrest us," said Brandon Ross, Gray's godbrother. "If they wanted to protect us, how do we have all these murders?" Another friend complained that the majority of the officers seem to be skilled only at humiliating, harassing, and beating people up. A third complained that most officers are outsiders, rather than members of the community they police; speaking over the loud din of the police helicopters circling overhead—an almost constant presence in the skies above Sandtown—he compared them to an occupying force.[8] Indeed, only a quarter of the city's police officers live within city limits, and that number is even lower (13 percent) for white officers.[9]

7   Author interview with Dr. Heber Brown, III, May 5, 2015.
8   Author interview with Brandon Ross and friends, May 27, 2015.
9   Nate Silver, "Most Police Don't Live in the Cities They Serve," August 20,

Living in a high-crime neighborhood notorious for its drug markets is like being in a fishbowl, Ross said. People like him don't have a fighting chance when it comes to questioning police tactics: "It ain't cops against robbers. It's cops against the community."

Police harassment and abuse in Baltimore aren't restricted to the city's poorest neighborhoods. Across the city, many African Americans have experienced unnecessary police stops and searches, unexplained harassment and abuse, and even illegal arrests. Abdul Jaami Salaam is a youth counselor who lives with his wife and three-year-old son on a quiet tree-lined street near Morgan State University. He was stopped in 2013 by two plainclothes policemen while driving home with his toddler and a trunk full of groceries. Officers Nicholas Chapman and Jorge Bernardez-Ruiz dragged him out of the car, threw him to the ground, beat him, and kept him in jail for forty-eight hours—allegedly for not wearing his seatbelt. Salaam filed a complaint with the Internal Affairs division of the police department but never received a response.

Two weeks later, the same two officers were patrolling the streets in the same neighborhood and pulled over an unlicensed cab operator named Tyrone West. West didn't submit easily after being dragged out of the car by his dreadlocks; a scuffle ensued, West was pepper-sprayed, and nearly a dozen more officers appeared on the scene, one of whom sat on West's back until he was no longer breathing. The police report claims he died of a heart attack. West's family members, bolstered by eyewitness statements, have refused this explanation and accuse the police of covering up a murder. Since West's death, his sister Tawanda Jones, an elementary school teacher, has led weekly protests calling for an independent investigation into her brother's death and for his killers to be prosecuted. Two years later, the family is still waiting. Meanwhile, Officers Chapman and Bernardez-Ruiz are still on the force.

Few in Baltimore are more familiar with the uphill battle for justice than Jones's and Salaam's attorney, A. Dwight Pettit, Jr. Pettit has sued dozens of police officers for misconduct and excessive force and estimates that his city leads the country in per capita incidents of police violence, owing in part to the lack of accountability for police abuse. When pushed, the city prefers to settle and, since 2011, has paid over six

2014, available at fivethirtyeight.com.

million dollars in over 100 police misconduct claims. [10] The errant officers themselves, however, rarely pay a price for their actions. According to Latoya Williams, a lawyer at Pettit's firm, the Baltimore police have "literally no one to answer to" and are rarely taken off the force in response to abuse complaints. [11]

The scale of the crisis goes far beyond a few bad officers. Pettit and Williams blame the widespread abuse on a "culture of lawlessness" within the police department that worsened markedly during the tenure of Mayor Martin O'Malley (1999–2007), who imposed a broken windows–style "zero tolerance" policy. As part of the war on drugs, police were empowered to make mass arrests for small violations. The rate of arrests was so high that nearly one in six Baltimore residents was arrested in 2005—100,000 people arrested in a city of 640,000. [12] This policy, according to Pettit, led to sweeping arrests without any probable cause and created a systemic attitude among the police that they "did not have to adhere to the constitution." [13]

Maryland state delegate Jill Carter, who represents West Baltimore and has often been the lone voice in Annapolis advocating police reform, agrees with Pettit, describing O'Malley as "savagely wrong on criminal justice issues." [14] At the height of enforcement of the zero-tolerance policy, it was common, according to Carter, for police to go to working-class

---

10   Mark Puente and Doug Donovan, "Brutality Lawsuits Continue in Baltimore, Site of Freddie Gray Death," *Baltimore Sun*, April 22, 2015. The total amount is relatively low because of a Maryland state law that caps monetary awards for claims against local governments at $200,000 per person.

11   Author interview with Latoya Williams, June 4, 2015.

12   The following year the ACLU and the NAACP sued the Baltimore Police Department for routinely making arrests without probable cause. In 2010, the city settled the lawsuit and publicly ended the policy. O'Malley, who was a Democratic candidate for the 2016 presidential election, has claimed never to have promoted aggressive policing and instead credits his policies with the drop in the murder rate. But many, including journalist David Simon, have refuted his claims. Simon, the creator of HBO's *The Wire*, alleges that the drop in the crime rate was creatively manufactured through "juking the stats." See Bill Keller, "David Simon on Baltimore's Anguish," Marshall Project, April 29, 2015, available at themarshallproject.org.

13   Author interview with A. Dwight Pettit, Jr., May 7, 2015.

14   Author interview with Jill P. Carter, June 4, 2015.

African American neighborhoods and simply arrest everyone they saw outside. According to the ACLU, in 2010, 92 percent of arrests for marijuana possession in Baltimore were of African Americans, even though rates of marijuana use are roughly equal among whites and Blacks. The police department evaluated officers' performances according to how many arrests they made, Carter explains, under the theory that "the more people we arrest, the less crime there will be, because no one will be on the streets." The results are unsurprising: an explosive rise in incarceration, a generation growing up with criminal records, the dismantling of communities, the shattering of trust in the police, and a police force trained to focus on the quantity and not the quality of arrests.[15]

"Numbers, number, numbers. They're so skewed on the numbers game in Baltimore, you're never going to get quality arrests, you're never going to get anybody above street level." Joe Crystal is a former detective in the Baltimore Police Department's elite counter-narcotics unit. We were lying prone on the rooftop of a tall residential building looking over a low-rise housing project across the street. This was one of Crystal's surveillance spots, where he would spend hours watching small drug deals and waiting to see if it could lead him to somewhere bigger.

"Look, over there, you see those guys on the corner? And the other guy walking towards them? Watch closely." Crystal wanted to show me how easy it was to spot a deal from this vantage point. Within minutes there was an exchange and the man who had approached left quickly. "See? I told you! They always walk faster after a deal, that's how you know." We watched as the man disappeared down a narrow path and then behind a corner, his pace hastening with every step. He wouldn't waste time arresting anyone here, Crystal said. "Wait and watch and investigate, that's policing, not this numbers game."[16]

Crystal, the son of two New York City police officers, joined the Baltimore Police Department in 2008 and rose quickly through the ranks. He loved his job and the pace of life in Baltimore and was an avid fan of the HBO's *The Wire*. But in September 2014, he was forced out

---

15   American Civil Liberties Union, "The War on Marijuana in Black and White," ACLU Foundation, May 2013.

16   Author interview with Joe Crystal, May 9, 2015.

after blowing the whistle on police misconduct. On October 27, 2011, Crystal had watched a veteran sergeant allow an off-duty officer to take Antoine Green, a small-time drug dealer they had just chased down and arrested, out of the police van and back into the house where they had apprehended him. There he heard the officer beat the handcuffed Green and watched as they brought him back out, disheveled and limping. When Crystal complained to another sergeant, he was warned to stay silent and told that his career "wouldn't be worth shit" if he snitched. But Crystal couldn't let it go. This wasn't the kind of policing he wanted to do.

He spoke to a friend at the State's Attorney's Office, and the two of them pressed charges. Over the next two and half years, Crystal was routinely harassed and threatened by his colleagues, treated like a pariah for snitching, and abandoned by the police union (who chose instead to publicly defend the sergeant whose misconduct he had reported). When he called for backup, his calls were ignored. Someone left a dead rat on his car. The message was clear, and after a jury found both the sergeant and the officer guilty, Crystal and his wife moved as far away as they could. They now live in rural Florida, and Crystal works as a security guard for a fraction of the pay he got in Baltimore.

Cyrstal has no regrets, and his experience has made him empathize with people in Baltimore who don't trust the police. "I can relate," he said, adding that testifying against the police was the scariest thing he's ever done. "Across the board, there's no accountability: they just turn a blind eye and sweep things under the rug."

Crystal is a rare breed: a cop with a conscience, and one who's willing to pay a heavy price for breaking the infamous blue wall of silence. He's the kind of cop people on the streets of Baltimore respect and admire and many would love to have return.[17] But while scanning every visible corner of the housing project, tracking the movements of people from twenty floors above and seeking discernible patterns in their actions, even Crystal viewed everyone in the crosshairs of his binoculars as an object of suspicion.

---

17   See, for example, J Broody's petition on Change.org to reinstate Crystal, available at change.org/p/the-baltimore-city-police-department-repair-community-relations-and-rehire-joe-crystal?

A car pulled up on the far corner; a man approached it deliberately and leaned casually over the driver's window. A few minutes later a young child ran up to the man by the car, and then back into a building. "He's probably the runner, delivering the drugs," Crystal said. At that moment an elderly couple emerged from the car, arms full of grocery bags, and walked into the projects. "Oops," he said, as his eyes settled on a new target. He pointed to the right at two boys sauntering down an empty sidewalk, patches of green sprouting up through its cracks. "Those two, I'll bet they have something on them. Look at how they're walking. Like they've got something to hide."

Crystal emphasized that he would never arrest anyone simply based on these unsubstantiated suspicions. But he's seen police in Baltimore arrest people on less, he said, what with the pressure on officers to get as many arrests as possible. And his candid reactions to the people on the sidewalk below were an unexpected window into the zero-tolerance style of policing, demonstrating how easily a community can be stripped of all nuances and framed in a single, unforgiving light.

Doing police work in Baltimore (as in most American cities) still relies on the broken windows model and, as a result, the hyper-surveillance of one community in particular: working-class African Americans. When the police are trained to watch for certain suspicious behaviors, and they primarily watch people from one community, and those behaviors considered suspicious include walking too quickly or standing for too long, sitting alone too quietly or hanging out too noisily with others, driving too fast or running too suddenly, then every move made by members of this community can easily conjure up the subtext of a larger drug deal, the context for an unfolding crime, a pretext for arrest, probable cause.

This is how an entire community can be criminalized, and could reveal in part why Gray was chased down, beaten, "folded up like a pretzel," and arrested outside the Gilmore Homes on that fateful morning of April 12, 2015, when all he had done was make eye contact with a police officer and then run as fast as he could.[18]

*   *   *

---

18   Author interview with Kevin Moore, an eyewitness to Gray's arrest who filmed it on his cellphone.

The tragic death of Freddie Gray and the uprising it spawned exposed so much of the systemic racism, inequality, and police violence in Baltimore to national scrutiny that it has created small but significant openings for change. The six police officers involved in Gray's death were formally indicted in June 2015, despite a smear campaign against Mosby's charges by the police union. When Attorney General Loretta Lynch visited Baltimore to investigate the police department, grassroots activists working to end police brutality, including Tawanda Jones and Heber Brown, met with her. Whereas in the spring of 2015 the Maryland state legislature rejected seventeen bills introduced by Delegate Carter to reform the criminal justice system and reduce the oversize influence of the police union, there appears, at the start of 2016, to be an appetite for some modifications. But until the broader culture of police impunity and the systematic criminalization of Black lives is addressed and changed, alongside a fundamental transformation of the economic priorities of the city to remedy the deep structural inequalities in Baltimore, the broad constellation of factors leading to the rebellion remain unchanged. Perhaps it will soon be time for another uprising.

~

Anjali Kamat is a journalist with *Fault Lines*, a current affairs documentary program on Al Jazeera America and Al Jazeera English. Her film on police killings in Baltimore was first broadcast on Al Jazeera America on June 17, 2015. The views expressed here are hers alone.

6. TOTAL POLICING AND THE GLOBAL SURVEILLANCE EMPIRE TODAY: AN INTERVIEW WITH ARUN KUNDNANI

Jordan T. Camp and Christina Heatherton

Arun Kundnani is the author of The Muslims Are Coming: Islamophobia, Extremism, and the Domestic War on Terror *(Verso, 2014) and has written extensively on topics such as race, Islamophobia, political violence, and surveillance. A former editor of the London-based journal* Race & Class, *Kundnani currently teaches in the Department of Media, Culture, and Communication at New York University.*

Heatherton: Broken windows policing and community policing are often presented as domestic issues. Your work forces us to understand these policing models in the expanding context of counterterrorism. For someone new to these questions, how would you describe US policing as a global issue?

Kundnani: When I was researching the book *The Muslims Are Coming*, I interviewed FBI agents working on counterterrorism in different parts of the US. It became clear that their work could only be understood within a global context. For example, there are a number of people who have military backgrounds and have served in the war on terror in Iraq, Afghanistan, Somalia, and so forth. Inside their field offices, there are clocks on the wall set to each of the US time zones as well as to the times in Iraq and Afghanistan. These give you a sense of the mental geography in which they are working. Agents in counterterrorism investigations will also accompany the military on raids in Iraq and Afghanistan. So even though the FBI is meant to be a domestic law enforcement agency it has this global footprint. You see the same thing with the New York Police Department, which has offices around the world.

Looking at the infrastructure of policing and the flows of data being collected within the US, it is clear that they are completely integrated within global structures of surveillance. This has been made apparent with the Edward Snowden revelations.[1] There are also multiple examples of surveillance technologies developed for use in Iraq and Afghanistan which then flow back for domestic use in the US: things like social network analysis software, sensor technologies, or drones with the capacity to suck up wi-fi data. These technologies are now going to be used in the policing of protests in the US, and so forth. These are some ways in which the US military's global footprint and domestic law enforcement are connected.

Camp: NYPD commissioner William Bratton recently announced the creation of a new counterterrorism unit called the "strategic response group," which he describes as "designed for dealing with events like our recent protests or incidents like Mumbai or what just happened in Paris."[2] How do counterinsurgency and "counter-radicalization" inform domestic policing?

Kundnani: The notion of radicalization has become the main way in which counterterrorism is understood in the US. It blurs the distinction between what might conventionally be described as criminal activity and what might conventionally be defined as expressive activity, which is supposed to be protected by the First Amendment. In this blurring, Muslim religious and political expression are deemed to be signs of future terrorist risk. This demonstrates a shift away from "reasonable suspicion" that someone is involved in crime as a basis for investigation. We're moving away from that to a notion of "risk" and trying to determine what kind of risks certain populations represent. Within

---

1   Laura Poitras, Marcel Rosenbach, Michael Sontheimer, and Holger Stark, "How the NSA Helped Turkey Kill Kurdish Rebels," *The Intercept*, August 31, 2014.

2   Quoted in J. David Goodman, "Bratton Says Terrorism and Protests Will Be Handled by Separate Police Units," *New York Times*, February 2, 2015.

this model, dissent becomes criminalized in the name of national security, and the term "terrorism" becomes a means of criminalizing various kinds of political opposition, dissent, or insurgency.

The new counterterrorism unit under Bratton likewise assumes an overlap between protest and acts of spectacular political violence. Of course, the violent events he was referring to—the attack on Charlie Hebdo in Paris in 2015 and the Lashkar-e-Taiba attack on Mumbai in 2008—are rare. In the absence of having much to do, this unit will inevitably be spending its time policing protests. It will be doing so with the legitimacy of counterterrorism, which gives it additional powers to criminalize. Of course, this is nothing new. There is a long history of policing in the US operating through a counterinsurgency logic that essentially sees protest as a kind of warfare. This goes back to COINTELPRO and all the other kinds of linked strategies to criminalize the American Indian Movement, Puerto Rican nationalists, the Civil Rights Movement, and so forth.[3]

Camp: In a recent article co-authored with Deepa Kumar, you explain how the NYPD's aggressive racialized surveillance of Muslim Americans has authorized monitoring of all political activities, reviving Cold War strategies that criminalize dissent. What links can you draw between NYPD intelligence units and the history of countersubversion?

Kundnani: In the late nineteenth century, the NYPD had Red Squads dedicated to the political policing of the Left. In post-9/11 New York, there is a clear continuity in practices such as the construction of vast databases of information on people's activities, surveillance of communities for their purported ideologies, the use of informants, and the deployment of agents provocateurs to criminalize legitimate political activity. What Deepa Kumar and I are saying is that there is a recent history of these practices in relation to Muslim Americans, but also that there are continuities going back to the policing of Black protest; the policing

---

3   Ward Churchill and Jim Vander Wall, *The COINTELPRO Papers: Documents from the FBI's Secret Wars against Dissent in the United States* (Cambridge: South End Press, 2002).

of labor, particularly through the first half of the twentieth century; and the policing of various kinds of anti-imperialist movements. Every time these things happen we tend to think they are unprecedented, so explaining that history was important to us.

We also wanted to demonstrate that this kind of surveillance, which comes out of political policing, is also a means through which race itself is reproduced. By defining a community as "suspect," you construct a racial lens through which that community is viewed. There's a very important book by criminologist Paddy Hillyard called *Suspect Community*. Hillyard looked at the experience of the Irish in Britain in the 1970s and 1980s and discovered that the Irish "community" in England did not pre-exist police surveillance but was itself constituted through the interrogation process, both in the minds of the police and of their targets. The police picked up people who happened to be Irish, interrogated them and found out who their relatives and friends were, and then worked their way through those networks. Eventually, this method of investigation produced in the minds of the police a picture of the "community" as a network of suspicious persons linked together by various social relationships. At the same time, this experience of policing also bound together those targeted as a community with a shared experience of being rounded up. Hillyard's point is that the community is forged in the police cells. The surveillance practices of the police are integral to the construction and reproduction of the Irish as a racial group. That, I think, is something that can be generalized.

What it means to be a Muslim in New York now is in part defined by the experience of being an object of this surveillance gaze, which is also a kind of racialized gaze. This is what is linking together what would otherwise be very different experiences of being, say, an African American Muslim in Harlem, or a suburban Pakistani Muslim. There's not much that links these people until they are lumped together by all being under surveillance by the NYPD. This is simplifying things a little, but I do think there's something important to be said about how surveillance actually creates a racialized identity.

Heatherton: The war on terror has devastated many innocent lives, particularly those of people profiled as Muslim. Yet, as many organizers have argued, the emphasis on innocent victims has also narrowed the discussion and produced mixed results. Efforts to clear people of guilt who "do not deserve" state repression can unwittingly reinforce the idea that some people do deserve such treatment. Can you discuss the strengths and the weaknesses of the innocent victim narrative?

Kundnani: There's an obvious tension. There is a temptation to say that in order to reach a mainstream audience, we need to find a kind of "perfect victim." But when you look at who's being criminalized domestically in the war on terror as far as Muslims are concerned, more profound questions are raised beyond those of innocence or guilt. We don't have a very good grasp of what is essentially a political issue. We can imagine that terrorists are all evil fanatics driven by some kind of religious madness, but by and large the people who are getting sucked into this are teenagers who are not especially religious. They have a narrative that the West is at war with Islam, and they believe that they should be combatants in that conflict. Until we comprehend that framework of militarized identity politics, we're looking for a notion of religious fanaticism that actually has little to do with terrorism.

Camp: Your book describes how the fantasies of state intellectuals have produced the very thing they purport to confront. Can you explain?

Kundnani: This is the key point. We are producing the very thing that we think we are fighting. This happens in at least two ways: either through the use of informants to entrap people who would otherwise not be involved in any kind of plot, or through foreign policies that generate political contexts in which violence becomes more likely. That's the tragedy of it. This conflict looks like it could last as long as the Cold War because we keep manufacturing the enemy we're fighting. The foreign policy establishment has a conception of the world in which resistance to US empire cannot be confronted directly and is instead viewed through a racial lens. In responding to racial fantasies of its own making, the US empire ends up producing the very violence it fears.

Heatherton: A report in the *New Statesman* gave an example of Westerners ordering copies of the book *Islam for Dummies* before they left to join ISIS.[4]

Kundnani: Absolutely. All the reports that are coming out from ISIS show that those who go there lack any kind of religious sophistication. What is driving a young kid to leave Britain and travel to Syria are the images of violence available online. They show Muslims being victimized in very violent ways either by the West or by people who are seen as proxies for the West. Or they show a path towards heroism. The way in which that kid is being recruited is basically the same way that kids are recruited to join the US military. You use victimhood, you use heroism, and you glorify violence.

Heatherton: FBI director James B. Comey recently addressed the tension between African Americans and law enforcement. While he admitted a troubling legacy of racism by law enforcement, he also rehearsed an old argument that Black people grow up in "environments lacking role models and good education and decent employment." His comments echo British officials' attempts to address the "cultural issues" or lack of "proper upbringing" among British Muslims. Can you talk about the implications of this culturalist framing?

Kundnani: There's a tendency to use culture as a way to depoliticize issues that are about power. Whether people are speaking about Muslim communities in Britain or the US or about other racialized groups, the formula is, "The problem is rooted in *their* culture, not in *our* politics." When applied to Muslims, this involves seeing Islam as a "backward" cultural force that completely determines everything Muslims do,

---

4   Mehdi Hasan, "What the Jihadists Who Bought 'Islam for Dummies' on Amazon Tell Us about Radicalization," *New Statesman*, August 21, 2014, available at newstatesman.com.

irrespective or social or political circumstances. This then implies measures to "integrate" Muslim populations into what are considered to be the "superior values" of European or Western society. Political conflicts around racism and imperialism are thus transformed into debates around values and cultural integration. There's a long history of that in Europe, which ultimately goes back to European colonialism.

In the US, though there's a slightly different dynamic, there's also a long history of saying that Black people are in poverty because of the "dysfunctional Black family" or other cultural reasons. This is still a powerful narrative today. You even hear it from Obama. Essentially it's the same culturalist response to what are actually political issues rooted in histories of oppression.

Heatherton: In the wake of the police killing of Mark Duggan in August 2011, a cycle of rebellion rocked British cities. William Bratton was brought to London as an advisor. How do we understand the export of US policing practices to the UK?

Kundnani: When British politicians or people in leadership positions import ideas from the US, they usually win support from most of the establishment. The US is seen as almost the definition of innovation in policing, so there's been a constant stream of imports from the US to Britain. In the late 1990s we imported the "zero tolerance" slogan from you. We got all these things a few years after they hit the US. "Broken windows" has been floating around as a slogan that the British police occasionally invoke. The Mark Duggan killing was part of a much older pattern of people, especially Black people, dying in the custody of the police in Britain, as a result of chokeholds, the use of pepper spray, and so forth. Historically, only a small number of police officers have been armed in Britain but we're moving towards a police force that is increasingly armed.

The uprising and grassroots response to Mark Duggan's death sprang from people's repeated experience of racist violence from the police. Mark Duggan was killed in Tottenham, where people had been campaigning for decades around cases of Black people being killed in police custody, going back to at least the 1980s. What happened in 2011 was a crisis in the sense that the police felt they were no longer in control of the streets. They wanted to bring in a new kind of formula to reassure the power brokers and the wider public that they were still in control. In that context, Bratton became an attractive figure to call in.

The slogan that came out of that collaboration was not "broken windows" but something called "total policing," which sounds as bad as it is. It's a continuation of a much longer trend of integrating the police into other spheres of public service provision. This is one flow that actually moved the other way across the Atlantic. This tradition of creating partnerships between the police and other agencies, whether social services or schools, is something that has come over to the US after having been in Britain for a much longer time. Integrating law enforcement surveillance into all of these other spheres that serve purposes very different from policing is dangerous. Youth workers, for example, have been expected since the early 1990s to be the eyes and ears of the police. They are supposed to collect information about young people through a model of risk assessment, rather than criminality. They then share that information with the police. That's the policing model we've had since the early 1990s. Total policing is an outgrowth of that.

Camp: That reminds me of a quotation by a state official suggesting that "counterinsurgency is armed social work."[5]

Kundnani: Yes, absolutely. It's not a coincidence that it's the same formula. This model of policing comes out of the counterinsurgency model used in Northern Ireland. The counterinsurgency practices implemented by the British army in Malaya and in Kenya were reproduced in Northern Ireland from the early 1970s onward, during the conflict between the Provisional IRA and the British army. Because Northern Ireland had a higher level of formal democracy relative to Kenya and Malaya, the intelligence gathering could not be done overtly through the army. Instead, it was integrated into all these other public services. The first principle of counterinsurgency is that you set up a comprehensive response that integrates all government departments.

---

5   David Kilcullen quoted in Laleh Khalil, *Time in the Shadows: Confinement in Counterinsurgencies* (Stanford: Stanford University Press, 2013), 49.

A child protection officer in social services plays as much of a counterinsurgency role as a police intelligence officer. In the early 1980s, after the urban uprisings in England, the head of the Northern Ireland police became the chief constable of the Metropolitan Police in London. These ideas from Northern Ireland were then imported into mainstream policing in England. Legislation was introduced to facilitate this transition so that the police began to integrate into all of these other departments.

Heatherton: So would you say that flows of policing knowledge draw from the present war on terror as well as from established colonial legacies?

Kundnani: Technologies and practices that have been developed in contexts where the US has a presence overseas are brought back into the US and then, in turn, Europe imports them. No doubt all kinds of other places around the world, like Brazil, import them as well. But within that, there are other flows of ideas, technologies, and practices that have been innovated in Britain or Israel and flow to the US. I think the US is still seen in Britain as the best place to look for ideas, but occasionally it happens the other way around.

For example, the kind of "partnership" policing model that I mentioned earlier, with its roots in counterinsurgency, is being imported from Britain. Here Britain likes to think of itself as Greece to the US's Rome. There's a feeling that, while Britain may no longer run its own empire, it retains a historically informed expertise in defeating anticolonial opposition that has been built up over a much longer period than that of the US. When I was doing research in Washington, DC, I was amazed by the number of British people in the national security think tanks. Their tone was always one of having the greater historical depth needed to run a colonial program.

Camp: Your colleague at *Race & Class* A. Sivanandan has often argued that capital "requires racism not for racism's sake but for the sake of capital." This implies that the struggle against racism requires a radical anti-capitalist struggle. Could you talk about how

the fight against policing and surveillance is, therefore, a necessary part of a larger struggle against racial capitalism?

Kundnani: The racist and imperialist violence upon which capitalism depends cannot be acknowledged in liberal society so it is transferred onto the personality of racial "others" and seen as emanating from "outside" the social order. Surveillance and policing structures are then established to catalogue, monitor, and disrupt those dangerous "others." This is a key part of the history of capitalism. But I don't think we've fully grasped the dramatic transformation that has happened in the last decade or so in regards to this global surveillance infrastructure. I don't think the post-Snowden debate has really grasped it. The questions about privacy and better encryption do not really address what is essentially an infrastructure of empire. This is about the politics of a neoliberal empire, but one that is unstable and therefore feels the need to know everything that's happening all the time, to preempt possible disruption and opposition. More than ever, the question of surveillance is at the heart of how capitalism is reproducing itself now.

The post-Snowden debate also has not been able to grasp the way that race is central to surveillance. If you look at how the NSA is responding to the allegations, it's by saying, "You, as an average American guy, don't have to worry about surveillance. We're only going after the bad guys who are the terrorists, the foreign spies, and so forth." This is a racially coded way of reassuring the majority of Americans. That part of it never gets discussed. We much prefer this "Big Brother" account of NSA surveillance, where everyone is equally under surveillance, but that's not how it works. The danger of describing the NSA in terms of a Big Brother image is that you end up saying that the problem is mass surveillance of everyone, which can carry the implication that "targeted" surveillance is fine. But, in practice, "targeted" surveillance could mean collecting data on everyone in Yemen, or the entire Muslim population of the US.

In terms of organizing I think we want to come at this in a completely different way. We can focus on the fact that specific groups are having their lives totally transformed as a result of surveillance. How do we then build on that very specific experience and create alliances with communities that have been experiencing it for decades, like African Americans? These should be our starting points in organizing. Ultimately, though, the struggle against surveillance cannot avoid confronting capitalism itself.

7. *MANO DURA CONTRA EL CRIMEN* AND PREMATURE DEATH IN PUERTO RICO

Marisol LeBrón

By the late 1980s, there was no question that Puerto Rico's economy had run out of steam. The economic growth produced during the mid-twentieth-century "golden age" of Puerto Rico's neo-colonial development scheme, known as Operation Bootstrap, was a distant memory. High levels of unemployment and a growing informal economy with all of its attendant problems had created a general sense of insecurity among many Puerto Ricans—a sense that the state would not or could not provide and protect. From the front page of the island's daily newspapers to conversations around countless kitchen tables, and reports produced by financial firms, academics, and government entities, the consensus was clear: the island was in crisis.

Although Puerto Rico's circumstances were somewhat unique given its status as a territorial commonwealth of the United States, Puerto Rican elites and policy makers responded to this crisis by implementing punitive strategies and promoting carceral logics that resembled those taking hold in other sites around the globe. Paralleling the growth of carceral and neoliberal regimes of dispossession in the United States and internationally, Puerto Rican officials turned to policing in an effort to maintain "order" and manage populations rendered redundant, and therefore dangerous, within racial and capitalist systems of value. The rise and consolidation of punitive governance on the island hardened hierarchies around race, class, spatial location, gender, sexuality, and citizenship status. The result is that some of Puerto Rico's most vulnerable have been, and continue to be, exposed to intense harm at the hands of both the state and their fellow citizens.

In this essay, I examine how punitive policing in Puerto Rico has rendered certain populations vulnerable to premature death through logics and practices of dehumanization and criminalization.[1] Punitive policing in Puerto Rico is an essential component of a racist, neocolonial, and capitalist system that functions through the unequal distribution of resources and opportunities. Rather than providing safety, policing as a form of crisis management has deepened existing societal inequalities and further limited life chances in Puerto Rico's racially and economically marginalized communities. I focus on *mano dura contra el crimen*, an anti-crime measure that sought to eliminate drug trafficking in Puerto Rico by explicitly targeting public housing and other low-income spaces around the island for joint military and police raids during the 1990s. In doing so, I seek to demonstrate how policing resulted in increased harm and vulnerability to premature death in marginalized communities. Punitive policing measures like *mano dura* both intentionally and unintentionally perpetuated forms of race- and class-based violence and exclusion, the effects of which continue to be felt in Puerto Rico to this day. *Mano dura* promoted an uneven distribution of risk, harm, and death by tacitly allowing the proliferation of violence within and against economically and racially marginalized communities. While law enforcement agents enacted violence against public housing and *barrio* residents as part of *mano dura contra el crimen*, police and other state officials also positioned the alarmingly high levels of drug-related violence and death occurring within the confines of these classed and racialized spaces as a necessary by-product of the island's "war on drugs." In this way, police interventions—both those hailed as "successful" in protecting *el pueblo puertorriqueño* (the Puerto Rican people) and those during which police deliberately "failed" to prevent violence related to the informal drug economy—resulted in greater exposure to harm and death for racialized and low-income populations.

~

---

1   I draw on scholar and activist Ruth Wilson Gilmore's definition of racism as "the state-sanctioned or extralegal production and exploitation of group-differentiated vulnerability to premature death." Ruth Wilson Gilmore, *Golden Gulag: Prisons, Surplus, Crisis, and Opposition in Globalizing California* (Berkeley: University of California Press, 2007), 28.

The anti-crime logics, measures, and rhetoric associated with *mano dura contra el crimen* arose during a moment of intense insecurity on the island. During the late 1980s, Puerto Rico was described in the local press as a nation under siege from violent crimes associated with drug use and trafficking. Fear of carjackings, armed robbery, and getting caught by a stray bullet from drug-related shoot-outs punctuated everyday conversations, while news of bloody "massacres" over *puntos*, or drug points, dominated the headlines.[2] As crime rates increased during the 1980s, the island's middle and upper classes blamed the urban poor for the chaos unfolding around them, presuming that they were involved with crime and the drug economy. With legislative support, middle-class and wealthy Puerto Ricans turned to private security firms to fortify their homes and keep potential threats at bay. On May 20, 1987, the Puerto Rican legislator approved Law 21, known as the Controlled Access Law, which allowed municipalities to grant permits to residential communities that would restrict pedestrian and vehicular traffic. Gates and controlled access points would monitor entries and exits, thus, presumably, controlling crime. Fortified enclaves proliferated around the island in an attempt to identify, screen, and exclude those Puerto Ricans perceived as dangerous and undesirable.

With Puerto Rico's middle- and upper-class citizens barricading themselves against street violence in controlled access fortifications, violence became concentrated in many of the island's poorer areas, particularly public housing and predominately Black barrios. For the most part, police considered these areas to be *zonas calientes*—hot zones of illegality that police, politicians, and social scientists deemed both physically and morally dangerous—and allowed violence to proliferate there. Signaling an uneven terrain of justice and legality to both residents and non-residents alike, such spatial taxonomies served to decontextualize, normalize, and justify the forms of racial and economic violence enacted against barrio and public housing communities.[3] Labeling these

---

2   On the ways the Puerto Rican press began to categorize "massacres," see Jorge L. Giovannetti, "Puerto Rico: An Island of Massacres," *Global Dialogue: Newsletter for the International Sociological Association* 3, no. 5 (2013).

3   My thinking about spatial taxonomies is informed by Denise Ferreira Da Silva, "Towards a Critique of the Socio-logos of Justice: *The Analytics of Raciality* and the Production of Universality," *Social Identities* 7, no. 3 (2001): 441. Emphasis in original.

communities as *zonas calientes* promoted a popular understanding of these spaces as inherently violent and pathological, rather than as sites that had been engineered, in a sense, to concentrate the various forms of harm associated with the island's informal drug economy. Government neglect and the segregation of low-income, racialized communities, pre-dating but intensified by measures such as the Controlled Access Law, played a significant role in generating the conditions of socio-spatial isolation that allowed the informal drug economy and its attendant violence to become concentrated in low-income and racialized neigh-borhoods around the island.

Although the violence associated with the island's booming informal drug economy was most acutely felt in low-income and predominately Black and Brown areas of the island, there existed, nonetheless, a pre-vailing sense that crime was "out of control" and that everyone was at risk. This growing public concern over violence and crime crescendoed when, at the close of 1991, Puerto Rico experienced a record number of robberies, carjackings, assaults, and murders. Pedro Rosselló, a former pediatric surgeon who had risen through the ranks of the pro-statehood party, kicked off 1992 by unveiling his course of treatment for Puerto Rico's ailing body. During the gubernatorial race, Rosselló vowed to wield a "*mano dura*" against crime and do whatever it took to restore peace to *la gran familia puertorriqueña* (the great Puerto Rican family). Rosselló seized upon the "talk of crime" that was circulating among citi-zens and in the popular media in order to cement his position as a "law and order" candidate.[4] He justified his drastic approach by positioning violent crime as penetrating all aspects of daily life and touching every family on the island. Rosselló declared, "We live in a Puerto Rico where every day more Puerto Ricans are killed, and where even in our own homes our families are not safe. In essence, we are living in a crisis, an emergency. Faced with this crisis we must act firmly, with extraordinary measures."[5] Rosselló's rhetoric redefined daily life on the island as marked by victimization or potential victimization at the hands of violent crimi-

---

4   See Teresa P. R. Caldeira, *City of Walls: Crime, Segregation, and Citizenship in São Paulo* (Berkeley: University of California Press, 2001), 1–2.

5   Joel A. Villa Rodríguez, *Crimen y Criminalidad en Puerto Rico: El Sujeto Criminal* (San Juan: Ediciones SITUM, Inc., 2006), 252. Translation my own.

nals. Rosselló's rhetorical reconceptualization of the citizen as a victim of crime not only redefined the legal process and the appropriate conditions for government intervention, but also created consensus as well by appealing to existing hierarchies of value governing those worthy and unworthy of protection, and from what forms of violence, on an island that imagined itself to be besieged from within.[6] Rosselló's promises of a swift, *mano dura* approach to crime provided populist cover for an increasing fortification of the urban landscape driven by racist and classist underpinnings.

Shortly after Rosselló was elected governor, he and police superintendent Pedro Toledo unveiled Operation Centurion, the most visible component of *mano dura contra el crimen*, in which they deployed the National Guard to assist in civilian policing efforts. On February 25, 1993, Rosselló signed an executive order activating the Puerto Rican National Guard to assist police in maintaining public security and quelling drug-related crime.[7] Initially seen patrolling public spaces of leisure such as beaches and malls, the National Guard's presence quickly became concentrated in public housing complexes after the first joint police and military raid at the Villa España complex on June 5, 1993. The pre-dawn raid at Villa España was the first of more than eighty raids carried out between June 1993 and March 1999. During these raids, police conducted searches, confiscated contraband, and interrogated residents while the National Guard provided logistical and tactical support in the form of soldiers, helicopters, military vehicles, technology, and weapons. The National Guard was also responsible for setting up surveillance, establishing checkpoints, and constructing a perimeter fence. The perimeter fences built during *mano dura* incursions into public housing, coupled with the simultaneous rise in private gated communities, further enclosed low-income Puerto Ricans and concentrated the violence of the island's war on drugs. The police and National

---

6   See Jonathan Simon, *Governing through Crime: How the War on Crime Transformed American Democracy and Created a Culture of Fear* (Oxford: Oxford University Press, 2007), 109–10.

7   Pedro Rosselló, *Executive Order of the Governor of the Commonwealth of Puerto Rico to Order the Activation and Utilization of the Personnel and Equipment of the National Guard of Puerto Rico (OE-1993-08)*, February 25, 1993.

Guard soldiers occupied the raided complexes for weeks until a security force of part-time police and private security guards were able to set up a permanent presence.

With *mano dura*, Rosselló and his administration deployed seemingly populist discourse about the security of the population in order to marshal support for militarized policing that would further segregate low-income populations and expose them to even greater levels of violence in the name of saving them from violence. But while police violently intervened in low-income and racialized communities, sometimes harming and killing residents, it is primarily the ways in which *mano dura contra el crimen* sought to *concentrate* death and violence that most reveals the genocidal logic that haunts policing on the island.

One year after the implementation of *mano dura contra el crimen*, Governor Rosselló and police superintendent Toledo could be seen in the press almost daily touting the successes of their tough-on-crime approach. They boasted of decreases in the number of carjackings and assaults, and assured the public that the fight against drugs and crime was being won with every public housing project occupied and every *punto* dismantled. Indeed, if one looks at the rates of *Delitos Tipo 1*, or Type One offences, after 1992, there appears to be a decrease in most categories, seemingly giving credence to the narrative of *mano dura*'s incredible success (Table 1).

The daily lives of many Puerto Ricans, particularly those living in economically and racially marginalized areas, reflected a very different

Table 1 *Delitos Tipo 1* recorded in Puerto Rico, 1990–2000

Year	Murder & Homicide	Forcible Rape	Robbery	Aggravated Assault	Burglary	Larceny-Theft	Motor Vehicle Theft
1990	600	426	20,923	7,963	34,781	39,795	19,883
1991	817	424	20,003	6,901	33,649	38,916	19,021
1992	864	433	24,242	6,747	35,415	42,315	18,858
1993	954	401	18,181	6,806	33,636	43,468	17,589
1994	995	396	17,626	6,384	31,160	42,062	17,641
1995	864	324	15,753	5,509	27,689	39,960	15,989
1996	868	316	13,900	5,063	27,866	35,652	16,123
1997	724	278	13,642	4,952	26,942	32,715	15,623
1998	652	243	11,448	4,096	24,512	30,493	15,576
1999	593	223	9,827	3,563	23,033	30,206	14,435
2000	695	228	8,757	2,726	21,057	28,940	12,976

Source: Junta de Planificación de Puerto Rico, "Informe Social: Criminalidad en Puerto Rico años seleccionados" (May 2003).

reality, however. While *mano dura* may have resulted in an overall decrease in certain serious crimes, especially property crimes, it provoked an *increase* in homicides: 1993 witnessed 954 murders and 1994 saw the highest number of murders in Puerto Rico's history at that time, with 995 registered. The homicide rate decreased in 1995 but only to a still-alarming 864 murders, the same as recorded in 1992. Further, criminologists and demographers have suggested that there were significantly more homicides in the mid- to late 1990s than those recorded, but police manipulated statistics in order to support the story of *mano dura's* success. In their study of homicides in Puerto Rico, Judith Rodríguez and Alma Irizarry demonstrate that there is a significant discrepancy between the number of murders registered by the police and the number documented by the Department of Health, the latter which is significantly greater in the years immediately following the implementation of *mano dura contra el crimen* (Table 2).[8] As Rosselló's administration and police officials celebrated the safer Puerto Rico achieved by *mano dura*, images of young men slain in battles over turf haunted the nightly news and provided stark reminders of the intense vulnerability and proximity to violence that many Puerto Ricans continued to experience.

Table 2 Discrepancies in the Reporting of Homicides in Puerto Rico, 1990–2000

Year	Homicides reported by Police (P)	Homicides reported by Dept. of Health (DH)	(P)–(DH)
1990	600	583	17
1991	817	803	14
1992	864	851	13
1993	954	959	−5
1994	995	1017	−22
1995	864	929	−65
1996	868	928	−60
1997	724	881	−158
1998	652	819	−167
1999	593	705	−112
2000	695	698	−3

Source: Rodríguez Figueroa and Irizarry Castro, *El Homicidio en Puerto Rico: Características y Nexos con la Violencia* (2003).

8   Judith Rodríguez Figueroa and Alma Irizarry Castro, *El Homicidio en Puerto Rico: Características y Nexos con la Violencia* (San Juan: Universidad Carlos Albizu, 2003), 31 and Appendix B, Table 35.

Mano dura contra el crimen did not make the streets any safer. Instead, it maintained and contributed to high levels of violence in low-income and racialized areas during the height of police intervention into the drug trade. Police and military intervention resulted in increased drug-related homicides and violence, especially in 1993 and 1994, as incursions into public housing and low-income barrios disrupted the normal drug trade. Police intervention and arrests resulted in the abandoned *puntos*, which led to violent competition among dealers for these newly available spaces. As dealers were locked up or killed, the street price of narcotics increased to cover the new costs of doing business. In 1995, the constant drug raids triggered a scarcity of cocaine, driving the street price up from $10 to $30 a gram and provoking desperation on the part of both dealers and users, which, in turn, contributed to more violence and crime.[9] While public feelings and official discourse trafficked in the assumption that drugs and violence lurked at every turn, the effects of drugs and violence in the wake of the raids remained overwhelmingly concentrated in low-income and racialized urban areas, and the movement of drug points continued to follow well-established patterns of spatial inequality and social abandonment. In other words, while a few enterprising dealers and gangs may have ventured out and expanded into entirely new territory in an effort to stay ahead of the raids, most dealers moved around within already established circuits of the drug market—spaces that were becoming smaller, scarcer, and deadlier with each subsequent police intervention.[10] It is important to note that this phenomenon is not unique to Puerto Rico. "Ghetto sweeps," which sought to apply increasing pressure on drug dealers and users operating within public housing and low-income, predominately Black communities, proliferated during the 1980s and 1990s. With names like Operation Hammer (Los Angeles), Operation Pressure Point (New York City), Operation

---

9   Edwin González, "La Maldad dentro de la bolsa," *Claridad*, April 7–13, 1995, 14.

10   While the island's rural interior witnessed a growth of drug dealing and drug use during the *mano dura* era, the bulk of activity surrounding the island's informal, drug-based economy continued to occur in the island's metropolitan areas of San Juan, Ponce, and Mayagüez. The bloodiest battles over *puntos* continued to be seen in the San Juan area—due, perhaps, to sheer population density.

Sting (Miami), Operation Snow Ball (Orange County, California), and Operation Clean Sweep (Washington, DC), these drug raids provoked tremendous violence with no evidence, or negligible evidence, that drug use and dealing decreased in response.[11] Puerto Rico's *mano dura contra el crimen*, therefore, exists in relationship to a larger pattern of genocidal policing that marked the US-led global war on drugs, although it cannot be reduced to merely an importation of US punitive policy.

Police pointed to the constant movement of drug dealers from *punto* to *punto* as evidence of *mano dura's* success. According to police officials, one of the goals of these raids was to eliminate drug trafficking not only by disarticulating the *puntos*, but also by making *puntos* increasingly difficult for dealers to operate and maintain, thus forcing them to move around and engage in bloody battles over territory. Police knew that the pressure of constant raids would result in more competition between the gangs and therefore more murders, but this increased violence was positioned as a necessary evil in their efforts to eradicate drug dealing and restore a sense of "peace" to the "decent" people of Puerto Rico. As police superintendent Pedro Toledo put it, "There could be an increase in gangland killings as *puntos* are eliminated. However, we'll continue to hit them wherever they go, keep them on the move, make it tough for them until they have to give up and go out of business."[12]

The relationship between police raids and increased violence, particularly violent death, had been identified as an issue earlier under Governor Hernández Colón's administration when police first started to sporadically raid spaces associated with low-level drug dealing. Pushed to explain the spike in homicides and violence despite increased police action and intervention, Hernández Colón said,

> What is happening is that we are having more success in our strategy of penetrating the projects to eliminate the drug points, in many cases arresting those who control the drug points. This has unleashed struggles in other areas or territories or between people who work for the

---

11   See Christian Parenti, *Lockdown America: Police and Prisons in the Age of Crisis*, 2nd ed. (New York: Verso, 2008), 58–60.

12   Gino Ponti, "Rio Piedras Project Taken over in 7th Police, Guard Raid," *San Juan Star*, June 16, 1993, 10.

individual arrested to take control [of the *puntos*] and this is generating bloody battles between [drug gangs] and [as a result] we are seeing
many murders.[13]

The growing number of homicides related to battles over *puntos* became
a macabre hallmark of success, rather than a sign of failing police strategy. Both success *and* failure on the part of the police in controlling the
violence generated by the *puntos* produced even greater violence and
insecurity for low-income and racialized populations living in so-called
zonas calientes.

Part of *mano dura contra el crimen*'s strategy of controlling drug trafficking and drug-related violence on the island, then, included the tacit
acceptance of continued and, indeed, elevated levels of harm and death
directed at low-income and racialized individuals, particularly the poor,
young Black and Brown men who labored in the informal economy.
No only did state officials tolerate their deaths—or let them die in the
Foucaldian sense—but their strategy of promoting and exacerbating the
already tense competition over *puntos* created conditions that positioned
violence and death as necessary outcomes of police intervention. That
mano dura would drive up the death toll among individuals involved
with the drug economy was therefore, for policy makers, a foregone
conclusion.[14] Said differently, the deaths that *mano dura* ostensibly pre-
vented, or sought to prevent, were not the deaths of those involved in
the informal economy; in many ways, this was not the intention. While
there is no clear evidence that the state actively planned to harm or kill
individuals associated with the informal drug economy through police
intervention, it is clear that state officials knew that *mano dura* would
provoke more deaths. While, in a strict sense, the state may not have
premeditated their deaths, it did deliberately advance informal and
formal policies that "let" these alleged dealers die. Regardless of intent,
mano dura evidences a genocidal continuum of logic and practice, given
the death it allowed, provoked, and *naturalized* as an outcome.[15]

---

13   Nilka Estrada Resto, "Cosecha Fatal de Plan Anticrimen," *El Nuevo Día*,
August 5, 1992, 5. Translation my own.

14   See John D. Márquez, "Latinos as the 'Living Dead': Raciality, Expendability,
and Border Militarization," *Latino Studies* 10, no. 4 (2012): 484–5.

15   On how an emphasis on intent rather than outcome helps to obscure structural

Racial, spatial, and economic inequality are among the structural forces that enabled and contributed to the genocidal logics that drove *mano dura contra el crimen*. In *mano dura* coalesced a history of neo-colonial population management, intense anti-Black racism, anti-poor discrimination, and urban segregation that defined the mostly young Black and Brown men from public housing and barrios who labored in the island's drug economy as threats to *el pueblo puertorriqueño* that needed to be extinguished. Indeed, as Ismael Betancourt Lebrón, police superintendent under Governor Hernández Colón, reportedly remarked, "The punishment of the drug dealer is that at any given moment he can get shot in the head, but that's not my problem."[16] Betancourt Lebrón's comments index a growing frustration with the informal drug economy on the island that was unleashed in the form of violence and dehumanization against low-income Puerto Ricans, whose involvement with the drug trade was assumed. *Mano dura contra el crimen* seized upon and institutionalized these popular notions of "deserved" violence and proximity to death. The deaths of individuals involved with the informal drug economy were positioned as unconnected to the police's duty to protect all citizens—*not their problem.*

In 1994, following the raids in the working-class community of La Perla and the Llorens Torres and Nemesio Canales public housing complexes, murders multiplied in the adjacent areas of Old San Juan, Punto Las Marías, and West Hato Rey as dealers were displaced and competed over control of *puntos*. Captain Charles Pérez, commander of the Barrio Obrero police precinct, which had also seen a rise in homicides due to displaced dealers moving into the area, said, "It's like when you move into an old house that's full of rats. What happens when you move in? The rats go running out all over the place."[17] While Captain Pérez's metaphor attempted to capture the quicksilver nature of the *puntos* and their mobility, he inadvertently elucidated *mano dura*'s prevailing logic of dehumanization and disposability that allowed and encouraged

forces, see Laura Pulido, "Rethinking Environmental Racism: White Privilege and Urban Development in Southern California," *Annals of the Association of American Geographers* 90, no. 1 (2000): 17–19.

16 Villa Rodríguez, *Crimen y Criminalidad en Puerto Rico*, 246–7.

17 Karl Ross, "Project Crime Spilling into Tamer Areas," *San Juan Star*, n.d., 3, 8.

drug dealers to eliminate each other. The idea that criminals and drug dealers were outside the bounds of normative Puerto Rican society guided the logic of *mano dura* and justified the brutal force utilized during the incursions as well as the deliberate inaction on the part of law enforcement and politicians in the face of an increasingly volatile drug economy affecting some of the island's most vulnerable communities. As Governor Rosselló told the people of Puerto Rico, "habitual criminals" were nothing but "garbage," killing the island's youth with drugs.[18] The deaths of young people affiliated with the island's drug trade did not represent a cause for alarm or even a need for a reevaluation of police strategy—these were not human lives lost, but rather garbage that had been disposed of or rats that had been exterminated. In Puerto Rico, a political and popular rhetoric that dehumanized and vilified drug dealers and users as "monsters," "animals," and "garbage" and positioned them as a threat to *el pueblo puertorriqueño* allowed for the creation of law enforcement policies that protected some lives at the expense of others. The devaluation of their lives and deaths naturalized the uneven distribution of opportunity and harm and reinforced the genocidal notion that not all lives are livable and not all deaths grievable.[19]

An analysis of *mano dura contra el crimen* in Puerto Rico brings into sharp relief the multiple ways in which punitive policing functions under the auspices of keeping populations safe, in fact creating only a thin veneer of security by casting certain populations as disposable and dangerous and thus containable and eliminable. Through both official and unofficial methods of policing initiatives like *mano dura*, the state functions to further devastate already racially and economically marginalized communities. Moreover, the violence enacted through *mano dura* itself cannot be contained only to questions of street violence and police brutality. The police occupation of public housing complexes around the island marked residents as "unruly subjects," which hardened existing prejudices and made it increasingly difficult for them to access a range of economic and social opportunities. Further, those involved in the island's drug trade who were arrested during *mano dura's* incursions into the

---

18   "Al que no quiere caldo," *El Nuevo Día*, August 22, 1993, 3.

19   Judith Butler, *Precarious Life: The Powers of Mourning and Violence* (New York: Verso, 2006), xv.

puntos might have escaped death on the streets at the hands of a rival or an overzealous police officer only to encounter it in the island's prisons. In this way, we must consider the various forms of harm that policing enacts in marginalized and vulnerable communities and the ways in which it contributes to limited life chances and proximity to premature death. Only by acknowledging the ways in which these genocidal logics in fact *drive* punitive policing practices in vulnerable communities—and are not punitive policing's unintended and regrettable by-products—can we begin to work towards forms of redress and repair.

~

Marisol LeBrón is an assistant professor in the Department of American Studies at Dickinson College. An interdisciplinary scholar trained in American Studies and Latina/o Studies, her research focuses on social inequality, policing, violence, and protest in contemporary Puerto Rico.

8. POLICING THE CRISIS OF INDIGENOUS LIVES: AN INTERVIEW WITH THE RED NATION

Christina Heatherton

The Red Nation is a Native-led council of Indigenous and non-Indigenous activists committed to the liberation of Indigenous people and the overthrow of colonialism and capitalism. Based in Albuquerque, New Mexico, the council centers Indigenous agendas in direct action, advocacy, mobilization, and education from the perspective of the Indigenous Left. Members Melanie Yazzie (Diné), Nick Estes (Lakota), Sam Gardipe (Pawnee/Sac and Fox), Paige Murphy (Diné), and Chris Banks were interviewed in June 2015.

Heatherton: As of 2014, New Mexico has led the nation with the highest rate of police killings. The Albuquerque Police Department has one of the highest rates of fatal police shootings, eight times as high as the NYPD. Native people are statistically most likely to be killed by law enforcement. How do you explain this violence against Native communities here in New Mexico?

Estes: The Red Nation was partially formed out of the anti–police brutality movement. All of us here were involved in some way. For Native people in Albuquerque, forms of everyday police brutality are largely about the policing of Indigenous bodies in a space. It follows the thinking that Native people don't belong in this space. The police, especially the Albuquerque Police Department, manage the crises of colonialism, colonization, and occupation through the constant criminalization of Indigenous bodies, especially homeless and poor people. Settlement and colonization are never complete processes; they always have to be reenacted. Policing this crisis of Indigenous lives happens in the present and also in the future.

Yazzie: Colonization presumes the disappearance and the finality of settlement, but Indians are ubiquitous. The fact that we're present makes us anachronisms. We're not supposed to be here, but we're here in really large numbers. That increases the amount of violence necessary to contain us. This violence is not just from the cops, but also from citizens. Last summer two Diné men known as Cowboy and Rabbit were brutally beaten to death. This violence obviously doesn't only affect Native people; other homeless people and poor people of color especially are treated as totally disposable. Native people here experience the violence of anti-Indian common sense as an everyday thing. We call Albuquerque a border town since the city is surrounded by Indigenous land and has a large Indigenous population inside it—55,000 Native people, maybe more. As a border town it's also an important site in the production of anti-Indian common sense.

Heatherton: How do you define anti-Indian common sense?

Yazzie: Nick and I developed the concept by drawing on Dakota scholar Elizabeth Cook-Lynn, one of the most important scholars in Native American intellectual history in the last forty years. She coined the term "anti-Indianism," which she defines as "that which treats the Indians and their tribes as if they don't exist." She also describes it as that which disavows and devalues Indian nationhood—which demonizes and insults being Indian in America. Through the term, we can see how the weight of history is placed upon Native people's shoulders, as if anything bad that has transpired is our own fault.[1]

Estes: One way we use anti-Indianism as common sense draws from Antonio Gramsci, the Italian Marxist theorist who described "common sense" as an ideology not necessarily actively theorized but more like a knee-jerk response. People don't necessarily think that Indians aren't supposed to exist, it's just normalized in how they perceive their reality.

---

1   Elizabeth Cook-Lynn, *Anti-Indianism in Modern America: A Voice from Tatekeya's Earth* (Urbana: University of Illinois Press, 2001), x.

People can celebrate and mourn the passing of the Indian, but they can't actually confront the existence or the persistence of Indigenous life in cities because Indians don't "belong" here.

Heatherton: How do you confront anti-Indian common sense here in Albuquerque?

Gardipe: For the Indian on the street, we don't have a place to actually exist or have social lives and hash things out within the Indian community. We have a place here that's more or less a tourist attraction with Pueblos. It's basically full of artwork, pottery, and food supposedly made by Natives of the Southwest. However, if a street person walked in, he'd probably be turned away, because he's seen as an embarrassment to Natives. I get a little scrutinized when I walk in there because I have long hair and I'm obviously an Indigenous person, but I'm not a "mainstream Indian." They like to see the ones in suits and ties with short hair.

Heatherton: Your group often uses the term "unnatural deaths" to place the police killings within a larger political economy of extreme poverty, unemployment, and homelessness. How do you understand these connections?

Estes: Private property has more value and sanctity than Native lives. Unnatural deaths result from private property laws that prohibit everyday behavior in public. Whether it's eating, sleeping, defecating, urinating, having an untreated mental illness, for example, these behaviors are all criminalized because they are enacted on somebody else's property. Being unable to sleep, stop, drink, rest, or urinate are forms of what could be considered torture. When Native people enter Gallup or Albuquerque, they're made to stay in constant motion. Because of property laws, they can't loiter, panhandle, sleep in public, or perform basic bodily functions because these are all criminalized behaviors. As a consequence they have to constantly be moving. People walk up to ten or twenty miles a day. Often people can't sleep within the city where they have access to resources such as shelter, food, or other basic needs. They end up going to what people here call "the bush." We've found that a lot of people die as a result of this constant movement and constant policing because they are forced to live outside of society, on the outskirts of the city, while actually depending on the city for life.

An unnatural death can mean anything from dying from exposure, which happens quite frequently, to being beat up by vigilantes or by the police, possibly resulting in some sort of injury that means they can't work and therefore lose their job. It could mean getting their personal identification confiscated and destroyed by the police and losing the ability to work, access to medical services or secure housing. When we talk about unnatural deaths, it can be anything from the extreme forms of violence to the "slow death" of poverty or homelessness that always goes unaccounted for.

Banks: The pervasive view in Albuquerque is that the right place for Native people is on the reservation. If Native people are off the reservation, they seem to have no claim to rights or to citizenship. Police uphold this view that Native people have no rights they are bound to respect. Native people are seen as a disposable part of the population. This is related to the federal government's lack of respect for the sovereignty of Native land, which they view as existing for plunder. In their view, either the Native population will be exploited for their cheap labor or they will be absorbed by prisons. In that way, they have everything in common with other oppressed nations living in the United States, such as African Americans and Latinos. Thinking about them as a disposable part of the population explains their targeting by the police. The *Albuquerque Journal* recently reported that 12 percent of Native adults in Albuquerque experience chronic homelessness, which is a crisis if there ever was one. No one in the city is sounding the alarm or asking how we can mobilize resources to address this.

Murphy: I grew up in a border town in Gallup. It's common to see homeless Natives walking in the street. It's normal to see Natives sleeping on the street. In the news, it's normal to hear about homeless Natives dying due to exposure, especially in the wintertime, Native people freezing to death in the cold. No one really thinks twice about it, because it's an everyday normal thing—the violence that saturates a town like Gallup.

When I see Native people homeless in a town like Gallup, what I see are the failures of capitalism. You've got all of these different failures of capitalism: people who don't have access to jobs, people who don't have access to health care, people who don't have access to education. You just fall into these cracks. I guess you could call them pipelines to incarceration or to homelessness. Gallup is dire and decaying. When you see a town like that, you have to start questioning the system that allowed these things to happen, a system that will turn its back on Natives while they're in these dire circumstances. I see it in my families.

This is why I really like the Red Nation, because we all have these same stories. Every Native person that I meet knows what it's like to have alcoholism rip and tear your family apart. Every Native woman I have ever met has been sexually assaulted. They say that the statistic is three out of four Native women—

Yazzie: One in three.

Murphy: One in three. They say that one in three women are sexually abused in their lifetimes, but it's definitely higher than that. A lot of the Native people I know who have been sexually assaulted don't report it. I didn't report it when it happened to me. These numbers are extremely high. In a town like Gallup, a lot of women go missing. There are thousands of Native women who have gone missing and people don't talk about it. It's not breaking news. None of these problems get any attention. If they were to get attention, then you'd have to say, "Capitalism is failing." Capitalism has always failed Native people.

Yazzie: It's premised on our elimination.

Murphy: Exactly. These circumstances are dire. People are dying every day. Despite the rate of violence, there's no mobilization. No one is going out in the street. People are so used to it that their reaction isn't outrage. My mom tells me, "This is just the way it is. It's always gonna be this way." But by existing, we discredit the system and question the system. That's why I'm involved in the Red Nation.

Heatherton: Like the Black Panther Party, the Red Nation also has a ten-point program. Your fifth point is "an end to the discrimination, persecution, killing, torture, and rape of Native women." Can you say more about how this is central to your program?

Yazzie: I'm an Indigenous feminist. As I'm one of the co-founders of the Red Nation, there was no way this was not going to be in the agenda. That's the simple answer. All of the different subjects that we've included, whether it's LGBTQ2 (Lesbian, Gay, Bisexual, Transgender, Queer or Two-Spirited) people, women, the poor, the youth, and so forth, all of these groups are categories of Indigenous subjects under occupation by the United States that are completely marginalized and silenced. They are marginalized not just by the common sense of settler colonialism but also within Indigenous-led social movements. You never see young people or women or the poor or trans Native people at the helm of these movements. Traditionally, they are very patriarchal and quite sexist forms of social organizing. We are foregrounding these voices not as a simple politics of representation as though we merely needed someone with a uterus. We're feminists. That means we organize ourselves to confront the heteropatriarchy in organizing culture as well as in tribal government structures. We recognize the logic of heteropatriarchy as a form of violence disproportionately enacted on feminized bodies, whether Native women's bodies, queer bodies, or other Indigenous bodies.

Estes: I've been involved in a lot of environmental movements back home, especially in the anti–Keystone XL Pipeline movement. One thing I find fascinating is how non-Native people gravitate towards Indigenous causes that are "safe." They go to sites of extraction where the exploitation and monetization of nature is comprehendible to them. But capital is also reproduced in urban centers like border towns. Four out of five Native people live in urban centers. What would it mean if those same allies who came out to places they consider "Native spaces" instead came to places that aren't considered Native spaces, like Albuquerque? What if they rallied around us every time a Native trans woman was murdered on the street? Or every time a child was victimized in school? What if they protested every time a woman was violated in some way? If there was that same kind of reaction, in a city or a border town, what would that mean? The reason why Native youth, Native LGBTQ, Native women are central to these struggles is that they are made vulnerable by capital, not just at the sites of extraction, but also at the sites of its reproduction, the urban centers where a majority of Native people live.

Yazzie: Capital is reproduced through colonial violence. If you center the life of a Native trans sex worker, and there are many in Albuquerque, that person will have a subject position that has been reproduced through colonial violence. The logic of capital as it's reproduced through that person, or through a Native woman's body, is going to be so much more visible than when it appears in a white man or in many cases a Native man. In the Red Nation we are forced to talk about all of these forms of violence at the exact same time, because that's literally how people live their lives.

Heatherton: Like the Black Panther Party, your ten-point program also includes a demand for appropriate education, health care, social services, employment, and housing, what you call a "living social wage." How is this demand central to your organizing against capitalist colonialism?

Estes: The first point of our ten-point program is the reinstatement of treaty rights. That's what makes American Indians, Native people, distinct. Our treaty rights don't begin or end on the reservation boundary. When we cross the reservation boundary, we do not lose our rights. In Albuquerque alone there are 291 reasons why this is important, all based on treaties, because there are 291 federally recognized Native nations living in Albuquerque right now. That is a very powerful thing, politically speaking. Those are 291 guarantees for adequate health care, adequate education, and adequate social services. Those are basic human rights, and they aren't anything new. When we talk about the not-so-sexy battle for health care and education, it's based on treaties. That's where we're drawing our inspiration from when we talk about health care. Police brutality is more mainstream now. It's a really important struggle because of the ways in which we're having this conversation. We also need to do the hard groundwork of guaranteeing that these historic rights and historic obligations are fulfilled to keep a bare minimum of life and dignity for Native people.

Heatherton: The very last line of your ten-point program is "For Native peoples to live, capitalism and colonialism must die."

All: Yeah!

Banks: The Red Nation came into existence to fill a void. We wanted to provide a vehicle for struggle, to mobilize Native people, and, in a way, to be a catalyst to bring people into motion to fight. Like Paige said, homelessness, lack of access to health care, and poverty are often talked about as irrational outcomes of a rational system. Our perspective is the exact opposite, that these are actually quite rational outcomes of the irrational system that we live in.

This ten-point program, specifically the call for a living social wage, is a programmatic demand that serves the purpose of building into people's consciousness that these are not entitlements or the privileges of the few, but really human rights. We demand and fight for them, but we also believe that the current system will not actually be able to grant them. Our demands and our fighting will expose the system for what it is. They will expose the limits of the "democracy" that we live in and the limits of the capitalist system. That's really our goal.

Yazzie: Native people aren't living if we're living to die. We're produced so that we can reproduce the violence necessary for the accumulation of capital that is never ours. The capital is for a small group of people. We use the term "meaningful standard of living" in point eight of our ten-point plan. "Life" is at the root of that point because we mean it. Native people aren't living. In the capitalist-colonialist system, we are really only born so that we can be churned up, spit out, bludgeoned to death, killed by exposure, ripped apart by dogs, run over by cars, mangled by alcohol, or raped several times in our lives. That's really what life is like. That's not living. A meaningful standard of living would be a really basic step to allow Native people to begin to develop enough well-being to mobilize in any sort of way, and to create the kind of change we're envisioning in the Red Nation. We're not the kind of activists who say, "Our vision is to end colonialism and capitalism, and the way to do this is to burn down buildings, or whatever."

Murphy: Really? That's why I joined.

All: [*Laugh*]

Yazzie: We start where we're at. Where we're at sucks. It's incredibly violent. We want to allow Native people to live and to breathe just a little bit. We're genuinely interested in mobilizing poor people. We're a bunch of Marxists. We have a materialist approach, not an idealistic approach. We care about people. If you care about people then you have to deal with the messiness of life.

Estes: An idealized position envisions Native people as living this "authentic" Indigenous life, riding bareback in the mountains with the wind flowing through their hair, herding sheep, and hunting a buffalo, all at the same time. Despite the popular imaginary, four out of five Native people do not live on reservation land. That is a reality we have to confront. Albuquerque is Indigenous space. Gallup is Indigenous space. Rapid City is Indigenous space. The demands for reasonable housing, a living social wage, adequate social services, and adequate health care are not unreasonable. They are very, very reasonable. They are basic human rights that can be fulfilled. This is the richest, most powerful country in the world and it has people living in fourth world conditions. That's where Indigenous peoples are. To even begin to imagine an alternative future, an alternative to capitalism, an alternative to colonialism, and to facilitate that end, you have to have the ability to live. It's a future-oriented project. We're actually continuing a long struggle of Native people and moving it into the future. We're very progressive in that sense. We also understand that we want to work from the material conditions in which we find ourselves, not some imagined, idealized past where we're riding bareback, herding sheep, and killing buffalo.

Heatherton: All at the same time.

Estes: All at the same time.

Heatherton: You have a wonderful saying that "solidarity is not hard." Why is this an important organizing principle?

Murphy: The labor movement in the 1930s started off with a program like ours. This was a time of intense struggle. Workers got together. They put a list of demands together, including unemployment benefits and social security. This was really the work of the communists. At the time, people thought that these demands were totally unrealistic. But they won them through intense struggle. When all the workers stand together, it radicalizes people. You're able to see the system in a real way. If workers withhold their labor, then the capitalists have no power. We're materialists. We're Marxists. This program is a starting block to what we're trying to achieve. People may see things like access to education, free health care, social services, unemployment, and think that it will never happen. Through intense struggle and by bringing people out into the streets, we will be able to turn these demands into reality.

Estes: We've all worked in solidarity with Palestine, with the #BlackLivesMatter movement, and with other police brutality movements as well. When someone puts out a call, you respond. It's not about serving yourself as an individual. It's about using your body as a vehicle, putting it in the street, or writing a letter, or whatever, and standing behind other oppressed groups of people. I don't know any other way to explain it except that "solidarity is not hard." Get your shit together and get out there.

Murphy: Now more than ever, people are starting to bridge struggles together. We've done a lot of work around Palestinian solidarity, Muslim solidarity against Islamophobia, and against police brutality. All of these struggles are related. Everyone is fighting capitalism in their day-to-day lives whether they want to admit it or not. When you're struggling to make rent, you're fighting against capitalism. When you're looking for a job and you can't find one, you're struggling against capitalism. People every day are fighting against capitalism. When we link these struggles, that's when they're able to see it.

Yazzie: Another group we're building right now is Diné Solidarity with Palestine, since you can't end the occupation in Palestine unless you end the occupation of Indigenous land in the US. It's a globalized system of settler colonialism. If we're going to engage in solidarity, we have to center the Indigenous agenda. That's what the Red Nation is about. No one else centers the Indigenous agenda. It always gets lost or marginalized. If we actually center our own agenda and proceed with solidarity efforts from that position, what does that look like? I'm not terribly interested in solidarity paradigms that don't center Indigenous interests or an Indigenous critique of colonialism and capitalism.

Banks: We approach our work by thinking about how our activities can deepen the multinational character of an anti-racist struggle. We don't water down demands for self-determination, we try to raise the consciousness of the broader social justice movement. The Red Nation is trying to fill a vacuum, not just within society but also within the existing social justice movement that only pays lip service to the Native struggle. We're trying to build unity on a much different basis, on a deep understanding of self-determination, and that doesn't contradict in any way the need to build a broad-based, multinational, working-class movement.

Heatherton: Final thoughts?

Estes: Settlement is never a complete process, and we're here to make sure that it never gets completed. Colonization is a failed project, because they didn't kill us all.

Yazzie: That's why they have to constantly police us.

Estes: It's through 500 years of resistance that we have our existence in the present. That's what keeps us going. It's a beautiful thing, as much as it condemns us to this constant struggle. It's something that has to be fought. Otherwise, what did our ancestors die for?

II. BROKEN WINDOWS POLICING AS NEOLIBERAL URBAN STRATEGY

9. POLICING PLACE AND TAXING TIME ON SKID ROW

George Lipsitz

E very day one of the largest concentrations of police power anywhere in the world descends on a tiny, one-square-mile zone of
downtown Los Angeles. Police officers assigned to patrol the Skid
Row section of the city routinely wreak havoc on the lives of the 15,000
low-income and no-income people who inhabit this fifty-block area. In
a part of town where thousands of people are houseless and nearly three-
quarters suffer from physical or mental disabilities, police officers harass
and humiliate residents by incessantly checking pedestrians for outstanding warrants. They issue citation after citation for minor offenses
like jaywalking, sitting on the sidewalk, sleeping in public, holding an
open container of liquid, possessing small amounts of drugs, and failing
to appear in court to answer previous charges. In one instance, officers
cited a local resident for littering when the ash from his cigarette landed
on the sidewalk. Physically disabled residents using canes, walkers, and
wheelchairs have been cited and arrested for crosswalk violations because
they did not clear the intersection completely before the traffic signal
changed. Fines assessed for these trivial pedestrian violations range from
$159 to $191 per offense, a huge burden for people on fixed incomes
that generally range from $221 to $850 per month.[1] Those who cannot
pay the fines are often arrested and incarcerated for both failure to pay
and the initial offense.

Stopping, searching, citing, and arresting poor people for minor
offenses is part of the broken windows policing strategy championed

---

1 Los Angeles Community Action Network, "Community-Based Rights
Assessment: Skid Row's Safer Cities Initiative," December 2010, 1.

by New York City police commissioner William Bratton, who brought these practices to Los Angeles as chief of police between 2002 and 2009. Broken windows theory understands minor "quality of life" offenses such as loitering, drinking in public, and disorderly conduct as evidence of a disregard for law that undermines neighborhood pride and accountability, leading to more serious crimes. The approach, however, treats symptoms rather than causes. It is not the windows that have been broken, but rather the promises of full citizenship and social membership allegedly guaranteed by the 1866 and the 1964 Civil Rights Acts; the Thirteenth, Fourteenth, and Fifteenth Amendments to the Constitution; and the 1968 Fair Housing Act.[2] As a report by the Berkeley Law Policy Advocacy Clinic explains, "quality of life" is the wrong term for these policies to invoke "because there is no evidence that such laws improve the quality of life for anyone, and certainly not for homeless people."[3] Broken windows policing compels impoverished people to spend money on bail bonds, legal transcripts, appeals, attorneys' fees, and visits to prisons. Mass incarceration drives children into foster homes, interrupts work histories, and disrupts social networks. Jail time and fines increase the likelihood of eviction and shelter insecurity, and each eviction imperils future housing opportunities.

Local, state, and federal authorities spend six million dollars every year to pay for the deployment on Skid Row of a special force of fifty police officers and an additional twenty-five narcotics control agents. These expenditures leave less revenue available for safe and affordable lodging, accessible trash cans and restrooms with working sinks and toilets, medical care, and drug treatment and rehabilitation.[4] Moreover, the stop-and-frisk policies and the arrests that accompany them on Skid Row actually promote *disrespect* for the law: they rely on racial profiling,

---

2   Tom Hayden, "Dismantling the Myth of Bill Bratton's LAPD," *The Nation*, December 6, 2013.

3   Berkeley Law Policy Advocacy Clinic, "California's New Vagrancy Laws: The Growing Enactment and Enforcement of Anti-Homeless Laws in the Golden State," February 2015, 6, available at law.berkeley.edu.

4   Los Angeles Community Action Network, "LA Is 'Crafting a New Plan' for Skid Row—Unfortunately in Reality It's Just Talking Points," July 21, 2014, available at cangress.org.

provoke frequent, random, and indiscriminate confrontations with citizens who have engaged in no criminal activities, and make residents feel like interlopers in their own neighborhoods. Police stops, questionings, and arrests interfere with people's daily routines, while constant disruption and dispersion fragment social ties. Scholarly studies show clearly that harassment and discrimination make people frustrated, angry, fearful, sad, depressed, detached and isolated.[5]

The Los Angeles Police Department has boasted that its officers made 5,000 arrests on Skid Row in a four-month period in 2006–7. In 2013, 14 percent of the people arrested in the city of Los Angeles were homeless, a percentage that represents nearly 15,000 people.[6] In theory, officers can stop and question someone legally only if they have reasonable suspicion that the person has committed a crime. Individuals stopped by officers on Skid Row, however, reported that they were not questioned about crimes, that the officers immediately asked them other kinds of questions about their parole and probation status. In some cases, the officers checked names against lists of people with outstanding warrants and detained those with a name that corresponded to one on the list without explaining the original stop.[7] In addition, the property rights of people on Skid Row are not respected. Until an injunction by a federal judge in 2011 put an end to the practice, police officers routinely confiscated the meager private possessions of houseless people, claiming that blankets and clothes on the sidewalk were litter or constituted fire hazards. Despite the court's ruling, city officials continue to disregard the property rights of houseless people. A recently proposed amendment to the city ordinance regulating property on sidewalks would give those cited only twenty-four hours to move their possessions to private

---

5   John Mirowsky and Catherine E. Ross, *Social Causes of Psychological Distress*, 2nd ed. (New Brunswick, NJ: Aldine Transaction, 2012), 17; Amy Schultz, David Williams, Barbara Israel, Adam Becker, Edith Parker, Sherman A. James, and James Jackson, "Unfair Treatment, Neighborhood Effects, and Mental Health in the Detroit Metropolitan Area," *Journal of Health and Social Behavior* 41, no. 3 (September 2000): 316.

6   Gale Holland, "Why Most of the $100 Million LA Spends on Homelessness Goes to Police," *Los Angeles Times*, April 17, 2014.

7   Richard Winton and Cara Mia DiMassa, "Skid Row Cleanup Is Challenged," *Los Angeles Times*, March 3, 2007.

storage facilities (which do not exist in the area and which the residents could not afford to use even if they did). The proposed amendment forbids citizens to move their possessions to a different public place, which would force houseless people to carry everything they own on their person twenty-four hours a day.[8]

These policies of aggressive policing purport to protect poor people from crime, but in most cases, the only criminal charges that emerge are the ones that the officers bring against the residents they claim to be protecting. Aggressive policing subjects houseless people to unprovoked abuse and undeserved humiliation. A survey among residents of Skid Row in 2009 found that 89.3 percent reported being stopped and questioned by police officers, 82.8 percent reported that they had received citations, and 82.1 percent reported that they had been arrested. Respondents expressed more fear of harassment by the police than fear of criminal acts by other residents, a fear borne out by statistics that revealed a higher frequency of police harassment (37 percent) than assault (24 percent) or robbery (18 percent).[9] A 2010 survey revealed that more than 50 percent of respondents reported being arrested in the previous year and losing housing, social services, or jobs as a result. Nearly half of those surveyed said that they had been verbally or physically abused by law enforcement officials while being cited for jaywalking, sleeping on the sidewalk, and other nonviolent offenses.[10]

The pervasive stops, citations, arrests, convictions, jail sentences, and fines meted out to Skid Row residents in response to minor, alleged offenses bring major collateral consequences. Interactions with officers tax the time of poor people, disrupting social networks and interrupting daily routines. The punishments meted out in the form of monetary fines and jail terms lead to a host of other extrajudicial punishments. For example, a record of arrests, even arrests that do not lead to charges or convictions, creates new impediments to securing jobs, housing, and

---

8   General Dogon, "Keep Ya Hands Off My Property!" *Community Connection*, April–May 2015, 5.

9   Los Angeles Community Action Network, "Community-Based Rights Assessment: Skid Row's Safer Cities Initiative," December 2010, 4.

10   Heather Timmons, "A Fatal Police Shooting Shows How the 'Safer Cities' Initiative in Los Angeles Failed Skid Row," *Quartz*, March 2, 2015.

social services. People who plead guilty to sitting on the sidewalk when they have nowhere else to go can discover later that this "record" becomes a barrier to securing shelter and employment. People who have jobs risk being sent to jail if they do not appear in court, but they risk being fired by their employers if they miss work to do so. Incarceration can lead to temporary suspension of income support for children and disabled adults. People can be denied public housing because of an arrest record.[11] The criminalization of poverty and its collateral consequences create ever increasing and cumulative vulnerabilities for Skid Row residents.

Aggressive policing takes time and wastes time. Officers incessantly interrupt and disrupt poor people's lives with perpetual rounds of stops, questions, frisks, arrests, and incarcerations. Nearly all of the charges brought against houseless people by police officers and prosecutors are, in essence, poverty violations. They are crimes of condition rather than crimes of conduct. The same "offenses" would not attract any police attention at all if they took place in suburban cul-de-sacs, college fraternity houses, or on the docks of private yacht clubs. Police officers on Skid Row do not so much fight crime as fabricate it. They increase the misery of residents, undermine their dignity, and make their everyday lives chaotic. They produce a kind of anarchy in the name of order.[12]

This aggressive policing works in tandem with neoliberal neighborhood development policies by which the city is governed and which work to create a calculated ungovernability in the lives of poor people. It is not the criminality of Skid Row residents that gets them arrested, but rather their powerlessness—their status as people *with problems* but *without property* who inhabit an area that wealthy elites wish to redevelop. As far as city officials are concerned, houseless people are in the wrong place at the wrong time. In order to make Skid Row and nearby

11   Berkeley Law Policy Advocacy Clinic, "California's New Vagrancy Laws," 28; George Lipsitz, "'In an Avalanche, Every Snowflake Pleads Not Guilty': The Collateral Consequences of Mass Incarceration and Impediments to Women's Fair Housing Rights," *UCLA Law Review* 59 (2012): 1746.

12   I am using the word "anarchy" here to refer to a chaotic state of disorder, not to impugn the long and honorable traditions of political anarchism and their admirable visions of human freedom. The phrase "anarchy in the name of order" comes from Karl Marx, *The Eighteenth Brumaire of Louis Bonaparte* (New York: International Publishers, 1994), 73.

areas of downtown more attractive to investors and owners, city officials seek to make the area unlivable for poor people. By aggressively policing their spaces and disrupting their daily routines, they hope to displace and dispossess houseless people, to make them and the problems associated with their presence disappear. Affluent loft dwellers living in the condominiums they have purchased are viewed as desirable residents of the area. Impoverished tenants renting rooms in single-room-occupancy hotels or displaced people attempting to survive on the streets are seen as illegitimate, undesirable, and disposable. Pets are permitted in loft condominiums but banned in single-room-occupancy hotels. Overnight visitors are welcome to stay with the owners of lofts but not with tenants in the hotels. The city builds dog parks with fountains to enable the pets of people living in lofts to relieve and refresh themselves, but it does not provide sinks or toilets for those who live on the streets.[13] Municipal officials welcome the owners of newly purchased lofts to the neighborhood but describe the renters and the houseless as "transients," even though many of them and their families have lived downtown for decades. The authorities appreciate the exchange value of the neighborhood as a site for increased returns on investments but dismiss the use value of the neighborhood for poor people who rely on the services, social networks, and emotional ecosystems it supports.[14]

Almost all of the residents of Skid Row have extremely limited incomes and are vulnerable to exploitation by employers and landlords. More than one-third of the Skid Row residents are houseless, and almost all of the rest suffer from chronic housing insecurity. In the city of Los Angeles as a whole, more than three-fourths of the estimated homeless population of 82,000 people lacked access to a shelter bed in 2013, requiring them to live outside all the time.[15] People wind up on Skid Row because wages are too low, because affordable housing is

13   Monica Lomeli, "White Nostalgic Redevelopment: Race, Class and Gentrification in Downtown Los Angeles," (PhD diss., University of California Department of Sociology, 2014).

14   For a discussion of the importance of use value and exchange value in urban life, see John Logan and Harvey Molotch, *Urban Fortunes: The Political Economy of Place* (Berkeley: University of California Press, 2007).

15   Berkeley Law Policy Advocacy Clinic, "California's New Vagrancy Laws," 5.

in short supply, and because the social safety net has been shredded in order to subsidize tax breaks for the wealthy. Housing insecurity is a personal problem, but it has structural causes. It is produced by policies that discourage affordable housing, that protect predatory lending, that promote gentrification, that drive people out of public housing, and that sanction the conversion of apartments into condominiums. Nationally, veterans have at least a one in ten chance of becoming homeless. In Los Angeles, 18 percent of the homeless population is made up of military veterans.[16] People newly released from jails or prisons have a one in thirteen chance of becoming homeless.[17] The war on drugs, the prohibitive costs of drug treatment and rehabilitation, mass incarceration and the collateral consequences of a criminal conviction exacerbate housing insecurity. In the state of California, 10 percent of parolees live on the streets. In Los Angeles, ex-offenders comprise an estimated 30 to 50 percent of the houseless population.[18] Legislatures allocate extravagant sums of money for policing and prisons, but not enough for education, physical and mental health care, and job training. Government officials neglect enforcement of civil rights laws, leaving members of aggrieved and stigmatized groups vulnerable to discrimination. In a city that is less than 10 percent Black, some three-quarters of Skid Row residents are African American.[19] Nationally, Black families turn to homeless shelters at a rate seven times higher than white families.[20]

Housing insecurity on Skid Row is a product of the cumulative vulnerabilities and injuries caused by centuries of city, state, and federal housing policies that have promoted and subsidized asset accumulation for whites while confining communities of color to means-tested public housing.[21] Long histories of racial zoning, restrictive covenants, racial

---

16   Timmons, "A Fatal Police Shooting."

17   Berkeley Law Policy Advocacy Clinic, "California's New Vagrancy Laws," 4.

18   Alina Ball, "An Imperative Redefinition of 'Community': Incorporating Reentry Lawyers to Increase the Efficacy of Community Economic Development Initiatives," *UCLA Law Review* 55 (2008), 1897.

19   Lamp Community and the Los Angeles Community Action Network, "The Safer Cities Initiative Is a Failed Policy: End Human Rights Violations and Build Housing Today," 2008.

20   Berkeley Law Policy Advocacy Clinic, "California's New Vagrancy Laws," 4.

21   Melvin Oliver and Thomas Shapiro, *Black Wealth/White Wealth: A New*

steering, blockbusting, mortgage redlining, and predatory lending have relegated people of different races to different places. They have produced "sorted-out" cities characterized by polarized zones of affluence and abandonment.[22] The aggressive policing of place and time on Skid Row by the haves who govern individualizes the disorder created by the histories of structural racism and systemic class exploitation. Presuming that people who *have* problems *are* problems confuses the consequences of poverty with its causes. Policing poor people and taxing their time appear as cheaper options to city officials than building affordable housing, providing physical and psychological health services, enforcing civil rights laws, and paying workers a living wage. In the long run, however, policing poor people, taxing their time, and dispossessing and displacing them create enormous social and economic costs. These practices produce many of the non-normative behaviors they purport to prevent.

The dispossession, displacement, and desired disappearance of Skid Row residents in Los Angeles form part of a broader pattern of neoliberal accumulation by dispossession that affects the entire country. The privatization and fiscalization of urban development relies upon a fragmented, delinked, and devolved state dedicated to protecting the propertied and the privileged but increasingly unwilling and even unable to meet the needs of the majority of the population.[23] For over four decades, cuts in social spending coupled with massive subsidies for expensive but ineffective privatization schemes have undercut the real wages and quality of life for the overwhelming majority of the population.[24] Neoliberalism promotes the hoarding of resources, revenues, amenities, and opportunities in prosperous communities and

---

Perspective on Racial Inequality (New York: Routledge, 2006); Chad Freidrichs, dir., *The Pruitt-Igoe Myth* (First Run Features, 2012), DVD.

22   Mindy Thompson Fullilove, *Urban Alchemy: Restoring Joy in America's Sorted-Out Cities* (New York: New Village Press, 2013), 108.

23   Clyde Woods, "Do You Know What It Means to Miss New Orleans? Katrina, Trap Economics and the Rebirth of the Blues," *American Quarterly* 57, no. 4 (2005): 1012; David Harvey, *The New Imperialism* (Oxford University Press, 2003), 67; Naomi Klein, *The Shock Doctrine: The Rise of Disaster Capitalism* (New York: Metropolitan Books/Henry Holt, 2007).

24   Henry Giroux, "The Occupy Movement Meets the Suicidal State," *Situations* 5, no. 1 (2013): 14.

the concentration of nuisances, hazards, and inconveniences in places inhabited by the poor.[25] It elevates the potential exchange value of Skid Row over its use value. Its utility as the home of a social world for a population with nowhere else to go counts for nothing from a neoliberal perspective. Its potential as a site for new development and investment is all that counts from a perspective that sees all space as only market space. Similarly, the historical causes of the concentration of poverty or the historical uses of the neighborhood by its diverse population can be disregarded from the neoliberal perspective, because the only time that counts is the area's possible future as a site for profitable returns on investment. Thus, houseless activists and their allies on Skid Row not only confront powerful entrenched economic and political opponents, they must contend with the privileging of market place and market time over social and historical place and time.

Neoliberalism promises prosperity but produces austerity. It lauds the work ethic but wages war on working people. It lauds the ideal of small government yet relentlessly expands the state's expenditures on incarceration, military intervention, and business-related infrastructures. These contradictions run the risk of producing an angry, embittered, disillusioned, and disaffected public. Yet for precisely that reason, punitive policies towards the poor serve pedagogical and political as well as economic purposes. Punitive policies that criminalize poverty deflect attention away from the failures of neoliberal policies. By inciting fears and stoking the flames of moral panic about crime, disorder, and welfare dependency, leaders of the public and private sectors alike win popular consent for policies that only benefit the rich. For that reason, they need campaigns against the homeless as part and parcel of a coordinated strategy designed to encourage people to fear open and democratic public spaces, to seek controlled and guarded environments from which the poor have been expelled.

In order to police place, the authorities also tax time. Every encounter with police officers reminds Skid Row residents that they do not control the places they inhabit, that they live in spaces of hierarchical surveillance and regulation rather than nurturing mutuality and reciprocity.

---

25   Robert Reich, "The Secession of the Successful," *New York Times Magazine*, January 20, 1991.

Living overpoliced and underprotected on Skid Row means having to stop time, waste time, and serve time. The great organizer Cesar Chavez used to say that the rich have money but the poor have time. He meant that time spent by workers educating, agitating, organizing, and mobilizing could offset their opponents' material advantages and attendant political influence. The experience of poor people on Skid Row, however, demonstrates that the rich control even time. Residents of single-room-occupancy hotels, for example, encounter "the twenty-eight-day shuffle." The shuffle takes place in response to California state laws that extend certain protections to tenants once they have lived in their dwellings for thirty continuous days. Status as "thirty-day" tenants means they cannot be evicted without due legal process. Evicted tenants are entitled to monetary relocation assistance ranging from $2,000 to $5,000 depending on their vulnerability. In order to avoid liability for these obligations, some apartment owners move tenants every twenty-eight days from one room to another, from one hotel to another, or from one room back into the same room. Sometimes they simply evict the tenants. Being forced to move every four weeks adds to the instability and insecurity in the lives of Skid Row residents. This unwanted mobility fragments friendship networks and shatters support systems, inhibits the establishment of stable routines, and promotes transience. Twenty-eight-day evictions defy the spirit and intent of the law but are not considered quality-of-life crimes by the police officers who patrol Skid Row. The Los Angeles city attorney's office did initiate one prosecution in 2006 that accused hotel owners of harassing and intimidating their customers, locking them out of the rooms they had rented, and illegally evicting tenants without paying relocation fees in order to facilitate the conversion of a hotel into luxury loft apartments. Two years later, the owners agreed to a settlement that required them to pay civil penalties, reimburse the city's investigative costs, and establish a $700,000 restitution fund to pay relocation fees. Yet despite the pervasiveness of the twenty-eight-day shuffle, the city attorney admitted that as far as he knew, this was the first successful prosecution of the practice anywhere in the state.[26]

---

26   Richard Winton and Cara Mia DiMassa, "City Targets 'the Shuffle' on Skid Row," *Los Angeles Times*, March 23, 2006; Sherri M. Okamoto, "Hotel Owners Settle Suit with City over '28-Day Shuffle,'" *Metropolitan News-Enterprise*, March 14, 2008.

Private landlords who disrupt the lives of Skid Row residents by per-petrating the twenty-eight-day shuffle clearly violate the law. Instead of policing and prosecuting these malefactors, police officers and city attorneys compound the instability of poor people's lives by perpetrating shuffles of their own under the cover of law. Between 2000 and 2015 arrests for vagrancy in California increased by 77 percent, even though arrests for public drunkenness declined by 16 percent and arrests for dis-orderly conduct decreased by 48 percent.[27] These are arrests caused by *not* moving, by the "crimes" of standing, sitting, resting, sleeping, lodging, or camping in public places. Houseless people are expected to constantly "move along" in public even if they have nowhere to go. As Western Regional Advocacy Project spokesperson Paul Boden explains, "Everyone sleeps, eats, and sits, but only some get tickets or go to jail for it."[28]

As Becky Dennison of LA CAN argues, the actual lawlessness that exists on Skid Row "is almost entirely people preying on the poor and the homeless." The "worst criminals on Skid Row," she insists, are slum-lords, but it is harder and more expensive to prosecute them than the homeless.[29] An investigation conducted in 2007 by social service and activist organizations found that the average cost to the city of pros-ecuting one slumlord was $232,000, and that prosecuting all known slumlords in the city would cost between $344 and $462 million dol-lars.[30] While working with the tenants of the Regent Hotel, activists from LA CAN found that the building suffered from insect infestation, mildew, missing screens and windows, broken elevators, chipping and peeling paint, inadequate heat and hot water, and dangerous ongoing construction work. The tenants suffered from asthma, depression, rashes, rat bites, staph infections, respiratory problems, colds and coughs, throat and ear infections, and eye irritations. Conditions like this exist throughout Skid Row and the Los Angeles area, but law enforcement

---

27   Berkeley Law Policy Advocacy Clinic, "California's New Vagrancy Laws."

28   Eric Ares, "The Right to Rest Act Stays Alive," *Community Connection*, April–May 2015, 9.

29   Okamoto, "Hotel Owners Settle Suit," 1.

30   Albert Lowe and Gilda Haas, eds., *The Shame of the City: Slum Housing and the Critical Threat to the Health of LA Children and Families* (Los Angeles: Strategic Actions for a Just Economy, 2007), 4.

officials have decided that it is homeless people who should be prosecuted for diminishing the local "quality of life."[31]

Policing place and taxing time are instruments of class rule, but they
are also technologies of white supremacy. The existence of Skid Row,
the persistence of ghettos and barrios, and the unequal distribution of
amenities, advantages, hazards, and nuisances to differently raced neighborhoods testify to the spatial dynamics that link race to place. The
taxing of time on Skid Row evidences a similar temporal dimension to
racial oppression.[32] While poor people have to waste time and serve
time because of the metaphor of the broken windows, actual broken
windows sit unrepaired. A study by the National Fair Housing Alliance
revealed that broken windows on bank-owned, foreclosed property in
Black communities are repaired less often and more slowly than those
in white communities; bankers value white property more highly than
Black property.

The different iterations of broken windows policing in cities around
the world endanger vulnerable people. People locked out of opportunities are locked up in detention centers, jails, and prisons to protect the
locked-in advantages of the privileged and powerful. When police officers in Los Angeles fan out across Skid Row each day to harass houseless
people, they act not as individuals but as part of a national and international pattern organized around the needs of neoliberalism. More than
an economic theory and its attendant practices, neoliberalism is also a
historical conjuncture in which specific social subjects are produced and
reproduced through specific social practices. The activists, advocates,
and allies who campaign for houseless people's "right to the city" thus
confront not only investors and law enforcement officers, but also a way
of thinking and a way of life promoted by the neoliberal social warrant.

Social warrants are widely shared assumptions about what is permit-
ted and what is forbidden, about who is included and who is excluded.
They are rarely written down, argued about, or even openly proclaimed.
Yet they constitute the common sense assumptions of an era. They are

---

31   Lowe and Haas, *The Shame of the City*, 17.

32   National Fair Housing Alliance, "Here Comes the Bank, There Goes Our
Neighborhood: How Lenders Discriminate in Treatment of Foreclosed Homes," April
22, 2011.

embedded so thoroughly in social practices and social relations that they seem natural, necessary, and inevitable. A social warrant functions as a de facto social charter that contains foundational principles about obligations and rights. In order to refuse the unlivable destiny to which neoliberalism has consigned them, Skid Row activists in Los Angeles find themselves compelled to raise demands and programs that challenge the social warrant of neoliberalism, that call into question the legitimacy of the entire system. People who are relatively more privileged than Skid Row residents might convince themselves that minor reforms can make their lives better, but the eyewitnesses to mass displacement, dispossession, and disempowerment have no such luxury. They require radical changes in social policies and social values simply to survive.

A neoliberal society needs to naturalize exploitation and hierarchy, to elevate internalized desires for advantages and wealth over mutual recognition and respect, to create spaces structured around the imperatives of hostile privatism and defensive localism, and to stoke exaggerated fears of difference in order to mobilize resentment, contempt, and anger towards vulnerable populations and render them disposable, displaceable, and deportable.[33] The spatial imaginary that flows from campaigns proclaiming a right to the city for all, on the other hand, proceeds from very different premises. Houseless activists, advocates, and allies seek to elevate use value over exchange value, to discover hidden value in undervalued places and undervalued people, to create new democratic opportunities, to share responsibility for common problems, and to promote mutuality, accountability, stewardship, and respectful interactions across social divides in order to generate new practices, new perceptions, new polities, and new politics.

Activist groups like the Los Angeles Community Action Network need to win short-term gains within the existing social warrant while at the same time setting in motion forces that can lead to a new social warrant. The organization has secured important victories against the excesses of the present system. One campaign stopped the Community Redevelopment Agency's City Center plan that would have eliminated

---

33   See Barbara Tomlinson and George Lipsitz, "Insubordinate Spaces for Intemperate Times: Countering the Pedagogies of Neoliberalism," *Review of Education, Pedagogy and Cultural Studies* 35, no. 1 (2013): 3–26.

3,000 badly needed affordable housing units in the downtown area. Another ended the practice by landlords of charging tenants fees for hosting family members, friends, and caregivers in their dwellings. Lawsuits against illegal evictions secured some $3 million in compensation to low-income people. The Community Watch program that monitors police behavior has protected residents from brutality and mobilized them to work together as an alternative security force in the neighborhood.[34] In the long run, however, it will not be enough to curb the excesses of developers without questioning the very logic and premises of neoliberal development. It will not suffice to rein in the excess brutality of police officers and security guards without questioning why the reigning definition of security protects investors and owners at the expense of the safety, peace of mind, and well-being of all residents. As a consequence, the organization augments its short-range projects with efforts to deepen democratic desires and capacities in the long term. LA CAN's mission statement proclaims the group's intentions to organize and empower residents to change the relations of power that shape life in the community, to create an organization and organizing model that eradicates the ways in which race, class, and gender oppressions prevent communities from building true power, and to eliminate the multiple forms of violence used against and within the community that maintain the status quo. Transitional goals on the way to achieving these long-term objectives include opposing the criminalization of poverty, supporting women's rights, insisting on adequate housing as a human right, and securing access to healthy foods.[35]

LA CAN counters the social warrant of neoliberalism by championing the interests of renters over those of owners and investors.[36] In the face of urban planning that promotes the city mainly as a site for profitable returns for private investors, LA CAN seeks to channel public investments to projects that benefit ordinary people, that create housing stability without fear of displacement, that promote strong neighborhood social ties through public activities and events, that provide

---

34   See the Los Angeles Community Action Network website at cangress.org.

35   Los Angeles Community Action Network, cangress.org.

36   Pete White, "Transforming Our Communities, Transforming Ourselves," Center for Black Studies Research (Santa Barbara, CA), May 9, 2015. Author's notes.

freedom from fear of police officers, that support affordable, accessible, and effective public transportation, that lead to healthy conditions within and around homes and all living spaces, and that enable access to physical and mental health care, fresh foods, and parks and recreation.

For groups like LA CAN, developing a new social warrant requires the development of oppositional understandings of time and place by raising what might seem like illogical demands. City officials assume that safety on the streets requires more stops, frisks, arrests, and incarcerations. LA CAN and its allies argue that funds now expended on law enforcement (an estimated $46 to $80 million on labor costs of arrests alone in 2013) should be used instead to build safe, clean, and affordable housing and to provide mental and physical health care.[37] They challenge their confinement to a small space in downtown Los Angeles by reaching out to a wider world in many ways, including sending houseless activist Deborah Burton to Geneva, Switzerland, to testify before the United Nations Human Rights Commission and inviting hip-hop legend Chuck D to stage a street festival on Skid Row so that people from other parts of town could witness the enduring humanity of houseless people in the face of inhumane conditions. At a time when neoliberal development schemes emphasize public subsidies for privately owned, controlled, and occupied places, LA CAN promotes the creation of a new public sphere that guarantees universal access to parks, grocery stores, and efficient public transportation. The group enacts the desired social relations that it envisions through the creation and maintenance of events, activities, clubs, and organizations that build strong social ties. In a city that treats people without property as a social liability, houseless activists demand recognition and promotion of community-level expertise and assets.

The logic of neoliberal capitalism within the US racial order permits groups to demand resources and recognition in limited ways. Activist groups can be viewed as representatives of individual stakeholders entitled to a better distribution of opportunities. Aggrieved racial groups are thus sometimes allowed to claim and compete for a more equitable share of available resources. Neoliberal logic does not, however,

---

37 Holland, "Why Most of the $100 Million L.A. Spends on Homelessness Goes to Police."

acknowledge a right to challenge the hegemony of market space and market time. It does not countenance democratic deliberation and decision making. It does not recognize the collective, cumulative, and continuing linked fate of members of aggrieved racial groups. It does not authorize popular control over the decisions that affect people's lives. Under these conditions, even those seeking to challenge the prevailing order find themselves echoing its assumptions and presumptions. Social scientists theorizing social movements assume that in order to succeed oppressed people must think like their oppressors, frame their demands in ways that secure approval from those in power, and create interest convergence by proposing schemes resonant with privatization and fiscalization, that primarily make money for owners and investors and only incidentally help the oppressed. This impoverished model of distributive justice limits members of aggrieved groups to seeking to become recipients of largesse from their oppressors. The work of LA CAN points in another direction. It seeks procedural justice as well as distributive justice, insisting on the right of aggrieved groups to speak for themselves, to participate in deliberative conversations and secure the power to make decisions about issues that concern them and others. Rather than positing a world made up of individual, self-interested market subjects, LA CAN speaks for and from the collective experiences with displacement and dispossession of communities of color.[38]

In Los Angeles, a city where people have been inculcated for decades with fear-laden fantasies about the poor, about the houseless, about people of color, about returning ex-offenders, about people with non-normative sexualities, brutal, punitive, and aggressive policing seems, to many, like a good thing. Many people consent to aggressive policing and the criminalization of poverty because they believe those policies will insure that they will be safe. Yet the pattern of policing that prevails on Skid Row and the urban interests it has been designed to protect create dangerous conditions for the neighborhood, the city, the state, and the nation. LA CAN and other activist groups championing the

---

38 On procedural and distributive justice, see Julie Sze, Jonathan London, Fraser Shilling, Gerardo Gambirazzio, Trina Filan, and Mary Cadanasso, "Defining and Contesting Environmental Justice: Socio-natures and the Politics of Scale in the Delta," *Antipode* 41, no. 4 (2009): 807–43, especially 826–7.

right to the city for all provide a humane, democratic, and just alternative to neoliberalism. They teach us that a new social warrant is possible. Through their emerging practices of procedural justice, they are planting the seeds of new ways of knowing, new ways of being, and new ways of making decisions about rights, resources, and recognition that push back against the oppression and theft of our time and offer a glimpse of an alternative to the calculated cruelties that permeate our lives.

~

George Lipsitz, chair of the board of directors of the African American Policy Forum, is a professor of Black studies and sociology at the University of California, Santa Barbara. He is the author of many books, including *How Racism Takes Place* (Temple University Press, 2011).

10. ASSET STRIPPING AND BROKEN WINDOWS POLICING ON LA'S SKID ROW: AN INTERVIEW WITH BECKY DENNISON AND PETE WHITE

Jordan T. Camp and Christina Heatherton

Pete White is the executive director of the Los Angeles Community Action Network (LA CAN). Becky Dennison was co-executive director of LA CAN for fourteen years and recently became executive director of Venice Community Housing and an LA CAN Board member. LA CAN fights for the civil and human rights of the poor and predominantly Black and Brown residents in Los Angeles and based in Skid Row, the area with the highest concentration of poverty and policing in the country. The organization is engaged in a broad-based national alliance against the criminalization of poverty and for the human right to housing, health, full employment, and dignity.

Heatherton: Several high-profile, filmed police killings ignited the #BlackLivesMatter movement. Recently, Charly Leundeu Keunang, known as "Africa," was shot here on San Pedro and 6th Street, not too far from where we are sitting. Can you talk about the everyday violence and vulnerabilities people experience here on Skid Row?

Dennison: The police murders we've seen here on Skid Row are part of a nationwide trend. They are consistent with the level of force, animosity, and artillery that the police have been using against our communities citywide and here on Skid Row. The murder is also an outcome of broken windows policing, specifically the Safer Cities Initiative (SCI), a measure that has been in place since 2006 (though it was initially intended to last six months). SCI has produced an over-concentration of police that leads to constant interactions, harassment, unheard-of levels of citations and arrests, the highest use of force in the city, and a basic disregard for human life. People here have been completely dehumanized by this level of policing.

White: Charlie Keunang's murder by the LAPD has resonated in a moment in which Black lives are being devastated in public view. We are clear that police violence has been happening long before it was in everyone's home, on every TV screen, and all over the Internet. In thinking about violence we have to also think about structural violence, particularly the violence used to remove people from gentrifying communities. A few months ago, the Los Angeles City Administrative Office released an audit that showed that the city devoted $100 million dollars from its General Fund to homelessness last year; $87 million of that went to the police. That's more than $238,000 dollars a day. In the city of LA you could spend that money to build housing, so the lack of housing is clearly not about a lack of resources. We have to confront structural racism and the way it authorizes the removal of people, particularly Black people, by any means necessary, from any community, at any time.

Camp: When William Bratton was reappointed New York City police commissioner, Mayor Bill de Blasio cited Bratton's "success" as LA's police chief between 2002 and 2009. As a group working on the ground in LA before and after Bratton's time here, can you comment on the legitimacy of claims made by politicians and circulated in major news outlets such as the *New York Times* and the *Los Angeles Times* that Bratton-style policing improved "race relations" and made LA "safer"?

Dennison: The Safer Cities Initiative brought anywhere between 50 and 110 officers into the fifty square blocks of the Skid Row community. It was also supplemented and coordinated with parole and probation officers as well as the sheriff's department. There was a level of law enforcement in the community that nobody had ever witnessed before. Within the fifty square blocks of Skid Row, this deployment focused on a fifteen-square-block area where street homelessness is the most concentrated.

SCI was sold to the public by politicians and by Chief Bratton as a means of "making the community safer." I don't know of one person who lives in this community who believes that. People felt fear and apprehension about even walking down the sidewalk since the chances of getting stopped, cited, or arrested were so great. This is a police occupation, a way of enforcing spatial and racial segregation in downtown LA.

White: In 2004, Bill Bratton's road dog and business associate Dr. George Kelling came to Los Angeles and hosted a meeting in Central Division, a police station in downtown LA. In that meeting he essentially said, "Quality-of-life policing is not going to look good and it is not going to feel good, but we have got to gain the moral high ground. How we gain the moral high ground is by getting the media on our side." Public relations is at the core of broken windows policing, quality-of-life policing, and now community-oriented policing.

Bratton was also masterful at building coalitions of organizations around the city who formerly would have been critics of the police department. One example is the Advancement Project. When Bratton was in town they changed their business model. Connie Rice, their co-director, said this herself no less than six months ago at Ward AME Church. She said that when she started representing the police instead of representing Grape Street Crips, the courts gave her a different kind of respect. A lot of her business model is now closely linked with the LAPD. When Bratton returned to New York he flew Connie Rice out with him to pave the way. He took her on a press junket, to say: "This is civil rights LA. She is here to tell you that I have reformed a racist organization." Bratton's biggest asset is not that he's the nation's top cop—it's that he is the best hype man and public relations guru and politician we've seen in a long time.

Dennison: Bratton, both in New York and in Los Angeles, has also been one of the "leaders" in using policing as a tool of gentrification. He perpetuated that model of using the police to clear public space and also to clear people from their homes. That's what we have seen in the use of broken windows policing in public housing and in other neighborhoods throughout the country.

Heatherton: Skid Row is located in zones of international capital investment and is a stone's throw from a center of global finance. The fight for this space is a struggle over property with the backing and pressure of global capital. If it wasn't, the police response wouldn't have been so fierce. You at LA CAN are on the frontlines of a struggle against criminalization with global ramifications. What does this struggle look like from the perspective of Skid Row residents?

White: When Antonio Villaraigosa was mayor of Los Angeles, the question global investors kept asking him was about resources and buying land. Specifically, they asked, "What about Skid Row?" Villaraigosa and Bratton answered them by discussing a homeless removal strategy. The plan authorized the police to clear the land for global investment in this particular area. I know people like to think about this fight in a localized way, but we see this thing continuously repeating itself, from San Francisco to New York. The police are the frontline of defense so that investors can come in, spend resources, and buy up space.

The city is responding to the desires of big capital. You can see this in the Los Angeles Housing Authority's (HACLA) decision to redevelop Jordan-Downs, the Watts public housing project, or in the way that the civilian Police Commission consistently supports the LAPD's removal of people from this area. The global expansion of capital impacts the material conditions of people on the ground. Yeah, we've got the hipsters and many are racist, but the real support of gentrification comes from these larger racist structures.

Camp: The term "asset stripping" usually describes large-scale takeovers of companies, mass firings, and the selling of all of their assets. The late blues geographer Clyde A. Woods used the term to describe broken windows policing and redevelopment in Skid Row. Can you talk about how the poor encounter asset stripping on Skid Row?

Dennison: People in Skid Row are stripped of their entire history. Whether they are housed residents who have been homeless before, people assumed to be homeless, or homeless residents, they are stripped of their history and made into a simplified problem of mental illness and drug addiction. These are not the primary causes of homelessness. These narratives conveniently displace structural factors that cause homelessness, like the federal government's complete disinvestment in housing.

Both housed and homeless people in the neighborhood have also repeatedly lost their personal possessions. Sometimes this was because they were twenty-eight-day-shuffled out of residential hotels (displaced as a result of managers' attempts to dodge tenancy laws), or they were illegally evicted or arrested and had their possessions thrown away. We have videos of people screaming, "Those are my mother's ashes!" or "That's the only picture of my father!" as the police destroy their belongings. Physical assets are stripped in incredibly aggressive and violent ways.

White: Developers have tried to frame Skid Row as an empty, broken place where there is "nothing worth saving." One of the most effective things we did was encourage residents to introduce themselves as community residents of Skid Row. As a result, we immediately saw the narrative shift. The police started to say that they were "going after the criminal elements and not the poor people." We are still working to shift the narrative.

Dennison: When developers originally planned to eliminate all the residential hotels in the historic core, they labeled them as transient and prostitution havens. This narrative was so widespread that people outside the community didn't believe there were actually human beings living in these hotels. We started a housing preservation campaign where people testified about living in the neighborhood. They discussed living here, sometimes for several decades, and raising kids and grandchildren here. Everyone discussed their deep relationships to the place as Skid Row residents. This shifted the narrative.

Heatherton: Broken windows policing enacts a disproportionate level of violence against women of color and queer, trans, and gender-nonconforming people. How are Skid Row organizers working to confront the criminalization of gendered poverty?

Dennison: There is a level of violence against women, particularly trans women and sex workers, especially if they are homeless, that is serious and needs to be addressed. Talking with people in the community about these issues has led to some really difficult but good conversations about policing and safety.

A lot of residents thought SCI would make them safer but, as we have said, this type of policing does not address the issue of safety at all. For example, at the exact same time that SCI rolled out at a cost of $118 million for the first three years, the LAPD said they could not hire two new lab technicians to address the rape kit backlog. This means there is no follow-up for women in this community who report experiences of interpersonal violence. These populations also experience new levels of violence by police. There's an incredibly serious and escalating issue of police violence against trans women and particularly trans sex workers.

White: In Skid Row we have a sizeable transgender community, members of which experience policing in particularly traumatic ways. When a police officer stops a transgender person and demands to see an ID, and if, to that officer's mind, the ID doesn't match the person's gender, intense harassment and violence can result: everything from strip searches to the humiliation of having one's identity denied. It's oppressive across the board.

We believe that one way to encourage safety is to provide housing. Housing for all. We believe that safe spaces, green spaces, parks, educational opportunities, and occupational opportunities all represent what safety would feel like to us. We know there's $100 million, $87 million of which went to policing, that could have gone to solutions that encourage safety in an entirely different way.

Heatherton: LA CAN and many groups you work with have been criminalized for political organizing. Can you discuss this process on Skid Row?

Dennison: This is a problem that the LAPD perpetuates throughout the city. The criminalization of protest has been most heavy-handed and most intense towards the folks who have dissented against the Safer Cities Initiative, particularly residents of Skid Row. We have clear evidence about this targeting. It has not been without huge risks that residents have spoken out against the Safer Cities Initiative. We've had members unjustly arrested and charged with strikeable offenses. Almost every organizer or core member of the organization has been arrested. Some face charges, some do not. Someone is threatened with arrest every time there is a Safer Cities protest.

Most recently, there was a malicious prosecution of a sixty-year-old woman, who was a community organizer here. It devastated her entire life. It led to physical and mental health consequences from which she could not recover. She left community organizing because of it. There is a long history of criminalization of dissent in many movements. The recent crackdown in LA against folks who spoke out against SCI with the very simple message of "homes not jails" has been hard, firm, and sustained, and it has devastated folks' lives.

White: Targeting the organization was clearly meant to disable and dismantle it. It sent the message that other people should stay away, especially when we held big political events. Even when we weren't targeted as an organization, the streets were targeted. We would routinely see street sweeps on the same days that we held large actions as a way to deter anyone thinking about joining the growing movement. Our structure was targeted, our leadership was targeted, but the activities were also targeted in a way that punished the entire community if they dared to think about joining political organizing against capital and the police department.

Camp: In one interview, Bratton claimed that perceptions of the police in Black and Latino working-class neighborhoods belonged to the past, arguing that "police were used at the time of slavery ... and the Civil Rights era ... We were used as the instruments of segregation." Indeed, some members of the civil rights establishment, such as Connie Rice, assert that Bratton-style broken windows

policing has helped overcome mistrust of the police in Black communities. Do poor and working-class communities of color trust the LAPD more as a result of Bratton's time here?

White: In the aftermath of the murders of Walter Scott, Mike Brown, Ezell Ford, and others, there has been tremendous energy on the ground. People in LA are refusing to accept the notion that the police are somehow "better." In Skid Row we've been under no illusions that the police department has changed in any way. We think about the legacy of policing in this country, the same one that Bratton pointed out: their roles in catching enslaved people who had escaped, enforcing Jim Crow and the Black Codes, breaking labor struggles and unions, enforcing mass deportation during Operation Mojado, and decimating and dismantling the Civil Rights Movement and the Black Power Movement. When we describe "Negro removal" and gentrification as the same thing, with police on the frontlines, people understand. The question really becomes, who is selling the story? Who is giving the data that suggests otherwise? The resounding answer, of course, has to be a corporate media whose interests are tied to the removal of poor people from inner-city communities.

Camp: In what ways have you expanded the bandwidth of the community to organize on a broader geographical scale?

Dennison: We have had a community-based newspaper, the *Community Connection*, in circulation for a very long time; we also use social media and have some access to community-based radio. We've been telling our own news and counteracting the narrative of the mainstream media. The Western Regional Advocacy Project, which we're a part of, has really expanded the bandwidth of those opposing the criminalization of homelessness. In four different states, we had four substantive homeless bills of rights moving this year. Elected officials in Colorado are telling their colleagues for the first time, "This is the civil rights issue of our time. This is about racist policing. This is about segregation."

#BlackLivesMatter is the most recent example, nationwide, of people feeling an urgent connection to a movement. We're at a point of crisis that has existed for a long time but is now drawing new voices into the mix. It is good to see the new energy on the ground.

White: Publications like *Community Connection, Downtown Blues: A Skid Row Reader* (2011), and *Freedom Now! Struggles for the Human Right to Housing in Los Angeles and Beyond* (2012) did a lot to authenticate the struggle in classrooms and across the country. Films that we've been featured in, like *Lost Angeles* and others, have also reached out in ways that we never could have done as an organization. Our relationship with the hip-hop community, with Operation Skid Row and the Hip Hop Gods tour, situated us in a particular way in hip-hop culture that gave us some authenticity, both with the issues we're talking about and with our ability to connect to hip-hop music and culture.

I also believe that just being around here doing this work for so long and creating a body of knowledge has actually helped seed the field for some of the #BlackLivesMatter movement. We have been called upon since day one because of our history of fighting police repression in downtown LA as well as in the broader city. Those would be the ways I'd say we're linking up.

Heatherton: What can social movements around the world—from New York to Ferguson, from Baltimore to London and beyond— learn from the struggle in Skid Row Los Angeles?

White: We have to learn more from one another. We need to export our lessons quicker, both those that move us forward and those that move us backward, because we are definitely fighting the same system. It has been interesting to watch the Ferguson rebellion and see all the community demands and signs saying, "End Broken Windows Policing." It reinforces, to me, that we are all saying the same thing, but we are disconnected. We should really figure out how to expand our bandwidth, to communicate, to connect, and to build a larger national and international community around these issues.

Anyone Home, 2014

US National Guard passing through the intersection of Pennsylvania and North in West Baltimore, hours after Marilyn Mosby's May 1, 2015, announcement of charges against six police officers in the death of Freddie Gray.

Three young participants at an enormous "Victory Rally" across Baltimore, calling for justice for Freddie Gray, May 2, 2015.

A freshly painted mural commemorating Freddie Gray in the Sandtown-Winchester neighborhood where he grew up, May 8, 2015.

Members of the Chicago-based We Charge Genocide presenting evidence of police violence at the fifty-third session of the United Nations Committee Against Torture in Geneva, Switzerland, November 12, 2014.

The popular gay magazine *Christopher Street* often featured stories about the role of gay men in the changing real estate economy, including a special issue on gay life in New York that included the article "Can Gays Save New York City?" Cover of *Christopher Street* magazine, September 1977.

LAPD officer conducts arrest in Skid Row, Los Angeles, February 18, 2009.

William Bratton, who served as Chief of the Los Angeles Police Department between 2002 and 2009, in Los Angeles, May 1, 2009.

Los Angeles Community Action Network rally against the Safer City Initiative, September 25, 2008.

Members of the Red Nation march in front of pawnshop in Gallup, New Mexico, April 4, 2014.

Over ten thousand people gather in downtown Manhattan to protest after grand jury decides not to indict NYPD officer Daniel Pantaleo for the killing of Eric Garner, New York City, December 4, 2014.

Police officers raid Dr. Rafael López Nussa public housing complex in Ponce, Puerto Rico, May 31, 2002.

11. BROKEN WINDOWS, SURVEILLANCE, AND THE NEW URBAN COUNTERINSURGENCY: AN INTERVIEW WITH HAMID KHAN

Jordan T. Camp and Christina Heatherton

Hamid Khan is the lead organizer for the Stop LAPD Spying Coalition, an alliance seeking to confront and dismantle police surveillance, spying, and infiltration in Los Angeles. He is a member of the Los Angeles Community Action Network's Action Team and a board member for the National Network for Immigrant and Refugee Rights, Political Research Associates, and Youth Justice Coalition.

Camp: Why is Los Angeles such an important place to understand broken windows policing? How has the LAPD's broken windows policing extended into counterterrorism policing?

Khan: Broken windows theory is presented as a core justification for "preemptive policing." The Safer Cities Initiative (SCI), based on this theory, was launched in LA's Skid Row in 2006 under former LAPD police chief William Bratton. In that first year of SCI, people's lives were made so miserable because of the thousands of tickets police issued, based often on excessive enforcement of municipal codes, that they were forced to leave; the ones who stayed continue to face police harassment, brutality, and surveillance on a daily basis. The goal of these policies is to get rid of "undesirables."

Broken windows policing also set the stage for tactics, operations, and structures that are increasingly being adapted into counterterrorism policing. All models, including determinations of "suspicious activity" in counterterrorism policing, are built on attempts to predict future events. In 2004, Congress passed the Intelligence Reform and Terrorism Prevention Act, based on the theory that 9/11 had resulted from a breakdown in information flow between various agencies. The act required Homeland Security and various other agencies to create what was called an "Information Sharing Environment," meaning that local, state, and federal law enforcement agencies would file Suspicious Activity Reports (SARs) on observed and reported activities that can be shared amongst these agencies and private contractors through the Information Sharing Environment. The LAPD was the launching ground for the National Suspicious Activity Reporting Initiative, resulting in the issuance of Special Order 11 requiring LAPD officers to file SARs on any observed or reported "suspicious" behaviors or activities that might be connected to terrorism or crime. "Suspicious" behaviors included non-criminal behaviors, such as using cameras in public, using binoculars, taking notes, walking into an office and asking for hours of operation, and changing appearances. The "suspicion" cast on such benign daily behaviors opened the door for racial profiling and for using these activities as a pretext to open investigations on law-abiding citizens.

Heatherton: The Stop LAPD Spying Coalition seeks "to dismantle the use of militarized tactics by the police and an end of the surveillance state" and works in partnership with LA CAN, the Youth Justice Coalition, #BlackLivesMatters-LA, and others to achieve those ends. One militarized tactic you've challenged is mass arrests of peaceful demonstrators. What is the relationship between surveillance and the repression of political dissent?

Khan: In September 2012, the LA Police Commission approved new guidelines for intelligence gathering on political groups and others engaged in social justice work. These guidelines gave the LAPD extraordinary new powers and scaled back previous safeguards. There is no criminal predicate, meaning no pretext of reasonable suspicion is needed—anybody can pick up the phone and place an anonymous tip. Based on that tip the LAPD can plant an informant in an organization for six months, sometimes longer. Police can also take on different personas and identities to engage people through social media.

There are new tactics for mass arrests. During the mass protests in November 2014, the LAPD started issuing "rolling" dispersal orders, arresting uninvolved bystanders within or near the area. Another new practice of "kettling" saw the police surround two or three hundred people at a time, disrupting their protest and movement and preventing them from leaving the area. These tactics not only result in arrests but also intimidate people into staying away from any protests.

When you look at all of these moving parts, the structure that emerges is counterinsurgency: gathering information on people, tracking them and creating a record of their activities, creating new databases to house this information, disrupting people's movement, and eventually placing them and those around them under arrest. We cannot forget that these tactics and strategies are based on the methods of police Red Squads and the FBI's counterintelligence program (COINTELPRO) developed under J. Edgar Hoover to discredit, disrupt, derail, and neutralize social movements.

Camp: How have the tactics developed by the Red Squads in the past shaped the LAPD's surveillance of contemporary social justice movements?

Khan: The LAPD has historically been on the cutting edge of the funding and development of counterintelligence measures. The LAPD Red Squad, which engaged in covert and surveillance activities, actually predates the FBI. Red Squads originated after the 1886 Haymarket strikes in Chicago and were created by the Chicago PD in response not to a foreign threat but rather to labor organizing and grassroots movements. The LAPD's history is rife with extrajudicial, unconstitutional, illegal activity such as entrapment and planting of infiltrators and informants. In the 1980s, the LAPD's Public Disorder Intelligence Division was exposed for having opened files on 55,000 individuals which contained over two million documents. The bust revealed that nonprofits, the city council, and even former mayor Tom Bradley had been infiltrated. Surveillance is an ongoing process that has only intensified since 9/11.

Heatherton: You've written that war abroad means war at home. How do we understand this in relationship to the militarization of local law enforcement?

Khan: The connection between the war abroad and the war at home is tried and tested. There are so many examples in which the LAPD has trained groups in urban counterinsurgency tactics. In the 1980s it trained officials from El Salvador. More recently it helped train the Marine Corps for patrolling Al Anbar and other Iraqi provinces. The Israeli state has also played a key role in the development of counterinsurgency tactics. Bratton was one of the main people to establish these ties; he has helped transfer technology used in the open-air prisons of the occupied territories to US cities. Police officials from LA, St. Louis, and many other law enforcement agencies around the country have gone to Israel for training and to examine technologies such as drones for tracking and targeted killings—observing policing in a context free of US constitutional protections (particularly the Fourth and the First Amendments) to see how the use of technology and its justifications can be transferred to the US. When we talk about militarized policing we often are talking about police use of military weapons. We also need to think about how police increasingly describe the people they monitor as insurgents or enemy forces. These developments are very much in line with Israeli policing structures.

The LAPD gets close to 54 percent of the city's general funds in addition to the hundreds of millions of dollars in grants. Just like the military, they are recession-proof. Structurally the LAPD is one of the most hyper-militarized agencies, with a massive architecture of surveillance that operates similar to counter-insurgency forces.

Heatherton: What gives you hope at this moment?

Khan: The flipside of all of this surveillance and security is that it's coming from fears of an uprising or a rebellion. People are beginning to look at law enforcement and ask new questions. In Ferguson, for example, people questioned the heavily militarized presence at the protests. They are starting to fight not just for their individual privacy and security but against the broader structures that have created their inse-curity as well.

Law enforcement and other emergency preparedness agencies have received over $40 billion from the DHS since 2003, while the social safety net is being cut and scaled back. People are fighting against this disinvestment in their communities. Our task now is to build com-munity power. It's all about organizing. Our goal is to ultimately keep building that deep power and work to dismantle these destructive plans.

12. THE EMERGENCE OF COMMAND AND CONTROL POLICING IN NEOLIBERAL NEW YORK

Alex S. Vitale and Brian Jordan Jefferson

There has been a great deal of attention paid by scholars and activists in recent years to the problem of mass incarceration. The explosive increase in incarceration rates, especially for minorities, led sociologist Bruce Western to describe prisons as one of the central institutions in African American life and law professor Michelle Alexander to call this the era of the "New Jim Crow."[1] But unlike other major cities, New York City has relied on intensive and invasive policing to a much greater extent than mass incarceration in order to contain socioeconomic disjuncture. New York City's jail population dropped 55 percent from 1991 to 2014, and New York State's prison population has dropped 28 percent from 1999 to 2014. In fact, since 1999 the number of inmates under correctional custody in New York has decreased every single year with one exception (2006).[2] Conversely, between 1990 and 2000, the number of full-time employees working for the New York City Police Department increased by nearly a quarter, almost twice the rate of any other metropolitan city during that decade.[3] In this chapter we make the case that the NYPD's core policing strategies represent a shift: from an emphasis on using extensive imprisonment as the primary

---

1   Michelle Alexander, *The New Jim Crow: Mass Incarceration in the Age of Colorblindness* (New York: New Press, 2010).

2   New York State Department of Corrections and Community Supervision, *Research Report: The Foreign-Born, Under Custody Population, and the IRP*, 2011.

3   Bureau of Justice Statistics, *Police Departments in Large Cities, 1990–2000*, US Department of Justice, 2002.

tool of punitive social control towards the intense regulation of low-income communities of color as prisonlike spaces themselves. In this way, the reduction of incarceration rates is not necessarily a lessening of the burden of punitive social control, but instead an extension of the carceral state to the community, which broadens its reach into the lives of the vast majority of young men and increasingly women of color.[4]

Defining the Command and Control Strategy

Beginning in the early 1990s, New York City embarked on a grand new strategy in urban policing based in large part on the broken windows theory, which enforces a new moral order on the poor, a new public ethos of law and order, through police practices targeting low-level offences and non-criminal disorderly conduct. That mindset, combined with new technologies and management practices and driven by the neoconservative politics of first Rudolph Giuliani and then Michael Bloomberg, led to the development of a new form of policing we call "command and control." This term comes from management scholars who use it to describe public decision making in which power is vested in technocratic experts who, insulated from democratic oversight, make rules without public input. We are also drawing from academics and those in the civil liberties community who have used the term to describe the department's aggressive and inflexible handling of public demonstrations over the past two decades. In this chapter we shall argue that this nonnegotiable approach to imposing uniform behavior is indicative of the NYPD's *everyday* policing strategy, characterized by the intensive and invasive micromanagement of quotidian activities.

James Q. Wilson and George Kelling, the authors of the broken windows theory (which is really more of a hypothesis), have consistently said that they intended it to be applied proactively, but with discretion and tied to specific crime problems in accordance with the law. In practice, however, it has become a mostly indiscriminate zero-tolerance

---

4   Marie Gottschalk, *Caught: The Prison State and the Lockdown of American Politics* (Princeton: Princeton University Press, 2014).

system of punitive street policing.[5] A close reading of the theory in its original form and then as further described by Kelling and Coles and Wesley Skogan makes clear the intellectual basis for this more pernicious application of the theory—at root, a very conservative theory about human nature and the importance of the coercive power of the state in regulating the poor.[6] Wilson and Kelling had both been steeped in the neoconservative urban theory of the 1960s–80s. Close associates of Edward Banfield and Charles Murray, they were deeply skeptical of the ability of the poor to manage themselves in a civil manner. This was especially true following the Civil Rights era in which existing social systems such as Jim Crow no longer tightly regulated public behavior. The authors point to the increased individualism brought about by the social revolutions of the 1960s and 1970s as a chief source of the growing disorderliness of urban America. Crime and the decline of cities were tied to the moral failings of poor, mostly non-white communities. Left completely out of their analysis was the role of deindustrialization, urban disinvestment, and federal policies that encouraged middle-class white suburbanization and industrial migration to the South and West.

Broken windows policing came into vogue in New York only as a result of the precipitous increase in public disorder beginning in the 1980s with the rise of mass homelessness. The neoliberal reorganization of the city's finances following the 1970s fiscal crisis established a permanent austerity governance in which government-led initiatives to resolve social problems were deemed too expensive and possibly ineffective, and replaced by market-driven solutions, privatization, and attacks on public workers. That economic program in turn generated increased crime and social disorder, which engendered a neoconservative politics of punitive social control. While little acknowledgment has been made by the neoliberal camp of this causal relationship, neoconservative politics are the

---

5   George L. Kelling and James Q. Wilson, "Broken Windows: The Police and Neighborhood Safety," *Atlantic*, March 1982.

6   George L. Kelling and Katherine Coles, *Fixing Broken Windows: Restoring Order and Reducing Crime in Our Communities* (New York: Touchstone, 1998); Wesley Skogan, *Disorder and Decline: Crime and the Spiral of Decay in American Neighborhoods* (Berkeley: University of California Press, 1992).

most likely response to the economic and social consequences of neoliberal economic programs. As neoliberal austerity produced untreated mental illness, economic displacement, and mass homelessness, neoconservatives responded by demanding enhanced punitive action against the symptoms of this process: intensified policing of the mentally ill, poor, homeless, and unemployed, the alleged causes of economic and social breakdown in the city. This neoconservative turn was driven significantly by both business leaders and many community activists who had grown frustrated with the inability of liberal leaders to resolve these problems and weary of calls for tolerance while long-term solutions were pursued. As the number of people living in public spaces, often with mental illnesses or substance abuse problems, continued to grow throughout the 1980s, communities began to demand a more punitive government response. This is the political dynamic that ushered in two successive Republican mayoral administrations that spanned twenty years. Throughout this period, social problems were turned into criminal justice problems and the police were placed on the frontlines of managing them, while the broken windows theory provided the ideological justification and functional game plan.

The broken windows prescription for this breakdown of social order was the imposition of new standards of public civility by the police. This was to be done in theory through a gentle nudge or stern reminder, but if necessary (and more realistically) through arrest or other forms of coercion. The police, therefore, were placed in the role of arbiters of what was thought to constitute public civility. The result has been the broad criminalization of communities of color through a numbers-driven zero-tolerance approach to policing that undermines discretion and dramatically expands the role of police in the everyday lives of young people of color, homeless people, street vendors, sex workers, and others. In essence, it has become a system to micromanage these populations, not through the constant brutality that characterized earlier methods of policing the poor, but through more subtle but invasive tactics of creating hundreds of thousands of additional contacts between the police and the policed and dramatically expanding the number of people churned through the criminal justice system, even if only for short periods of time.

The emergence of command and control policing did not happen all at once, but rather as the result of a mixture of often contradictory agendas, institutional arrangements, and concepts. Core elements were first introduced during the Dinkins administration (1990–3), most notably in its efforts to establish an expanded police presence to manage quality-of-life issues such as squatting, window washing, panhandling, unlicensed vending, and prostitution. The administration's strategy in response to these issues was best articulated in its 1990 *Safe Streets, Safe Cities* omnibus anti-crime package, meant to quash disorderly conditions through a patchwork of new social services, programs for NYPD–community cooperation, and substantial increases in police deployment across the city.[7] Dinkins was receptive to the role social programs could play in juvenile delinquency prevention and launched several youth programs and agencies such as Job Opportunities for Youth (JOY), Youth Services (DYS), YOUTHLINK, and the Local Employment Action Program (LEAP) to provide over 4,000 youth with summer and part-time employment and 6,250 youth with drug prevention counseling and family intervention. *Safe Streets* also recommended reforming juvenile justice through the Peace Corps and the Annie E. Casey Foundation Juvenile Detention Alternatives Initiative to create community-based programs for at-risk and convicted youths.

But glimmerings of command and control policing shone in the administration's ambitions to flood the city with police officers, and were conveyed in police commissioner Lee Brown's (1990–2) blueprint for comprehensive NYPD reform in 1991. Brown suggested increasing the detective squad by 67 percent, patrol forces by 54 percent, enforcement strength by 50 percent, and community police officer (CPOP) personnel by 523 percent.[8] These increases were made in conjunction with the establishment of tighter links between the city government, police headquarters, local precincts, and discrete neighborhood areas so as to maximize the NYPD's ability to manage "problem epidemiologies." They reflected Brown's goal to mobilize the "total community for

7   David N. Dinkins, *Safe Streets, Safe City: An Omnibus Criminal Justice Program for the City of New York* (City of New York, 1991).

8   Lee Brown, *Policing New York City in the 1990s: The Strategy for Community Policing* (New York City Police Department, 1991).

an all-out collective assault" against disorder by "block-by-block polic-ing throughout the city." This approach resonated in city programs to increase NYPD staffing by 50 percent, increase the NYPD's presence in the subway system on approximately 100 trains, and merge the NYPD with the Housing Authority Police Department and the Transit Authority Police Department to form one "super police agency."[9]

These elements of command and control policing were augmented and institutionalized during the Giuliani administration (1994–2001), whose 1994 quality-of-life campaign unleashed NYPD forces on indi-gent persons across the city. For Giuliani, command and control became increasingly defined by the police department's nonnegotiable posture vis-à-vis the public, and growing distance from democratic control. Keeping Dinkins and Brown's emphasis on dramatically expanding the NYPD's public presence intact, Giuliani's 1993 campaign rhetoric stressed dismantling police-community cooperative programs on the grounds that they ensnared officers in a "convoluted academic science" incommensurate with law enforcement.[10] Giuliani instead stressed strict law enforcement solutions to quality of life and disorderly conditions. This was echoed in broader criticisms that NYPD's community-based initiatives created excessive red tape, and fostered animosity between community officers and regular squads.[11]

After Giuliani's departure, Michael Bloomberg's administration (2002–14) substantially intensified both the NYPD's public presence and its insulation from democratic checks and balances. His 2002 inau-gural speech assured that the city's police strategy would continue to operate unchanged, with its steady focus on aggressive quality-of-life enforcement and zero-tolerance policing. The administration intensified the NYPD's stringent regulation of behavioral and physical disorder, with Bloomberg claiming that his crime-fighting focus was one on "problem

---

9   See Dinkins, *Safe Streets, Safe City*, 1991.

10   Alison Mitchell, "Giuliani Urges Street Policing Refocused on Crime," *New York Times*, January 25, 1994.

11   Vincent Henry, *The Compstat Paradigm: Management Accountability in Polic-ing, Business and the Public Sector* (Flushing, NY: Looseleaf Law Publications, 2002); Paul E. O'Connell and Frank Straub, *Performance-Based Management for Police Orga-nizations* (Long Grove, IL: Waveband Press, 2007).

people and problem places." Moreover, the police department's withdrawal from public oversight continued during Bloomberg's tenure. The World Trade Center attacks on September 11th only reinforced the NYPD's progressively more insulated decision making, giving rise to the instatement of the Deputy Commissioners of Counter-Terrorism and Intelligence in 2002. Both offices expanded training, prevention, and investigations free from public oversight while increasing the department's discretionary authority.

The NYPD under Bloomberg-appointed commissioner Ray Kelly conducted several operations publicized as indicators of the new administration's commitment to continuing the aggressive quality-of-life enforcement of its predecessors. The 2002 Operation Clean Sweep was one such undertaking, based in aggressive policing of low-level offenses such as squeegee operating, panhandling, unlicensed peddling, public alcoholic consumption, marijuana smoking, public urination, and homeless encampments. The administration launched Operation Spotlight in the same year, which swept city streets for chronic misdemeanants—principally drug offenders, shoplifters, and prostitutes. Operation Impact was launched in 2003, deploying over 1,000 officers in high-crime areas and, in December of that year, was extended to disadvantaged "impact schools" through school safety agents, armed police, and metal scanning machines similar to the ones used to screen airline passengers.

Command and control policing is thus characterized by the city government's increasingly inflexible, intensive, and pervasive use of NYPD forces to regulate social order among the very groups overrepresented in the jail and prison system. The strategy situates law enforcement as the primary mechanism for managing social problems arising from the socioeconomic polarizations that had been developing since the mid-1970s, and eventually exploded across the cityscape. Each administration played a part in inching command and control objectives towards ubiquitous social control, making low-income areas more prisonlike in the process.

Command and Control Tactics

The command and control strategy incorporates a variety of intensive and invasive practices with different scalar and geographic applications, establishing an architecture of social control throughout the city. While the strategy revolves around the order maintenance concept of intervening with suspicious individuals, its application to entire populations and neighborhoods has become normalized and extended over the past twenty years. This approach has in turn converted areas of concentrated poverty into quasi-correctional spaces that are micromanaged by massive low-level arrests and summonses, intensified policing of disadvantaged youth in schools, broadly enhanced surveillance, and repressive policing of dissent.

Broken Windows

Broken windows policing came to New York in the early 1990s, about the same time it arrived in San Francisco and a few other cities. George Kelling and then chief of the Transit Police Department (TPD) William Bratton devised a large-scale "problem-solving exercise" for clamping down on underground vagrancy, panhandling, fare-beating and a range of incivilities which were coded as "illegal disorderly behavior."[12] On March 12, 1994, Giuliani's administration announced it would begin a citywide quality-of-life campaign by reinvigorating the effort to eliminate squeegee men once and for all, hunting down truant youth ditching school with new vigor, criminalizing graffiti, tearing down homeless encampments in parks and sprawled beneath bridges across the city, and aggressively targeting street-level drug dealing and prostitution. This aggressive dragnet approach was largely enabled by the widely touted Compstat database, which provides comprehensive precinct-by-precinct daily crime counts, creating an all-encompassing eye surveilling city disorder and a new brain trust for assessing the management of it. Zero-tolerance enforcement of minor legal violations, primarily targeting poor people of color, was recommended increasingly as a solution to a growing number of crime problems. This problem was exacerbated by

12   George L. Kelling, Michael Julian, and Steven Miller, *Managing "Squeegeeing": A Problem-Solving Exercise* (New York: Dinkins Archive, 1994).

Compstat's provision of hard data, which turned policing into a numbers game with the implementation of informal numerical productivity goals for officers that eventually morphed into full-scale quota systems.[13]

The expansion of broken windows policing meant a massive growth in citations and misdemeanor arrests. The number of summonses issued in a year mushroomed from 160,000 in 1993 to 650,000 by 2005. Misdemeanor arrests went from 129,000 to 227,000 during the same period, while felony arrests actually declined from 126,000 to 91,000. In the period from 2001 to 2013, 86 percent of these summonses were issued to minorities, even though they make up just 55 percent of the city's population. The most frequent offenses that resulted in summonses were drinking alcohol in public, disorderly conduct, urinating in public, and park code violations.

Stop, Question, Frisk

The NYPD's "stop, question, and frisk" (SQF) practice has garnered considerable public attention and is indicative of the NYPD's strategy of converting low-income Black and Brown neighborhoods into regulated spaces in which everyday activity is rigorously micromanaged. The practice is an extension of the powers granted to police in the Supreme Court's 1968 *Terry v. Ohio* ruling, which established that officers could detain, question, and search a person suspected of intending to commit serious crimes. The NYPD's use of SQF extends the *Terry* powers by turning streets into circuits of disciplinary management.

The SQF practice came to assume a primary role in the command and control strategy during Bloomberg's tenure and was used to regulate both low-income areas and everyday movements of Black and Brown men across the city. It was also a tactic used to manage suspect populations in more developed parts of the city, including youth of color, LGBT youth, sex workers, and any others deemed a threat to the new standards of public order and civility. Under Bloomberg's administration, stops rose by an average of 60,853 a year. Whereas his first year in office registered just under 100,000 stops, his penultimate year

---

13   John A. Eterno and Eli B. Silverman, "The New York City Police Department's Compstat: Dream or Nightmare?" *International Journal of Police Science and Management* 8, no. 3 (2006), 218–31.

registered well over half a million (SQFs decreased from the previous year in 2007 and 2012[14]). While the frequency of SQFs largely reflected crime rates over broad areas, NYPD presence is disproportionately stationed in minority communities.[15] Data on NYPD "trespass stops" has cast this place-based nature of SQF into sharper relief, showing that the department performed 369,000 stops on suspicion of trespassing in public housing units from 2003 through March 2010, yielding drugs and illegal contraband at a rate of 2 percent, and guns at a rate of 0.2 percent.[16] For instances of SQF overall between 2004 and 2013, the rate of gun confiscations was below 0.2 percent.[17] The stops are part of the NYPD's "vertical patrol" program, which polices public housing complexes, and are performed under the aegis of NYCHA's do-not-enter bylaws which ban nonresidents and non-visitors from public housing. The program directs officers to interrogate persons suspected of trespassing and, according to their discretion, demand identification or other proofs of residence. In New York City's densest cluster of public housing—the Brownsville section of Brooklyn—approximately 52,000 stops were performed from 2006 to early 2010. On average, Brownsville males in the fifteen-to-thirty-four age range were stopped five times annually during the same period.[18]

SQFs are also used to regulate the movements of Black and Brown males outside of economically depressed inner-city spaces and extend throughout the cityscape via citywide profiling. Between 2002 and 2012, 76 percent of nearly 5 million stops were conducted on Blacks and Latinos.[19] Data from 2004 to 2009 shows that during stops

14   New York Civil Liberties Union, "New York City Police Department Stop Question and Frisk Activity," *NCLU*.org, Jan. 1–March 31, 2014.

15   Matthew Bloch, Ford Fessenden, and Janet Roberts, "Stop, Question and Frisk in New York Neighborhoods," *New York Times*, July 11, 2010.

16   Al Baker and Janet Roberts, "Judge Criticizes Stop-and-Frisk Police Tactics in Housing Projects," *New York Times*, December 22, 2010.

17   Barry Paddock, "NYPD Cops Seized Nearly 400 Guns during Stop and Frisk Encounters in Past Year, Lowest Tally since 2003," *New York Daily News*, August 21, 2014.

18   Ray Rivera, Al Baker, and Janet Roberts, "A Few Blocks, 4 Years, 52,000 Police Stops," *New York Times*, July 11, 2010.

19   New York Civil Liberties Union, "Stop Question and Frisk Activity."

involving Black and Latino civilians, officers used force more than a quarter of the time, compared 19 percent of the time in stops involving whites.[20] Moreover, arrest rates among those stopped in this period were nearly identical irrespective of race: whites who were halted were arrested just over 6 percent of time compared to just under 6 percent of Blacks; 1.7 percent of halted whites were caught with weapons compared to 1.1 percent of Blacks. In fact, during Bloomberg's tenure, an average of 87.5 percent of those stopped have been innocent.[21]

This practice elicited attention from civil rights communities for its intrusiveness. In June 2012, tens of thousands marched against the practice, turning what had been a policing issue into a major civil rights concern. In 2013, mayoral candidate Bill de Blasio expressed significant concerns about the manner in which it was practiced and the extent of its usage and vowed to enact reforms. Candidate John Liu went so far as to pledge a total ban on its use. By late 2014, following de Blasio's election but before he had taken office and the *Floyd* suit (*Floyd, et al. v. City of New York*, a federal class action lawsuit against SQF) had concluded, SQF numbers began to drop precipitously. By mid-2014, the rate had dropped from over 500,000 a year to 50,000.

Schools

This hands-on governance of poor persons of color and the public space they inhabit extends into the educational system through the NYPD's deployment of thousands of personnel in disadvantaged schools to enforce behavior. The increasingly common use of police by urban public schools to handle disciplinary matters is at the forefront of what is often called the "school-to-prison pipeline," the zero-tolerance policies and practices in poor schools that increase the likelihood that students will be swept into the criminal justice system.[22] But it is also important

---

20   Jeffrey Fagan, "Expert Report," Floyd v. City of New York. 08 civ. 01034 (SAS). 2010.

21   New York Civil Liberties Union, *SSA Reporting on Arrests and Summonses, July 1, 2011–June 30, 2012*, 2013.

22   Sofía Bahena, North Cooc, Rachel Currie-Rubin, Paul Kuttner, and Monica Ng, eds., *Disrupting the School-to-Prison Pipeline* (Cambridge: Harvard Educational Review, 2012); Catherine Kim, Daniel J. Losen, and Damon T. Hewitt, *The*

to emphasize that under the command and control strategy, public schools in low-income areas have become mini criminal justice institutions themselves, sites where the NYPD exercises punitive control over student behaviors and movements.

School safety agents and police officers are the NYPD's blunt tool for clamping down on disruptive student behavior and enforcing a range of zero-tolerance practices. As the NYPD enforces school disciplinary codes, safety agents primarily police minor misbehaviors, including roughhousing, playing hooky, using profanity, and loitering. Agents' instruments for punishing such behaviors include a range of practices, such as summonses, citations, juvenile detention referrals, criminal charges, and arrests. The result is an even more meticulous regulation of behaviors in schools than on the streets, as school safety agents often bring criminal charges on youth for behaviors that would never be considered criminal for adults.

School safety agents' presence transforms disadvantaged schools into extensively regulated institutions with prisonlike features. Nearly 100,000 students pass through metal detectors before entering school.[23] Once inside, students in policed schools are enveloped in the presence of school safety agents whose tasks include patrolling hallways, offices, classrooms, bathrooms, stairwells, and outer perimeters for "developing situations."[24]

The disparate racial effects of the School Safety Division's (SSD) governance of public schools are clear. Black students were involved in 63 percent of school arrests and summonses in 2012, even though they made up less than a quarter of the overall student population. Black students were an astounding fourteen times more likely and Latina/o

---

School-to-Prison Pipeline: Structuring Legal Reform (New York: NYU Press, 2013); National Organization for the Advancement of Colored People. *Dismantling the School-to-Prison Pipeline.* New York, 2005.

23   New York Civil Liberties Union, "A Look at School Safety," 2013, available at nyclu.org/schooltoprison.

24   New York Police Department, *NYPD School Safety Agent Duties & Responsibilities: A Guide for DOE & NYPD Personnel* (2007); Vera Institute of Justice, *Reinforcing Positive Student Behavior to Prevent School Violence: Enhancing the Role of School Safety Agents* (New York, 2001).

students five times more likely than white students to be arrested in school.[25] This structure of disciplinary management, superimposed on a landscape of segregated education and stark racial and class inequities, has created an entirely new field of regulation of the city's marginalized outside of, and relatively independent from, juvenile detention centers, jails, and prisons.

Surveillance

Surveillance is another crucial feature in the command and control repertoire. The department's surveillance infrastructure has become increasingly dispersed throughout public space, while its command system has become increasingly centralized and insulated from public oversight. For one, the total count of public CCTVs (video surveillance) throughout the five boroughs has expanded dramatically over the last fifteen years, increasing from 769 in 1998 to 4,468 in 2005.[26] Today there are over 6,000 cameras throughout the cityscape, 4,000 in lower Manhattan.[27]

In addition to technology-based monitoring, the NYPD also practices aggressive forms of intel-based surveillance, actively targeting and tracking select social groups throughout the city. In 2005 the NYPD created a Demographics Unit to collect broad-based data on the activities of Muslims in restaurants, bookstores, college campuses, and religious settings. Most of this was done in the absence of any specific criminal allegation or suspicion, but instead was intended as baseline intelligence gathering that might either generate leads or provide useful information in future investigations.

The NYPD has also used social media to generate a list of over 28,000 alleged gang members. That list has been used to aid investigations and, presumably, to direct additional undercover and online surveillance.

---

25   New York City School-Justice Partnership Task Force, *Keeping Kids in School and Out of Court: Report and Recommendations*, 2013.

26   Loren Siegel, Robert A. Perry, and Margaret Hunt Gram, *Who's Watching? Video Camera Surveillance in New York City and the Need for Public Oversight* (New York Civil Liberties Union, 2006).

27   Jane C. Timm, "Drop a Bag in NYC? Cue the Bomb Squad," MSNBC, April 22, 2013, available at tv.msnbc.com.

The result is the NYPD's steady movement towards establishing an inescapable presence across public space and into the private realm as well.

Protest

Protest policing also became more intensive and invasive under both Giuliani and Bloomberg. Both mayors showed great contempt for the First Amendment but in distinct ways. While Giuliani's attempts to stifle speech are well documented, Bloomberg's control of dissent on the streets was even more intensive, as, for example, in his handling of the 2003 rally against the Iraq War, the protests at the Republican National Convention in 2004, and the Occupy Wall Street Movement of 2012.[28]

On February 15, 2003, one of the largest demonstrations in the city's history took place, with hundreds of thousands protesting the impending war in Iraq. As crowds spilled onto adjoining streets, police attacked them on horseback and with pepper spray and batons for the sole infraction of disrupting traffic, which resulted in numerous arrests, injuries, and lawsuits.[29]

In 2004, Bloomberg signaled that he would not allow protests to disrupt normal life in the city during the Republican National Convention. To accomplish this he utilized a series of intrusive and preemptive policing practices to surveil, infiltrate, and disrupt activity that the police thought might lead to disruptive street protests.[30] Every participant in several marches was arrested and people held for days

---

28   New York Civil Liberties Union, "NYCLU v. Giuliani: First Amendment Cases," October 1, 1999, available nyclu.org; Susan Sachs, "Giuliani's Goal of Civil City Runs into First Amendment," *New York Times*, July 6, 1998.

29   Christopher Dunn, Arthur Eisenberg, Donna Lieberman, Alan Silver, and Alex Vitale, *Arresting Protest: A Special Report of the New York Civil Liberties Union on New City's Protest Policies at the February 15, 2003 Antiwar Demonstration in New York City*, (New York Civil Liberties Union, 2003); Alex Vitale, "From Negotiated Management to Command and Control: How the NYPD Polices Protests," *Policing and Society* 15, no. 3 (2005): 283–304.

30   Jim Dwyer, "Records Show Scrutiny of Detainees in '04 Protests," *New York Times*, February 8, 2007; Dwyer, "City Police Spied Broadly Before G.O.P. Convention," *New York Times*, March 25, 2007.

on minor charges and in substandard conditions until the convention ended.[31]

Bloomberg also played a central role in undermining the Occupy Wall Street movement by ordering the police to tightly restrict the movement's activities and ultimately evict the encampment. Police used a wide variety of minor infractions to make arrests, apprehending people, for example, for using a bullhorn and writing on the sidewalk with chalk. When Occupy protesters marched without permits or defied police orders, they were met with pepper spray, mass arrest, and violence by the NYPD.[32]

Conclusion

We see that, in the beginning of the 1990s, government officials in New York City began to neutralize problems in the poorest areas by flooding them with NYPD officers. While arrests spiked in 1999, they quickly decreased at rates substantively faster than in other major US cities. At the same time, the deployment and activities of NYPD forces steadily expanded. The intensification of the command and control strategy relies on turning targeted spaces into quasi-correctional complexes, an extension of the carceral state.

New York City's relatively low incarceration rates over the past quarter century must be understood in relation to correlative increases in police activity in everyday public life. These dynamics have developed within the broader emerging consensus that has made criminal justice institutions the principal instruments for managing the slew of social problems erupting from neoliberal governance. Debates on whether or not intensive and invasive law enforcement is more preferable than mass incarceration thus skirt the more substantive issue of whether or not

---

31   Christopher Dunn, Donna Lieberman, Palyn Hung, Alex Vitale, Zac Zimmer, Irum Taqi, Steve Theberge, and Udi Offer, *Rights and Wrongs at the RNC: A Special Report about Police and Protest at the Republican National Convention*, (New York Civil Liberties Union, 2005).

32   Mike Bloomberg, "Mayor Bloomberg on Clearing and Re-Opening of Zuccotti Park," November 15, 2011, available at mikebloomberg.com.

New York City's socially and economically marginalized populations should be dealt with using criminal justice solutions.

~

Alex S. Vitale is associate professor of sociology at Brooklyn College and author of the forthcoming book *The Limits of Policing* (Verso). He also writes about policing for *The Nation, Al Jazeera America,* and *Vice News.*

Brian Jordan Jefferson is an assistant professor of geography and geographic information science at the University of Illinois Urbana-Champaign. He researches how criminal justice systems influence the production of US cities, and concepts of urban space in criminological thought.

13. BEYOND BRATTON

Ruth Wilson Gilmore and Craig Gilmore

> *The modern police system was designed to keep the marginalized in their place and to warn the poor of a fate worse than poverty.*[1]
> —Tony Platt

B

lackLivesMatter exploded into US and global consciousness by way of the Ferguson uprising against the police who killed Michael Brown. Founded when Trayvon Martin's killer went free, BLM came together to name and undo a general pattern: the state's central role in the destruction of Black lives.[2] As Tony Platt notes, the police dispense warnings to contain exclusion, abandonment, and change—using forms of speech, including killing, to make the message crystal clear.

Among the crises police interventions contain are legitimation crises, during which the foundations of the racial capitalist state apparatuses

1 Thanks to Vincent Brown, Avery Gordon, Judy Greene, David Harvey, Rachel Herzing, Laleh Khalili, Hamid Khan, Sónia Vaz Borges, Jack Norton, Cedric Robinson, Zubair Sayed, Jonathan Simon, Nikhil Singh, Mounira Solimon, Lucia Trimbur, Françoise Vergès, and Pete White for insightful conversations; to Plataforma Güeto—especially Flávio Almada and Rui Estrada—for inviting and challenging us in a Cova da Moura workshop with more than fifty activists; and to the editors of this book for their patience and vision. Tony Platt, "Obama's Task Force on Policing: Will It Be Different This Time?" *Social Justice*, February 28, 2015, available at socialjusticejournal.org.

2 Alicia Garza, "A Herstory of the Black Lives Matter Movement," *Feminist Wire*, October 2014, available at feministwire.com.

shake and crack. The lack of consensus about what the state should be or do requires greater coercion of some of that state's subjects. In the turn to neoliberalism, for example, the Thatcher and Reagan regimes manufactured legitimation crises designed to refashion the state—massively slashing the social wage by cutting welfare benefits, public education, and public housing, and smashing public and private unions, all the while lowering taxes on the rich and on corporations and increasing spending on military, police, and prisons.[3]

The institutional result of rhetorical but not real state-shrinkage, with its attendant devolution of obligations to more local levels or to parastate actors (such as charter schools or nonprofits), we have long called the "anti-state state."[4] What's most notable about the phenomenon is that those who seek to seize or maintain appointed or elected *state* office by campaigning against *government* exercise "relative autonomy" to consolidate power by strengthening—not dismantling—certain aspects of the state.[5] It doesn't get cheaper, and it doesn't, in the aggregate, shrink. However, the purpose and outcome of the anti-state state's crisis-fueled practice is to facilitate upward transfer of wealth, income, and political power from the relatively poor and powerless to the already rich and powerful.

The relatively powerless are not without social capacity, of course, and have fought to maintain, extend, and redefine access to health care, income, housing, public education, and life itself in urban and rural contexts. This ongoing struggle spans multiple regimes of accumulation and the policing apparatuses appropriate to them. Indeed, from the origin of professionalized policing in the early twentieth century, when Progressivism and Jim Crow arose as an interlocking system of benefit and exclusion, through the gendered racial and regional hierarchies of

---

3 Stuart Hall, *The Hard Road to Renewal: Thatcherism and the Crisis of the Left* (London: Verso, 1988); Neil Smith, *The New Urban Frontier: Gentrification and the Revanchist City* (New York: Routledge, 1996).

4 Ruth Wilson Gilmore, *Golden Gulag: Prisons, Surplus, Crisis and Opposition in Globalizing California* (Berkeley: University of California Press, 2007); Ruth Wilson Gilmore and Craig Gilmore, "Re-Stating the Obvious," in *Indefensible Spaces: The Architecture of the National Security State*, ed. Michael Sorkin (New York: Routledge, 2007), 141–62.

5 Nicos Poulantzas, *State, Power, Socialism* (London: New Left Books, 1978).

the New Deal, and on to the courtroom and legislative triumphs of the Civil Rights Movement, the location of the "thin blue line" has moved but never disappeared as a prime organizing—or disorganizing—principle of everyday life. In recent decades the rise of the anti-state state has depended on increased criminalization to mark the poor as ineligible for as well as undeserving of social programs. Under regime after regime, the politics of race define techniques and understanding, even though racial categories and hierarchies—at any moment solid—are not set in concrete.[6] If, therefore, as Stuart Hall painstakingly argued, race is "the *modality* in which class is lived," then mass criminalization, and the policing it depends on, is class *war*.[7]

Post-Ferguson, the #BlackLivesMatter uprisings and broad-based organizing have pushed some aspects of US policing to the brink of a legitimacy crisis. Complex and militant work against police violence since the shooting of Michael Brown challenges the normal support upon which police organizations depend. Mainstream media raise questions—long-standing among activists from Ida B. Wells to Angela Y. Davis—about the racism inherent in the purpose and use of saturation policing, mass criminalization, and mass incarceration as alleged "solutions to crime." Left-liberal magazines such as *The Nation* and *Rolling Stone*—not noted for deep or systemic critiques of US criminal justice—have gone so far as to call for the abolition of the police.[8]

But even in the face of mainstream criticism and so-called "bipartisan" calls for reform, has police legitimacy actually melted into air? Are we in the midst of structural change? If so, how and to what end does the anti-state state deploy ideological and material resources towards, around, or through the institutionalized forces of organized violence? How in particular have the police and their patrons responded to widespread

6   A. Sivanandan, *A Different Hunger: Writings on Black Resistance* (London: Pluto, 1982).

7   Stuart Hall, "Race, Articulation, and Societies Structured in Dominance," in *Sociological Theories: Race and Colonialism* (Paris: UNESCO, 1980), 341.

8   José Martín, "Policing Is a Dirty Job, but Nobody's Gotta Do It: 6 Ideas for a Cop-Free World," *Rolling Stone*, December 16, 2014; Michael Denzel Smith, "In Order to End Police Brutality, We Need to End the Police," *The Nation*, February 25, 2015. Not all the talk of abolishing police has come from liberals. See, for example, Mariame Kaba, "Summer Heat," *New Inquiry*, June 6, 2015.

condemnation of police violence and militarization, and offered solutions that threaten neither the power of the police nor the status of their patrons?

Police Violence / Police Legitimacy

Police homicides prove police violence in general, and police tanks emblematize police militarization in general—yet they are not the whole sordid violent tale. The righteous outrage against police murders and extra-heavy equipment enables a strange displacement (often unintended, yet also often cynically co-opted) of political focus from the necessarily systemic character of organized violence. This displacement results in partial containment of expansive, international grassroots work to weaken, in order to undo, contemporary police legitimacy. In other words, the techniques and ideologies of saturation policing and mass criminalization remain too frequently unacknowledged except at the margin, where minor tweaks (body cameras, a few dozen sentence commutations) focus energy and resources, ultimately changing little. What are the preconditions for individual killings and industrialized killing equipment? They include stop and frisk, widespread arrests, the issuance of massive numbers of citations, and the political culture of perpetual enemies who must always be fought but can never be vanquished. These preconditions, and the violence enabled and required to maintain them, will not change if an officer or two is indicted and a few tanks are dismantled for scrap metal.

Transfers and convergences between military and police have a long history. While dramatic objects such as Mine Resistant Ambush Protected (MRAP) vehicles command attention, what matters more in terms of police legitimacy and power are more subtle objects such as standard-issue handguns, or out-of-sight capacities such as computerized profiling. The United States not only dominates the planet militarily, it is also the world's principal manufacturer and purveyor of military equipment. The Department of Defense's 1033 program (dating from 1997) enables a tiny fraction of surplus warfare matériel to remain active. The corporations that sold military equipment to the

Pentagon don't get paid again when the Pentagon funds the transfer of such surplus to police. To kill, police use ordinary weapons—guns, batons—and weaponize ordinary things—hands, forearms, flashlights, trash bags, vans.

Any focus on military–police interdependence might usefully drill down through both equipment and ideology to reveal the underlying strategies and practices that rebuild rather than weaken legitimacy even or perhaps especially in a long moment of crisis. If the principal use of tanks and armor is to deliver a visual message via news and social media that those who demonstrate against police killing and other outrages are dangerous, then what is obscured behind that implicit narrative? What, in other words, do police organizations do to secure their foundational role? Both capitalization and institutional change provide insights, as the rest of this chapter will demonstrate.

The Los Angeles Police Department has long been at the vanguard of increased use of machinery in the place of putting more cops on the street with guns and clubs and radios. Whether the equipment was first designed for or acquired from the military or not, this process is "capitalization." Take the helicopter, now an almost clichéd symbol of high-tech policing: the LAPD purchased its first one in 1956—more than four decades before the Department of Defense's 1033 program began.[9]

The LAPD's capitalization intensified in the wake of the 1965 Watts rebellion. In the aftermath of Watts, the LAPD started the country's first special weapons and tactics (SWAT) team, which in its first deployment stormed the LA headquarters of the Black Panther Party for Self-Defense at 41st and Central in December 1969. The department also purchased more helicopters and other weaponry, cars, and vans, and acquired state-of-the-art upgrades in communications hardware and intelligence-gathering infrastructure. But even before 1965, "in the days when the

---

9   For a good overview of the current LAPD air force, see Hamid Khan, "LAPD Helicopters Flying Overhead Don't Deter Crime. They Antagonize Minorities," *Guardian*, March 12, 2015. Well-known depictions of the LAPD's choppers include: Kid Frost, *East Side Story* (Virgin Records, 1992); Ice Cube, "Ghetto Bird," *Lethal Injection* (Priority, 1993); Red Hot Chili Peppers, "Police Helicopter," *Red Hot Chili Peppers* (EMI Records, 1984).

young Daryl Gates was driver to the great Chief William Parker, the policing of the ghetto was becoming simultaneously less corrupt but more militarized and brutal."[10] That trend intensified post-1965, as Gates's LAPD repressed Watts through the "the paramilitarization of the police and the destruction of the community's radical fringe."[11]

Gates had deep ties to Parker, and his own years as chief were marked by both intensely modernized technology and thoroughly racist ideology, implemented by a succession of new programs such as Operation Hammer and new divisions such as CRASH—Community Resources Against Street Hoodlums, whose motto was "We Intimidate Those Who Intimidate Others."

The 1992 LA uprising, coming on the heels of Mike Davis's *City of Quartz* and after years of tireless organizing by the Coalition Against Police Abuse, produced a legitimation crisis for the LAPD.[12] Gates resigned from a lifetime appointment as chief of the LAPD two months after the rebellion. Attempting to regain some of its legitimacy, the city replaced him with Willie L. Williams, the first Black department head and the first chief to come from outside the department. Four years later, Bernard C. Parks became LA's second Black chief of police. Like Williams, he served only one term.

To replace Parks, Mayor James Hahn recruited former NYPD commissioner William Bratton. When Bratton took over, the LAPD had not significantly improved its reputation in Black LA since the days of Parker and Gates. Joe Domanick remarked that the LAPD's South Central style "wasn't policing, it was anti-insurgency run amok. Sheer brutality, suppression and force—those were the only things the LAPD thought people in South L.A. understood, and those were the only things the LAPD itself understood."[13]

---

10   Mike Davis, *City of Quartz: Excavating the Future in Los Angeles* (London: Verso, 1990).

11   Ibid., 294.

12   João Costa Vargas, *Catching Hell in the City of Angels: Life and Meanings of Blackness in South Central Los Angeles* (Minneapolis: University of Minnesota Press, 2006).

13   Quoted in John Buntin, "What Does It Take to Stop Crips and Bloods from Killing Each Other?" *New York Times*, July 10, 2013.

Bratton's political strategy to rebuild police power in Los Angeles involved two key approaches. The first consisted of intensive outreach to the old civil rights leadership and the press to emphasize the new LAPD's commitment to protecting poor people of color, and especially Black people, from violent crime committed by Black people. The second focused on significantly increasing the size of the police force, which Bratton justified by arguing that the LAPD's militarized history was the result of too few officers trying to police too much territory. By extension, according to Bratton, trigger-happy strong-arm policing resulted from feelings of vulnerability to street gangs on the part of thin-on-the-ground police personnel. Thus, to end police brutality Bratton's force required more police, and to achieve it the LAPD worked hard to transition the mainstream civil rights agenda *away* from opportunities for advancement and protections from calamity, and *towards* support of criminalization.

Of course, more cops don't arrive without adequate funding to pay for them. In 2004, Bratton gambled that city voters would approve Measure A, an attempt to raise sales taxes to hire 1,260 to 1,700 more police. The measure was defeated by an unusual but not unprecedented electoral alignment of two increasingly well-organized factions—anti-tax West Valley conservatives and anti-police people of color concentrated in South Central Los Angeles.

Bratton's outreach to the civil rights establishment paid more immediate dividends. While he achieved some success among the leaders of Black LA's biggest churches, his most important recruit was noted civil rights attorney Connie Rice, former co-director of the NAACP Legal Defense Fund's LA chapter and co-founder of the Advancement Project. As Rice tells the story, Bratton "persuaded me to put my complaints away and come inside the department, and I did. He gave me a parking space and a badge, and I haven't left."[14]

---

14   Connie Rice, remarks at "Bridging the Great Divide: Can Police–Community Partnerships Reduce Crime and Strengthen Our Democracy?" John Jay College, September 4, 2014.

Community Policing Reborn

In the decade-plus that Attorney Rice has had her badge and parking place, working closely with former chief Bratton and his successor, Charles Beck, she and her colleagues at the Advancement Project (AP) have built programs that Rice guarantees have eliminated the possibility of "another Rodney King riot" in Los Angeles.[15] Launched with a report called "A Call to Action: A Case for a Comprehensive Solution to LA's Gang Violence Epidemic," the AP plotted a long-term "Violence Reduction Strategy" to attack the "ten root conditions of violence" through providing services in five broad areas: "prevention, intervention, suppression, reentry and the equitable distribution of resources."[16]

The plan focused more narrowly on two targets: gang violence and domestic violence towards children. The strategy of suppressing gangs while strengthening families (rather than vice versa) embraced Moynihan's racist manifesto of blame, pretending that the patriarchal family might be free of violence if sufficiently "strong" while maintaining that street organizations, strong or not, could be a source of nothing but violence. The equitable distribution of resources took a backseat to gang suppression.

A dizzying number of new state and parastate agencies, tools, and initiatives have sprung from "A Call to Action," including Urban Peace, the Urban Peace Academy, the Mayor's Gang Reduction and Youth Development zones, the LA County Regional Gang Violence Taskforce, the Community Safety Scorecard, and, finally, the Community Safety Partnership (CSP).

Following Chief Bratton's penchant for hot-spot policing, the AP called for concentrating more violence-prevention resources in "the highest need communities."[17] As the five-year report makes clear, resources for gang suppression flow more easily to those neighborhoods than funds for job creation, programs like rent control, or subsidies that might enable struggling households to stabilize themselves.

---

15   Ibid.

16   Advancement Project, *A Call to Action: Los Angeles' Quest to Achieve Community Safety*, Los Angeles, 2013, 5ff.

17   Ibid., 44.

The crown jewel of the new programs—the one that will prevent any more "Rodney King riots"—is the CSP, lauded by the AP as the "Future of Suppression."[18] According to the AP, the new "strategic suppression" will replace "a counter-productive, overbroad suppression approach." The strategy? "CSP is unique for both HACLA (Housing Authority of the City of Los Angeles) and LAPD in its recognition that safety cannot be achieved through traditional policing, but instead requires *collaboration* among all stakeholders."[19]

In remarks at "Bridging the Great Divide," an exclusive policing conference held in New York City in September 2014, Rice detailed some of the CSP's mechanisms. The first order of business was to break down the "negative perception of law enforcement by the community."

Towards this end, LAPD selected new squads, each with exclusive responsibility to patrol one of four public housing projects. Each squad is teamed with Gang Intervention Experts, former and generally older gang members (OGs) now on the AP payroll. Their role is to facilitate relationship-building between the police and the policed, in order to "lower the level of perceived bias" among the policed.

According to Rice, the police and their retired gangster guides started with grandmothers in the housing projects, apologizing for acts of police violence against the elders' families and asking what needs the residents might have. Deteriorating eyesight? Diabetes? No computers for the grandkids to do their homework? LAPD delivered 800 pair of bifocals, arranged a medical van from the University of Southern California to do onsite diabetes screening, and bought and gave away $300,000 worth of tablet computers.

The goal of that largesse was to build trust.

Rice and others promote CSP as a new model that solves the legitimation crisis of US policing, and many see it as a seductive alternative to the militarization that has so damaged that legitimacy. "If you serve the community," says Rice, "the community will get to know you, and they will get to trust you; and if they trust you, maybe they'll pick up the phone when there's a crime … Just maybe the community would back

---

18   Ibid., 39.
19   Ibid. Emphasis added.

the police for a change."[20] However, the fact that officers of the LAPD, LA Sheriff, and other LA County agencies kill an Angeleno almost once a week significantly undermines CSP's ability to gain the trust of residents of the housing complexes.[21]

The Velvet Glove

The attempt to manage a police legitimation crisis through community-based policing is, of course, not new at all. The classic analysis of such campaigns remains *The Iron Fist and the Velvet Glove*, first published in 1975:

> Massive spending on military hardware, by itself, would not only fail to stop rising crime rates and urban discontent, but would probably serve to further alienate large sectors of the population. This approach stressed the need for police to develop closer ties to the communities most heavily patrolled by them. The emphasis began to be placed less on paramilitary efficiency and more on insuring popular consent and acquiescence.[22]

In the 1970s, LAPD rolled out community policing models in which "developing more intimate relations with people in the community" was a central goal, particularly in "poor and Third World communities" where police were central to maintaining order despite "increasing militancy and resistance to the police" in those neighborhoods.[23]

Across the United States, community policing experiments flowered. According to Platt and others most community policing projects shared two common factors: "One is to give people more responsibility in policing themselves—to bring people into active participation in the

---

20   Rice, remarks at "Bridging the Great Divide."

21   Youth Justice Coalition, "Don't Shoot to Kill: Homicides Resulting from Law Enforcement Use of Force within LA County, 2000–2014," 2014.

22   Tony Platt et al., *The Iron Fist and the Velvet Glove: An Analysis of the U.S. Police* (Berkeley: Center for Research on Criminal Justice, 1975), 54.

23   Ibid., 57.

policing process. The other is to encourage greater daily contact between the police and neighborhoods they patrol … Theoretically, with people's trust and participation, the job of the police will be less difficult."[24] While the community police experiments of the 1970s went far beyond earlier police efforts at public relations and crisis management, by attempting to enlist community members as extensions of the police web, two points stand out. First, the new relationships did nothing to disturb existing relations of coercive power and control. "From [the LAPD's] perspective, it is useful to decentralize police *functions* without decentralizing police *authority*."[25] Second, while the velvet glove's purpose was to soften the image of late 1960s and early 1970s militarized police, community policing spread across the country at virtually the same time as SWAT teams; thus, to be effective, the velvet glove—then as now—clothed an iron fist. Thus, for example, since the LAPD created SWAT teams in 1967, the use of those forces has risen from about 3,000 operations a year in the 1980s to 40,000 a year recently.[26]

Counterinsurgency

If CSP's emphasis on building relationships among specially detailed police and the housing projects they patrol isn't new, does it still provide an alternative to military policing?

No, it does not. In fact, the most notable innovations in the CSP model directly incorporate up-to-date military counterinsurgency tactics.

The importation of US military technique to domestic inner-city policing itself has a long and complex history, as many scholars have demonstrated. For example, Nikhil Singh shows the long articulation

---

24   Ibid., 63.

25   Ibid., 58.

26   Stephen Graham, *Cities under Siege: The New Military Urbanism* (London: Verso, 2010). The study Graham cites is Peter Kraska's *Militarizing the American Criminal Justice System: The Changing Roles of the Armed Forces and the Police* (Lebanon, NH: Northeastern University Press, 2001). For more on SWAT, see Joe Domanick, *To Protect and to Serve: The LAPD's Century of War in the City of Dreams* (New York: Pocket Books, 1994).

of late-nineteenth-century US imperial methods of insurgency suppression with changes in the structure and organization of domestic forces of organized violence.[27] Laleh Khalili reveals that military/policing practices imported from the Philippine-American war to the United States themselves grew out of US military experience fighting indigenous peoples in the colonization of the West.[28]

Platt and Takagi write of the "increasing militancy and resistance" to racist police violence—the broad range of activity and activism that put into crisis not only police legitimacy but by extension the racial capitalist state. To suppress spontaneous or consolidated opposition, the military techniques imported are generally those actively in use elsewhere. Seen in this light, the CSP resembles, not surprisingly, counterinsurgency campaigns operated by the US military in Iraq and Afghanistan. Stephen Graham argues: "'High-intensity policing' and 'low-intensity warfare' threaten to merge."[29] Indeed, they have merged.

CSP practice follows, nearly to the letter, the steps outlined by David Kilcullen, whom Khalili has dubbed "the counter-insurgency guru." The first move is to co-opt women.

These ideas are operationalized in the Female Engagement Teams in Afghanistan. Their mission is described as "non-lethal targeting of the human terrain" to "enable systemic collection of information from the female population in a culturally respectful manner to facilitate building confidence with the Afghan [or South Central] population."[30]

---

27   Nikhil Singh, "Critical Theories of Modern Policing," paper presented at "Resisting Arrest" conference, Department of Social and Cultural Analysis, NYU, April 11, 2015. See also Singh, *Exceptional Empire* (Cambridge: Harvard University Press, forthcoming); and Stuart Schrader, "Policing Empire," *Jacobin* (2014), available at jacobinmag.com.

28   Laleh Khalili, "Lineaments of Settler-Colonialism in Counterinsurgency Confinement," paper given at "The Scope of Slavery: Enduring Geographies of American Bondage," Harvard University, November 8, 2014. See also Laleh Khalili, *Time in the Shadows: Confinement in Counterinsurgencies* (Stanford: Stanford University Press, 2013).

29   Graham, *Cities under Siege*, 96.

30   Khalili, *Time in the Shadows*, 198.

Cops in South Central, like the military in Afghanistan or Iraq, work to win the hearts and minds of the grannies through the provision of goods and services—precisely the goods and services that the neighborhood has been starved of, thanks to the organized abandonment carried out by neoliberal firms and warfare states. Resources become, then, not the staff of life but the difficult-to-refuse inducements used to secure cooperation with the occupying army or police. Over the course of half a century, the LAPD has moved from Vietnam War anti-insurgency ("anti-insurgency run amok") to Iraq counterinsurgency. Khalili describes Kilcullen's predecessor John Paul Vann's impact on US strategy in Vietnam as:

> a rupture that framed—and continues to shape—the metanarrative of counterinsurgency … The story begins with a lumbering, conventional, and conservative counterinsurgent military using its firepower and technical prowess to bomb an unequal enemy into submission, all the while stoking native hostility not only with the force of arms but also its naïve racism. Then arrive unconventional—in both senses of the word—thinkers and military men, rebels who anger the bureaucracy around them, who, against their racist colleagues … look for more humane ways of acquiring local allegiances through virtuous behaviour, humility, and the provision of security (and resources and social goods.)[31]

The unconventional thinkers and military people are Bratton and Rice. The strategic hamlets are South Central housing projects. The reaction to overwhelming racist police violence produces, again, a velvet glove, but we must not ignore the fact that the glove remains a military-issue combat glove. Or that CSP, like the community policing initiatives of the 1960s and 1970s or Vietnamization, does not reduce police or military violence.

Rather, the new policing programs are intended to reduce "increasing militancy and resistance" in reaction to such violence—not only police killings but all of the violence on which mass criminalization depends. A large part of Bratton's cleverness has been to reinvigorate discourses

31 Ibid., 41–2.

of Black pathology, arguing that the numbers of Black people arrested, imprisoned, and killed by the police are not disproportionate. Rather, they are proportionate to the concentration of crime in Black neighborhoods and to Black victimization. Stopping and interrogating, arresting, and incarcerating so many Black people, Bratton argues, is the way to protect Black people. Gil Scott-Heron saw through an earlier iteration of organized violence targeting Black people, commenting on the benefits of Nixon's no-knock law for Black people: "No Knock, the law in particular, was allegedly legislated for Black people rather than, you know, for their destruction."[32]

Bratton and Rice are poised to lead the police through the current crisis of legitimacy towards a new, however temporary, stage of increased police power and prestige. The CSP velvet glove sheathes a centralized and high-tech iron fist. In other words, there's no movement whatsoever to shift power away from the police. Quite the opposite: the provision of necessary goods and services through the police—now often justified only as a means to reduce crime or violence—will further weaken what remains of the social welfare state and the neighborhoods that most depend on public services.

Devolution and Police Power: Organized Abandonment and Organized Violence in Racial Capitalism's Neoliberal Turn

> *A recurring problem, and not just limited to the issue of housing, is the lack of tools and resources available to municipalities when faced with a problem whose origin is global. Increasingly, conflicts specific to an urban area are caused by phenomena that exceed the formal powers held by municipal governments.*[33]
>
> —Ada Colau and Adrià Alemany

32   Gil Scott-Heron, "No Knock," *Free Will* (Flying Dutchman/RCA, recording, released August 1972).

33   Ada Colau and Adrià Alemany, *Mortgaged Lives: From the Housing Bubble to the Right to Housing*, trans. Michelle Teran and Jessica Fuquay (Los Angeles: Journal of Aesthetics and Protest Press, 2014 [2012]), 124.

> *I love the police because politicians are
> afraid of them.*
>
> —Connie Rice

Why does the racial capitalist state ever change? What accounts for variations? For convergences? To enhance their ability to extract value from labor and land, elites fashion political, economic, and cultural institutions. They build states. Tweak them. Aggrandize and devolve them. Promote and attack stories about why things should either persist or change. But even during periodic waves of abandonment elites rely on structures of order and significance that the anarchy of racial capitalism can never guarantee.[34]

At the same time, non-elites are never passive pawns. Ordinary people, in mutable diversity, figure out how to stretch or diminish social and spatial forms to create room for their lives—including building states to safeguard and more universally advance the general good, as happened in the US South among Black people during Reconstruction and during other revolutionary times in modern history.[35] In nonrevolutionary conjunctures some use elites' methods and join with dominating forces to get what they want, while others compel change from the ground up. Usually struggles combine top-down and grassroots efforts—part, as C. L. R. James remarked, of the exhaustive conservatism that underlies revolutions.[36] That said, in the long aftermath of the so-called golden age of US capitalism (c. 1938–1970), the increased vulnerability of workers and their communities, broadly defined across society and space, has resulted from purposeful abandonment organized by elites, as racial capitalism makes and consolidates the neoliberal turn.

The pattern of racial capitalism's contemporary class war in the over-developed world (imprecisely, the global North) closely resembles what

---

34 Clyde Woods charted this process across 130 years of Lower Mississippi Delta history. Woods extended these theoretical and analytical insights to policing in Los Angeles—a topic to which he turned his formidable intellectual energy late in his too-brief career. See Clyde Woods, *Development Arrested: The Blues and Plantation Power in the Mississippi Delta* (London: Verso, 1998).

35 See W. E. B. Du Bois, *Black Reconstruction in America* (New York: Atheneum, 1992 [1935]).

36 C. L. R. James, *Modern Politics* (San Francisco: PM Press, 2013 [1961]).

international financial institutions have longer demanded of the so-called developing world (loosely, the global South): limited states run by technocrat executives on behalf of local and transnational oligarchs and firms.[37] "Devolution"—the name for structural adjustment in richer, inequality-riven polities—consists of off-loading to increasingly local state- and non-state institutions the authority to allocate or withhold shredded social welfare, further restricting protections from calamity and opportunities for advancement. Municipalities encounter new obligations as unfunded mandates or tied to narrowly targeted funding streams. Therefore, devolution in action is a set of institutionalizing practices—a regime that, veiled by the rhetoric of "less government," specifically prevents the hands of the vulnerable from extracting the social wage from ever-deeper, tax-resistant pockets.

The social wage is public revenue (taxes and use fees) plus the deposits (gifts or bequests) stored in foundations and other tax-exempt, non-governmental institutions. "Welfare state" indicates a broad range of institutional, legal, and moral frameworks that temper racial capitalism's tendencies (monopoly and poverty) by downwardly redistributing a significant chunk of surplus money (and other resources such as public education, housing vouchers, and sometimes cheese). Neoliberalism's delegitimation and dismantling of welfare state capacities reallocates racial capitalism's accumulation crisis by taking resources from institutions, programs, streets, households, and lives, throwing all into permanent crisis.

Crisis, then, is organized abandonment's condition of existence *and* its inherent vice. To persist, systematic abandonment depends on the agile durability of organized violence. For example, by the year 1980, California's diverse economy was bigger than that of any of the other forty-nine US states and all but a handful of the world's nation-states. Throughout the next thirty years, through several booms and busts, the

---

37   See, for examples, Robert S. Browne, "Africa's Economic Future: Development or Disintegration?" *World Policy Journal* 1, no. 4 (1984): 793–812; Robert S. Browne, "Africa and the International Monetary Fund: Conditionality, a New Form of Colonialism?" *Africa Report* 29, no. 5 (1984): 14–18; Bobby M. Wilson, *America's Johannesburg: Industrialization and Racial Transformation in Birmingham* (Lanham: Rowman and Littlefield, 1996); Beverly Silver and Giovanni Arrighi, *Chaos and Governance in the Modern World System* (Minneapolis: University of Minnesota Press, 1999).

gross state product nearly doubled. Every bust destroyed jobs—shaking up households, communities, and productive regions and dropping more and more people into poverty. Every boom deepened inequality while padding the ranks of the very rich.

As capital strolled or ran away from paying a significant percentage of the state treasury's receipts, the sweep of Golden State policy shifted dramatically, bringing to an end the expansive Cold War–justified social investment in people, infrastructure, and innovation. Abandonment-induced anxieties about the future encouraged voters to punish elected officeholders by instituting tax limits and term limits—which, unsurprisingly if ironically, guaranteed that individual political ambition could only be realized through capitulation to the biggest checkbooks rather than the general desires of potential district voters.[38] These, combined with fiscal, procedural, and policy shifts, shredded protections from calamity and raised the sticker price on opportunities, all the while ideologically recasting public goods such as education, for example, as an individualized instrument. Worldwide today, wherever inequality is deepest, the use of prisons as a catchall solution to social problems prevails—nowhere as extensively as in the United States, led by California where, in turn, Los Angeles dominates.

The racial capitalist state's institutional capacities changed because, in the aggregate, capital succeeded in burdening workers and their communities with the costs of both downturns *and* surges in economic activity. By contrast, for a few prior decades the rising strength of workers had, again in the aggregate, compelled capital to smooth fluctuations by paying both higher wages and, important for this discussion, a significant indirect—or social—wage through taxes on profit. But now, states' rights, once the bulwark of US apartheid, have returned with a vengeance.

Thus, as we have seen in the case study, what Rachel Herzing terms "the Bratton brand" of policing developed in the context of ideological as well as institutional crises.[39] Capitalism saving capitalism from

---

38   Michan Connor, "Uniting Citizens after *Citizens United*," *American Studies* 54, no. 1 (2015): 5–27.

39   Rachel Herzing, "Resisting the Bratton Brand: Lessons from the US," Institute of Race Relations, 2011, available at irr.org.uk.

capitalism creates vulnerabilities and opportunities precisely because the intertwined imperatives of organized abandonment and organized violence are so thoroughly destabilizing. The motion affects everybody and everything.

In other words, racial capitalism's contemporary self-saving modality —cut costs and evade regulation by starving the welfare state and smashing regulatory and other barriers to rapid accumulation—has put all public agencies on notice by raising the anti-state hue and cry. As a result, in the general context of organized abandonment, all state actors, fighting their redundancy or seeking state power, try to expand their agency's scope and durability. Both the relative autonomy of the state *and* inter-institutional competition within states help us understand how this unfolds. The constant invocation of oligarchs' demands ("do more with less") belies behind-the-scenes scheming for comparative advantage that permeates what Toni Negri characterized in 1980 as "the crisis of the crisis-state."[40] Superficial instrumentality underlies *institutional* ambitions. The ruse is to appear compliant—act and sound anti-state —while achieving security towards the goal of absolute growth, in the process developing and sustaining the anti-state state.

Given the default legitimacy of "organized violence" in the range of obligations, responsibilities, and privileges characterizing the modern state, it might seem self-evident that in a time of abandonment police would come out well—compared with education or health or housing. But in fact, even the domestic agents of organized violence have consolidated and grown by re-legitimizing themselves institutionally and ideologically, certainly before 9/11 but even since then.[41] Such success takes a lot of work because institutional competition within states draws on varying constituencies who, at least in theory, might come together to achieve different outcomes.[42]

40   Toni Negri, "The Crisis of the Crisis-State," in *Revolution Retrieved: Writings on Marx, Keynes, Capitalist Crisis and New Social Subjects (1967–1973)* (London: Red Notes, 1988), 177–98.

41   For an overview of this shift, see the Policing Futures Institute volume: Joseph Andrew Schafer et al., *Policing 2020: Exploring the Future of Crime, Communities, and Policing* (Washington, DC: United States Department of Justice/Federal Bureau of Investigation, 2007).

42   James O'Connor, *The Fiscal Crisis of the State* (Piscataway, NJ: Transaction

Much to the dismay of libertarians who embrace devolution as a route to shrinking government absolutely rather than merely rescaling it, the dollar cost of the "anti-state state" hasn't diminished much, if at all. While attacks rage on non-discretionary spending (social security, medicare, and other entitlements), discretionary costs associated with the production and management of mass criminalization manifest most dramatically. Criminal justice spending has risen across the board, with most cost devoted to uniformed and civilian personnel, in the wake—not ahead—of decades-long drops in all kinds of crime.[43]

In addition, police departments have revised and expanded their remit, as the Los Angeles case study demonstrates.[44] The practice of agencies imitating institutional competitors in order to secure scarce dollars or secure reputational legitimacy is not new. Analytically, what's important is the interplay of fiscal, bureaucratic, and ideological capacities, as we shall see in the next section.

Structure and Flow

Inter-institutional competition and copying is hardly a feature specific to devolution. The contemporary dynamic brings to mind a—perhaps *the*—major change that occurred during and after World War II, at a time of state aggrandizement. To prevent the Department of War's normal postwar dismantling, military elites and industrial and political members of their bloc figured out how to use fiscal and bureaucratic

---

Publishers, 2001 [1973]). Certainly the case study alludes to such a failed possibility, and many organizations around the country have tried to build on the kinds of insights put forward by O'Connor, the late Dr. Eddie Ellis, and others. See, e.g., California Prison Moratorium Project, *How to Stop a Prison in Your Town*, available at calipmp.org.

43   As Platt and Takagi note, police personnel and equipment spending increased in the 1960s and 1970s, and the LAPD committed enormous resources to developing the first comprehensive computerized data management system. Tony Platt and Paul Takagi, "Intellectuals for Law and Order: A Critique of the New 'Realists,'" in *Crime and Social Justice*, ed. Platt and Takagi (New York: Macmillan, 1981), 32–4; LAPD website: lapdonline.org.

44   Schafer et al., *Policing 2020*.

capacities, developed for New Deal social welfare programs, to grow rather than wither the department.[45] They built and expanded bases, hired uniformed and civilian staff, promoted mass postsecondary education, established the Gunbelt, oversaw one of the US's biggest population relocation projects, and churned trillions of dollars through public and private research, development, manufacturing, and think-tank outfits—including universities—that together produced not only vast industrialized capacity for war-making but also the ideological and public relations methods to promote and naturalize this remarkable transformation.[46]

The military-industrial complex is the short name for all of these activities, relationships, people, and places, and one of its achievements was the creation of the Sun Belt—a political-economic region that produced a string of presidents: Johnson, Nixon, Carter, Reagan, Bush, Clinton, Bush. After Johnson, most candidates ran on anti-state platforms, and, having won, they all set about making the state bigger while destroying individuals, institutions, and initiatives that might improve working people's lives and hopes: radical anti-capitalist organizations, full employment, public sector unions, the short-lived "peace dividend," welfare rights, prisoners' rights, open immigration, public education, peace itself.

In the closing decades of the twentieth century, prison, policing, and related agencies of state and local governments have demonstrated patterning similar to that of the late 1940s Department of War. As we have seen, there's a more detailed history of police/military interaction. But for our purposes here the pattern of achieving legitimate stability is what matters. Police, prisons, and jails have consolidated their numbers, relevance, status, and capacity—sometimes competitively, but always with combined growth.

In other words, devolution creates its own intra-state struggle for dominance; in the same way that capitalist firms concentrate while extending their reach, so do institutions patterned on the capitalist

---

45   Gregory Hooks, *Forging the Military-Industrial Complex: World War II's Battle of the Potomac* (Champaign: University of Illinois Press, 1991).

46   Ann Markusen et al., *The Rise of the Gunbelt: The Military Remapping of Industrial America* (Oxford: Oxford University Press, 1991).

imperative to grow or die. Certainly, the rise of the voluntary sector, as Jennifer Wolch demonstrates in *The Shadow State*, shows how ordinary people built the capacity to withstand some aspects of organized abandonment and meet basic needs. A good deal of the contemporary social justice not-for-profit sector is heir to the desire—whether altruistic, cynical, or desperate—to demand or provide services externalized from the state.[47] In such a context it isn't a foregone conclusion that in current practice, whatever legitimacy the police and military might have in theory, they automatically will withstand pressure to shrink.[48] Rather, they make themselves ideologically and practically indispensable.

Indeed, while the postwar Pentagon successfully *imitated* fiscal and bureaucratic *forms* intended for social welfare agencies in order to expand its war-making abilities, today's crisis-driven agencies—including the Pentagon—strive to *absorb* their institutional rivals' *missions* in order to survive and thrive. Since the late 1970s, for example, the US Department of Education has punitively monitored selective service (military draft) registration, as well as certain kinds of drug convictions. What's more, it has its own SWAT team to bust alleged financial aid fraudsters. Federal and local housing authorities ration eligibility for shelter based on criteria unrelated to the need for affordable rent.

So it is with the police and military: police organizations are increasingly participants in social services as both coordinating forces and primary providers, at the same time that the Pentagon has developed its latest counterinsurgency doctrine to recast soldiers as door-to-door diplomats in camouflage.[49]

Thus, while organized violence gives police a modicum of institutional durability, that platform, combined with the bureaucratic and

---

47   Jennifer Wolch, *The Shadow State: Government and Voluntary Sector in Transition* (Foundation Center, 1990). For an elaboration on these themes, see Ruth Wilson Gilmore, "In the Shadow of the Shadow State," in *The Revolution Will Not Be Funded: Beyond the Non-Profit Industrial Complex*, ed. Incite (Boston: South End Press, 2007), 41–52.

48   Schafer et al., *Policing 2020*.

49   U.S. Army/Marine Corps, *Counterinsurgency Field Manual* (Chicago: University of Chicago Press, 2007). See also Joint Chiefs of Staff, *Counterinsurgency*, Joint Chiefs of Staff Joint Publication 3-24, November 22, 2013; Khalili, *Time in the Shadows*.

fiscal capacities required of contemporary departments, has enabled the people in blue to seize new opportunities to *manage* organized abandonment—to administer all aspects of pacification, as has happened in the capitalist workplace and related institutions during this period.[50] Who better positioned for such a role in the ambience of organized abandonment-related crises than the police, whose professional hubris in recent years, beyond the hosannahs of heroism, rests on the expensive and expansive development of technocratic expertise: logistics, big data, Compstat, so-called predictive policing? This, then, shows us the larger context for our case study, by pointing to where the police intersect not only with rival agencies, but also articulate with shadow state formations that might have arisen in opposition to policing but now slurp at a single trough.

But even the opportunism—if it can be thus styled—isn't cut from whole cloth. Rather, the precedent for the case study has decades-long roots that snake forward from the time the rate of profit in US capitalism began to fall and *de jure* US apartheid came apart. We have already referred to the Sun Belt presidents who established the LEAA and spread it via significant federal subventions for policing and prisons.[51] They also made widespread if patchy attempts to develop snitch culture as a condition of minimal local development dollars, especially the Weed and Seed program—surely a preview of federal, state, and foundation-funded "community reinvestment" cash currently trickling down.[52] Remaining traces of the long transition from state aggrandizement to anti-state devolution show quite starkly how the social wage

50   See David Gordon, *Fat and Mean: The Corporate Squeeze of Working Americans and the Myth of Managerial Downsizing* (New York: Free Press, 1996); Samuel Bowles and Arjun Jayadev, *Guard Labor: An Essay in Honor of Pranab Bardhan*, University of Massachusetts Amherst, Department of Economics Working Papers no. 2004–15 (2004), available at ideas.repec.org.

51   Naomi Murakawa, *The First Civil Right: How Liberals Built Prison America* (Oxford: Oxford University Press, 2014); Marie Gottschalk, *Caught: The Prison State and the Lockdown of American Politics* (Princeton: Princeton University Press, 2014); Judah Schept, *Progressive Punishment: Job Loss, Jail Growth, and the Neoliberal Logic of Carceral Expansion* (New York: New York University Press, 2015).

52   See the Urban Strategies Group, "A Call to Reject the Federal Weed and Seed Program in Los Angeles," Labor/Community Strategy Center, 1992.

remains centrally controlled even as it appears that localities choose how to participate in various aspects of public life. Participation in design, scope, and consequence is not open to democratic process, while at the same time both categorical *and* procedural constraints determine possibilities within narrowly defined funding allocations (underwritten by private foundation dollars) and the preferences of the most powerfully organized municipal agencies.

In 2011, California governor Jerry Brown's administration rolled out a "Realignment" program for the adult criminal justice system. Realignment follows to the letter devolution's underlying principles, and in California's case it recapitulates an earlier round that involved the care (and sometimes custody) of persons with mental health problems. The vast criminal justice project shifts authority for control and custody of people with particular conviction profiles from Sacramento to the state's fifty-eight counties, accompanied by a rhetoric of "closer to home" that seems amenable to something like more democracy. But as we have seen, the anti-state state is forcefully organized by centralization—ranging from strengthened and technocrat-heavy executive branches to mandatory minimums, through strong central command of police departments to categorical exclusion of millions of people from many aspects of normal life due to criminal records. California is also in the process of funding and building $2 billion in new prison capacity, and the counties are competing for state grants (initially funded by new state debt) to expand jail capacity. At the same time, the Golden State hosted a test run for the new, US-wide "bipartisan consensus on criminal justice reform," which purports to return to schools money long-since diverted to prisons. The first year's implementation produced about a dollar per student, and even that paltry amount requires school districts to be organized to acquire the resources that police and sheriffs are already prepared to absorb into their budgets.

Ideologically, which is to say in thought *and* everyday culture, the experience and normalization of the twin processes, devolution and centralization—patterned as they are by the sensibility of permanent crisis—shape structures of feeling and therefore to a great extent determine the apparent range of socially as well as politically available options. That dynamic, in turn, sheds light on why certain tendencies in scholarship and advocacy have risen to prominence in the dense context of many kinds of analysis and many varieties of advocacy. When Connie Rice dismisses a worry about police delivering social welfare to benefits-starved residents, claiming that "it's what the community asked for," we can see beyond the shadow of a doubt that the shadow state has been absorbed into the repressive function of the anti-state state, and neither devolution nor a new round of deliberate state growth will undo the relationships so firmly established—as naturalized as the Pentagon's role in many aspects of everyday industry, workforce development, land use, and knowledge production.

Conclusion

In May 1961, local Alabama law enforcement allowed Ku Klux Klan members in Montgomery and Birmingham to beat Freedom Riders and burn one of their buses, provoking the Kennedy Justice Department to intervene. Rather than relying on Ku Klux Klan violence to discourage and discipline Freedom Riders, which would invite federal troops, Mississippi governor Ross Barnett changed the plot. He effectively told the plantocratic state's paramilitary wing (the Klan) to stay home by promising that differently uniformed officers would take care of matters using arrest and imprisonment—in local jails and at the Parchman Farm state prison plantation. Seven decades of organizing against white mob violence protected by law enforcement and the courts, growing out of Ida B. Wells's proto-#BlackLivesMatter advocacy, had finally managed to crack the legitimacy of a certain kind of terror regime. In other words, Governor Barnett agreed to protect the Riders from mob violence but did so by enforcing Mississippi's laws, including segregation laws and long sentences.

> Well, we didn't have much trouble with the freedom riders. When they didn't obey the officials here in the City of Jackson in Hinds County, we just simply put them in jail, and when the jails were all filled and the mayor's chicken coops down on the fairground were all filled, there were thirty-two of them left, and it was my happy

privilege to send all of them to the State Penitentiary at Parchman and put them in maximum security cells. We put them in maximum security cells so they would be protected, you see. You haven't heard of any more freedom riders in Mississippi.[53]

The shift from state-sanctioned mob violence to arrest and incarceration is one mark of the transition from American apartheid. While the rural and urban Black freedom struggle created the crises that compelled the transition, the movement's interdependent ideologies and tactics ran up against counterrevolutionary forces that regrouped behind a blue line they could move at will. Eventually massive expansion and capitalization of local law enforcement, community policing, and accelerated criminalization produced a temporary stasis.[54] The legitimacy of the badge replaced the discredited Klan hood.

Yet the onslaught of police killings suggests as well that turning the extralegal into the legal, more than half a century later, internalized in police forces certain aspects of non-state organized violence that erupt with regularity in the context of the crisis state. How often do police killings happen? Twice a week? Once every twenty-eight hours? Or, as the *Guardian* newspaper shows for the year 2015, once every eight hours—all, we might say, in a day's work.

The Bratton brand developed out of the need, variously understood, to deal with and contain long-standing opposition to police killing and other police violence. Just as Mississippi's Barnett shifted practices during Jim Crow's death throes, such reforms are not only about policing. Mississippi passed right-to-work laws and cut income taxes the same year that the Freedom Riders arrived. As a result, it welcomed some of the first companies fleeing strong union states, and made nice with the federal government in order to position the Magnolia State to receive a steady flow of Gunbelt-directed federal dollars.

"Bipartisan consensus" around police reform has emerged and

---

53   Ross R. Barnett, oral history interview, May 6, 1969, available at jfklibrary.org.

54   See Platt and Takagi, "Intellectuals for Law and Order"; Murakawa, *The First Civil Right*; Khalil Gibran Muhammad, *The Condemnation of Blackness: Race, Crime, and the Making of Modern Urban America* (Cambridge: Harvard University Press, 2011).

flourished in the precise nexus of organized abandonment and organized violence. The specificities of the contemporary anti-state state do not stop with reinvigorated rights for states and localities. Rather, by recasting obligations and responsibilities of various levels of the state in a state of permanent crisis caused by the withdrawal of the social wage coupled with the withering of the paycheck, Bratton, Rice, and their ilk become the Tancredi of the racial state, insisting that "if we want to keep things as they are, things will have to change."[55] To whom, against whom, can one carry one's petition or raise one's fist?

Sparked by police murder, in the context of racial capitalism's neoliberal turn, the post-Ferguson movement may therefore be understood as protests against profound austerity and the iron fist necessary to impose it.[56] The movement's central challenge is to prevent the work from facilitating another transition in regimes of racist policing and incarceration, displacement, and disinvestment through formal but not transformative reforms.[57] James Kilgore, one of the first to write about police humanitarianism, recently warned how the "bi-partisan consensus on criminal justice reform" is actually a move towards what he, following Tariq Ali, calls the "extreme center."[58] The USA's extreme center is far to the right, especially when it comes to vulnerable lives. The truth of the matter is that a few high-profile sentence commutations, coupled with new offers such as body cameras, training books, even the occasional indictment or end to military surplus weapons transfer, will not de-weaponize the various capacities, reaches, and effects of the Bratton brand, as mass criminalization—and the straight-up human sacrifice it relies on, from Trayvon Martin to Sandra Bland—enables racial capitalism's death-dealing austerity.[59]

---

55   Giuseppe Tomasi di Lampedusa, *The Leopard* (New York: Pantheon, 1960).

56   Ed Vulliamy, "The Rebellion in Baltimore Is an Uprising against Austerity, Claims Top US Academic," *Guardian*, May 2, 2015.

57   Ruth Wilson Gilmore and Craig Gilmore, "ReStating the Obvious," in Sorkin, *Indefensible Spaces*. See also Woods, *Development Arrested*.

58   James Kilgore, "Obama, Mass Incarceration and the Extreme Center," July 21, 2015, available at counterpunch.org.

59   Ruth Wilson Gilmore, "The Worrying State of the Anti-Prison Movement," *Social Justice*, February 23, 2015; Marie Gottschalk, "The Folly of Neoliberal Prison

~

Ruth Wilson Gilmore is professor of earth and environmental sciences and American studies, and director of the Center for Place, Culture, and Politics at the Graduate Center of the City University of New York. She has published and lectured widely on racial capitalism, the changing role of the state, and carceral geographies. She is co-founder of several social justice organizations.

Craig Gilmore co-founded the California Prison Moratorium Project (http://www.calipmp.org/).

Reform," *Boston Review*, June 8, 2015; Kay Whitlock and Nancy Heitzeg, "Moneyballing Justice: 'Evidence-Based' Criminal Reforms Ignore Real Evidence," *Truthout*, March 29, 2015.

14. THEY'RE NOT SOLVING THE PROBLEM, THEY'RE DISPLACING IT: AN INTERVIEW WITH ALEX SANCHEZ

Steven Osuna

Alex Sanchez is an internationally recognized peacemaker and the co-founder and executive director of Homies Unidos in Los Angeles, an organization working for peace among Central American immigrant, gang-involved, and criminalized youth in the city. He is the recipient of a number of awards for his advocacy, including the Drum Major Award from the Martin Luther King Legacy Association, the Lottie Wexler Award, and the AGAPE Award. Sanchez was interviewed by scholar-activist Steven Osuna, an assistant professor of sociology at California State University, Long Beach. The interview was conducted on February 6, 2015.

Osuna: You co-founded Homies Unidos, a group devoted to youth empowerment, gang prevention, and human rights in El Salvador and LA's immigrant communities. What experiences brought you to this work? Can you talk about your arrival in LA from El Salvador?

Sanchez: My parents sent for me in 1979. I was seven years old. It had been five years since they left us in El Salvador. One day the people who I called Mom and Dad told me that my brother and I were going to go "a la USA." We ended up crossing with complete strangers. I remember the coyotes telling me to call them my parents, because if a gringo opened the door and I didn't, the gringos could take me away forever. To see a white man in uniform asking us, "Quienes son tus papas?" was scary. That was my introduction to white people, to the Border Patrol, and to authority figures who can take you away. In LA, we got into a blue Chevy pickup truck around Skid Row. My brother was sitting next to my father and I was next to my mother thinking, "Who the fuck are these people?" We felt like we had been sold or something.

In El Salvador we had space to run, but there was no space in LA. We lived in a one-bedroom apartment and played in the alley where all the *borachos* would piss. Going to school was a nightmare. I didn't want anyone to know I was Salvadoran because I was getting picked on. I would ditch school and go by my friend's house. There were all these guys there with long hair. They were Mara Salvatrucha Stoners 13 (MSS13), but I didn't know them. In junior high school, I got introduced to El Pepito from MSS13. When I heard him speak, using *voz* and all the slang that I hadn't used in years, I thought, damn, this guy is not afraid. I thought these were my people and they'd stand their ground. I didn't have relatives looking out for me, so I started hanging out with the barrio and getting involved. Eventually I jumped in.

Osuna: Your gang prevention work comes from your own involvement in gangs in LA and also being targeted by the INS and the LAPD. Can you talk about your early experiences with law enforcement?

Sanchez: I ran away when I was fourteen and became homeless. Eventually there were seven of us: five guys and two girls. We were all Salvadoran. We used to steal food to eat. We were into heavy metal and would use LSD. We were confronted by law enforcement all the time. I was arrested for stealing ham at a Jon's market. By the time they took me, they also had my homeboy who stole cheese. That's when I found out about immigration. At the station, they were going to release my homeboy to my mom, because no one came for him. But my mom only took me out and my homeboy ended up getting deported. He was probably around fifteen or sixteen. This was 1986.

We were into the heavy metal scene. We were called MSS13, Mara Salvatrucha Stoners. The 13 was originally because it was bad luck, Friday the 13, and so on. We didn't consider ourselves a gang; we were more of a rock group. We all had Levis, Vans, heavy metal shirts, and long hair. The cops would arrest anyone who fit that profile and log them as a member of MSS13. Soon we began to know our roles. We knew that people were getting picked up, framed, and turned over to immigration. Everybody that came out of juvenile hall started to develop a different attitude. The gang also changed its attitude from being a stoner group to an actual Sureño gang. They took out the S ("Stoners") from MSS13.

Osuna: You were also involved in gangs in El Salvador and were targeted by the Salvadoran national police and its death squads. How did those experiences come about?

Sanchez: In 1994 I went to prison and then got deported. When I got to El Salvador, I had no one waiting for me, but there were all these other guys who had also been deported. In the 1990s the US was deporting masses of people to El Salvador in order to destabilize the country. There was no infrastructure to receive these masses of people, especially from detention, immigration, and prisons. What did the government do? They used the old tactics of death squads. During the civil war in El Salvador in the 1980s, the US trained military officers at the School of the Americas. The death squads in the 1990s were a direct result of that training.

The violence I confronted in El Salvador was unlike any other kind. These death squads would kill people, decapitate them, and leave their bodies in the street. The butchering was being done by the government. They knew the shock it created. A connection between homegrown gang members in El Salvador and deported gang members came organically—it wasn't planned. We needed each other. I used to see these kids in El Centro (the center of San Salvador) dying in the street. People would push them off sidewalks and cops would push them into the alleys. These were street kids, *huelepegas* (glue sniffers). In 1994, two years after the war, these were the abandoned kids that no one gave a fuck about. Those kids saw young guys like us stand up against authority. They were attracted to it. They wanted to have that. They starting claiming MS, mimicking it. All of a sudden people were afraid of them. They were asking for money, and people started giving it to them. That went to their heads. People feared them now. To see empowered young men, after they had been treated like shit, was crazy. That's how it grew. They were kids in need.

Osuna: How did you understand the US involvement in anti-gang policies in El Salvador?

Sanchez: In 1994 when I arrived in El Salvador, there was a lot of commotion about NAFTA (the North American Free Trade Agreement) and the Zapatistas in Chiapas that I didn't understand. In 1995, there were talks about how violent El Salvador was and how violence was part of the culture. I didn't know at the time but this was happening during talks about CAFTA (the Central American Free Trade Agreement), an expansion of NAFTA. Investors felt the country was too dangerous, or at least the media portrayed it that way. Suddenly a group called La Zombra Negra showed up. They were all over the news describing how they were going to eradicate the gang problem and reduce violence in the community. They said they were going to give gang members five days to stop being gang members or they would start killing them. After five days, people starting getting caught, bodies were hung on lampposts, naked with shots in the back of the head, in ditches, all over El Salvador. This death squad wanted to clean the streets.

I didn't know how involved the US was in El Salvador. It wasn't until Rudy Giuliani traveled to El Salvador with the Manhattan Institute in 2003 that they started talking about this *mano dura* ("iron fist"). *Mano dura* became a broken windows policing strategy in El Salvador. Giuliani recommended the same policies to El Salvador to eradicate the gang problem as he had implemented as mayor of New York in the 1990s. *Mano dura* didn't come from President Flores. It came through these US consultants.

Similar *mano dura* policies were implemented throughout Central America. It was called *Plan Escoba* (Plan Broom) in Guatemala, and *Ley Antimaras* (Anti-gang Law) in Honduras. What led to its spread were documentaries, in particular National Geographic's 2006 *Most Dangerous Gang in the World*. This escalated recognition of the MS gang as a national and transnational threat and hasn't stopped since.

Osuna: You described *mano dura* in El Salvador as a broken windows policy. How would you define broken windows policing?

Sanchez: Broken windows policing is a tool that takes on a problem and then displaces it. Broken windows supposedly cleans up all the "scum" in a neighborhood, the gang members and drug addicts. But through broken windows policing we've seen a whole different plan develop called gentrification. In most neighborhoods where gang injunctions have been implemented, people have been displaced. These neighborhoods let crime rise to levels that reduce the market price. Investors come and buy buildings at lower prices and redevelop them. They sell them as lofts near the new metro stations describing them as New York–style living, especially in Koreatown, where I grew up. Displacement through broken windows policing has not reduced violence in LA, it has displaced it to other California cities like Lancaster, San Bernardino, Riverside, Palmdale, and Victorville. Gangs that used to be in areas where broken windows policing was implemented are now popping up in those places. They're not solving the problem; they're just displacing it.

Osuna: You spoke about the impact of US policies and consultants on anti-gang initiatives in the early 2000s. What does that relationship look like today?

Sanchez: El Salvador wants to become a tourist attraction, so they have new interest in broken windows policing and gentrification. The business sector recently invited Rudy Giuliani to return to El Salvador. I asked someone in El Salvador's government why they were repeating the same mistake. Why were they hiring people that have failed? Why did they think the US had a solution for the problem—especially in Los Angeles where there were 400 gangs fifteen years ago, and now there are 1,500? Did they consider that a success?

The whole reason gangs continue is because governments let them continue. Once Central American countries need investment, they start using policies that were implemented in the US to suppress gangs. In El Salvador, *mano dura* mass-incarcerated anybody with tattoos. But these policies have not worked. El Salvador hasn't enjoyed peace since before the war. The only thing that can achieve peace is the truce that has been created by two gangs in El Salvador. It has dropped violence to levels not seen since before the war. It was demonized by the US, which also demonized the gang truce in Los Angeles in 1992. That truce also dropped violence to low levels. But what happened? They destroyed it, they infiltrated it, and they trained people to stop a movement that could have excelled. In Los Angeles the gang problem has not been solved. Our Black and Latino youth are killing each other.

Osuna: How do you see Homies Unidos as a response to that?

Sanchez: Homies Unidos in LA speaks up against those things that wrong our community, such as police abuse and corruption. Taking on multibillion-dollar corporations that are behind gentrification, zero-tolerance initiatives, and broken windows policies is a tough battle. We have been successful in bringing consciousness to youth, one at a time, through families and schools. We're working with the Central American migrant youth who came in during the summer of 2014. We have been able to help them with the culture clash that they face. I feel that we can go to the Salvadoran government and tell them to try different models besides supporting law enforcement.

The criminal justice approach has been a failure. We need to look at this as a big community problem and show people that opportunities in employment, housing, and education, would eradicate the problem. It's complex, and it will take billions of dollars, but as it is we've been wasting billions of dollars on mass incarceration. When we realize that these are the real solutions, that's when we'll have true security.

15. RESISTING STATE VIOLENCE IN THE ERA OF MASS DEPORTATION: AN INTERVIEW WITH MIZUE AIZEKI

Jordan T. Camp and Christina Heatherton

Mizue Aizeki is the deputy director of the Immigrant Defense Project. She has been organizing for workers' rights, racial justice, and immigrants' rights since the 1990s. She is also a documentary photographer whose work appears in publications including American Quarterly, Colorlines, *and* Dying to Live: A Story of U.S. Immigration in an Age of Global Apartheid *(City Lights Books, 2008).*

Heatherton: The discussion of broken windows policing and mass incarceration is often divorced from discussions of immigrant detention and deportation. In this era of mass deportation, how would you describe this relationship?

Aizeki: Broken windows policing and immigration policing not only share similar targets—largely Black, Brown, and poor people—they also share a logic that criminality is innate to certain groups of people for whom excessive policing and punishment is justified to maintain social control. Harsh laws from 1996 enable the government to deport people, including legal permanent residents, for a wide range of offenses, such as turnstile jumping and drug possession. The war on crime and broken windows policing has provided a huge reservoir of people whom the government can target for exile as desired.

This era of mass deportation is a convergence of the war on crime, the war on terror, and the war on immigrants. The logic of war-making is to invoke a "state of emergency"—in this case from racialized threats to "security"—justifying a lack of rights and a massive, repressive policing and exclusion apparatus. Militarization becomes the solution to address the ever-expanding yet elusive threats allegedly embodied in certain populations (e.g., the poor, non-white, terrorist, gang member, or "illegal"). These wars—waged inside and outside US borders—are critical to how the United States maintains power, yet the US role in creating the instability that fuels mass migration is continually obscured. They reduce the state's responsibility to provide universal security (such as food, housing, jobs) and legitimate the state's version of "security" for privileged classes.

After 9/11, President George W. Bush brought anti-terror, anti-immigrant fervor into the militarization of the border and all areas of the country. Certain racialized groups were targeted as a particular threat to "security," much like under broken windows: in this case, the threats were primarily thought to be Muslim immigrants, border crossers and undocumented workers. The Obama administration has shifted the named target to "criminal aliens," "felons," and "gang members," and effectively used the ideological and material practices of the war on crime to fuel mass deportation—using a preemptive policing logic that immigrants with convictions, regardless of how minor or how old, remain perpetual threats to public safety. More people have been deported under Presidents G.W. Bush and Obama than all the previous administrations combined.

Camp: The Immigrant Defense Project (IDP) promotes justice for immigrants accused or convicted of crimes, those often deemed "undeserving." How have purported distinctions between "deserving" and "undeserving" immigrants come to be?

Aizeki: The "state of emergency" in which "undeserving immigrants" have been framed as a major threat to public and national safety is part of a continuum that has existed since the European settlement of what is now called the United States. Expulsion and exclusion are the fabric of nation-state building, essential to the creation and maintenance of a racialized national identity and intimately tied to US global and economic power. This is the underlying logic legitimizing border policing and mass deportation.

Consistently there are periods when certain types of people are characterized as undeserving of protection, freedom, and basic rights and thus must be controlled, excluded, and/or expelled—such as slavery, removal and genocide of Native Americans, internment of people of Japanese descent, forced removal of people of Mexican ancestry, and exclusion of Haitian refugees. Deportation has been used as a weapon against people with threatening political views, whether communists, Black nationalists, or labor organizers. Although the targets shift, the nation-state and maintenance of the status quo requires an "other" to shore up the "we."

Heatherton: How has the war on terror strengthened collaborations between local police departments and federal security agencies?

Aizeki: The war on terror has justified much repressive state action, fueling an extensive surveillance apparatus, widespread local and federal collaboration through fusion centers and joint task forces, and the most massive policing, prosecution, detention, and deportation of immigrants in history.

The Department of Homeland Security (DHS) has referred to local police as a "force multiplier"—an extension of the federal policing apparatus. This is a manifestation of the "new normal," the surveillance police state in which data, technology, equipment, and personnel are seamlessly shared between federal, state, and local agencies, creating additional challenges for protecting people and our rights.

Since 2013, US Immigration and Customs Enforcement (ICE) has monitored everyone entering police custody through a fingerprint-sharing program with local law enforcement. If ICE wants someone, they may request that the police notify them and possibly detain the person once they are released from criminal custody. IDP is increasingly hearing of ICE showing up in people's homes, homeless shelters, courthouses, probation offices, and at work sites—all facilitated by widespread info-sharing.

In another example, on top of growing gang sentencing enhancement policies and problematic gang databases, the government further expands criminalization by increasingly linking "gangs" to terrorism and trafficking, classifying some as transnational criminal organizations. Policing gang activity is now part of ICE's continually expanding mission; the agency formed a gang unit and routinely collaborates with local police. If they cannot show that the targets have gang affiliation, they try to prosecute them for immigration offenses, other criminal offenses, or deport them if possible.

Camp: Proponents of mass surveillance and data-sharing programs argue that these measures are unproblematic if you "have nothing to hide." Can you describe the impacts of these new technologies and surveillance capacities?

Aizeki: We should all be concerned about the implications for human and civil rights. One of the functions of surveillance is to reinforce the status quo. The surveillance state not only monitors where you are and what you are doing, but it also serves to limit resistance as anyone perceived, or entrapped, to be a threat to authority becomes a target.

Massive data collection and info-sharing has implications for privacy and personal security. Just like zero-tolerance policing, these practices are being exported around the world. At Mexico's southern border near Guatemala, with US collaboration and funding, the Mexican government has installed biometric kiosks that collect data on every migrant they apprehend that they then share with US databases. In Afghanistan, the US military collects biometric data, including fingerprints and iris scans, from people on the street. ICE also works with other countries to populate databases so they can deny entry or deport people wanted for criminal prosecution. This notion that we are all suspects, and that therefore they must have data on everyone, is increasingly being realized globally as well as locally.

Heatherton: What are the most pressing challenges facing the struggle against mass deportation? Where do you see opportunities for alliance building?

Aizeki: We've seen immigration detention and deportation reach historic highs. Immigrants with convictions are increasingly vilified, and the most prosecuted federal offense is now immigration-related. The scale of the apparatus presents a significant challenge. The DHS budget has more than tripled since its founding in 2003. The United States spends more on policing immigrants than on all other federal policing agencies combined (including the FBI and DEA).

Yet, despite the challenges, immigrants and allies are fighting back. Advocates have been fighting steadily for cities and states to stop collaboration between police and ICE. Hunger strikes in immigrant detention facilities are spreading across the country. Undocumented youth, workers, and other surveilled and targeted communities, are organizing to challenge the deportation regime. Steady organizing to challenge the prison industrial complex continues to create space to reverse criminalization and imprisonment. The increasing convergence of the immigration and criminal legal systems offers possibilities to join forces with those fighting for the rights of people with felony convictions and against racialized state violence. IDP continues to build with groups organizing immigrants from Latino, Black, Southeast Asian, South Asian, and LGBTQ communities who are facing deportation due to convictions. My hope is that together we can turn the tide in this fight before too long.

III. THE CRISIS OF BROKEN WINDOWS COMMON SENSE

16. COMMUNITY POLICING RECONSIDERED: FROM FERGUSON TO BALTIMORE[1]

Justin Hansford

During a first-season episode of *The Fresh Prince of Bel-Air* entitled "Mistaken Identity," a family friend asks Will and Carlton to drive his Mercedes to Palm Springs. When they get lost, two white police officers pull them over, accuse them of stealing the car, and arrest them. The police clearly had racially profiled them. In the final scene, Carlton tries to make sense of what happened by arguing that the police were just doing their job: "If we would have had a map, we wouldn't have had to drive two miles an hour trying to find a freeway entrance, and we wouldn't have been stopped ... The system works." Will responds, "I hope you like that system, because you'll be seeing a whole lot of it during your lifetime." Will then poignantly explains that no amount of preparation or adherence to the dictates of respectability politics can save Carlton—his Bel-Air address and glee club membership notwithstanding, being Black in the United States is enough to put a target on his back. "Not if I bring a map!" Carlton insists.

In February 2015, I testified at a listening session at President Obama's Task Force on 21st Century Policing. The topics were community policing and crime reduction. I felt like Will Smith in a room filled with Carltons. Government officials, police chiefs, academics, and church leaders insisted that if only the police embraced community policing, the crisis between law enforcement and the Black community would, essentially, end. The police chief of Sanford, Florida, where Trayvon Martin

1 Special thanks to Britta Thornton and Nailah Harper Malveux for research assistance, and to Derecka Purnell and Seema Sadanandan for providing helpful feedback.

was killed, boasted that local protests had subsided after Trayvon's death in part because community policing strategies had changed the public's perception of his department. One of his accomplishments, which he recommended to others, included hosting a "Sweet Tea Day" where police could chat with local activists, clergy members, and members of the chamber of commerce over tea.

I was appalled. Many at the task force session contended that the Ferguson uprising indicated the presence not of bad law enforcement practices but simply bad public relations. I reminded the task force that the United States has 5 percent of the world's populace but 25 percent of the world's inmates. The incarceration rate of 750 inmates per every 100,000 citizens is nearly eight times the rate of the nearest comparable nations: Russia, China, and Iran. Also, this mass incarceration is concentrated along the lines of race. The combined state and federal prison and jail population that is nearly 43 percent Black, in a nation that is only 13 percent Black overall.[2] Significantly, this is not due to pervasive Black criminality but pervasive police and prosecutor racial targeting. For example, research has shown that five times as many whites as Blacks use illicit drugs, but Blacks are sent to prison for drug offenses at ten times the rate of whites; Blacks make up 12 percent of the drug users, and 58 percent of those in state prison for a drug offense.[3]

The racialized nature of mass incarceration means that the United States imprisons more of its Black community than South Africa did at the height of apartheid.[4] The Malcolm X Grassroots Movement has reported that a Black person is killed by the police every twenty-eight hours, revealing that racialized killing by the state happens at a rate as alarming as racially targeted jailing.[5] Amazingly, this situation has not

2   Federal Bureau of Prisons, "Inmate Age," November 28, 2015, available at bop.gov; National Association for the Advancement of Colored People, "Criminal Justice Fact Sheet," n.d., available at naacp.org.

3   National Association for the Advancement of Colored People, "Criminal Justice Fact Sheet," n.d., available at naacp.org.

4   Michelle Alexander, *The New Jim Crow: Mass Incarceration in the Age of Colorblindness* (New York: New Press, 2010).

5   Malcolm X Grassroots Movement, "Operation Ghetto Storm: 2012 Annual Report on the Extrajudicial Killing of 313 Black People," April 7, 2013, available at mxgm.org.

abated at all in the year since Ferguson. To the contrary, extrajudicial killings by police have been on the rise since then—both the *Guardian* and the *Washington Post* recorded nearly 1,000 killings in the United States in 2015, more than three a day.[6] Is there enough sweet tea in the world to make this acceptable?

In the United States in 2015, it would be not only irrational for Black people to warmly receive the police at their doorsteps when they come bearing a sweet tea and a smile, it would be abjectly irresponsible. It is the police who unceremoniously usher boatloads of Black people into cages or to untimely meetings with the grim reaper every year. And those who survive do not emerge unscathed; they are left, like Will Smith, humiliated and searching for answers.

These facts did not persuade the decision makers at the task force hearing that day. When deliberations ended and conclusions were reached, in a long report that contained over a hundred citations my testimony was left out completely.[7] I blame myself, in part—perhaps I could have argued more effectively. But instead of emerging bitter and scornful, I left the task force worried and saddened. I believed then, and still believe now, that many in that room genuinely wanted to address the problems illuminated by the Ferguson uprising. They either concluded that the disparities were justified, that the problem was beyond their control, or that community policing was the solution.

A number of seemingly illusory arguments support this final conclusion. The term "community policing" denotes nothing in particular, but it hints at positive values such as community control and police de-escalation. In truth, however, community policing not only does little to help the problem, but as an ideological framework it is essential to support broken windows policing, mass incarceration, and America's system of anti-Black state violence.

---

6 Mapping Police Violence, "Police Violence Map," available at mappingpolice-violence.org; "The Counted: People Killed by Police in the US," *Guardian*, June 1, 2015; Sandhya Somashekhar, Steven Rich, "Final Tally: Police Shot and Killed 986 People in 2015," *Washington Post*, January 6, 2016.

7 President's Task Force on 21st Century Policing, *Final Report of the President's Task Force on 21st Century Policing* (Washington, DC: Office of Community Oriented Policing Services, May 2015), available at cops.usdoj.gov.

If we are going to succeed in creating livable environments that provide wellness instead of terror for people of color, what we need is not a change in the state's tactics but a change in the state's values. We don't care if the police smile and offer sweet tea—the racially targeted jailing, killing, and attempts to force Black people into submission through the use of violent state power must end.

What Is Community Policing?

The idea of community policing emerged primarily in response to the social movements of the 1960s.[8] After generations of state repression produced racial unrest in Detroit, Watts, and other cities across the country, police recognized the need for a change in tactics. Building upon a wistful desire to return to the halcyon days of "Officer Friendly" walking the beat, reformers promoted the idea that increased community contact would result automatically in increased community trust and goodwill.

The refrain of "community policing" itself strikes a seductively democratic tone. Who wouldn't want police to engage with members of the community? The Department of Justice has declared that community policing "promotes organizational strategies, which support the systematic use of partnerships and problem-solving techniques, to proactively address the immediate conditions that give rise to public safety issues such as crime, social disorder, and fear of crime."[9] Benign homilies, yes, but look closer.

First, who comprises "community" in community policing? The term could be delineated using ethnicity, age, city, neighborhood—even Facebook friends or Twitter followers. The difficulty in finding community is not a coincidence. Much authentic communal feeling has been strategically dismembered over the years by policing practices. These practices have included the use of informants against friends and family members and the ejection of people from public

---

8   Kristian Williams, *Our Enemies in Blue: Police and Power in America* (Boston: South End Press, 2007), 204–22.

9   Office of Community Oriented Policing Services, *Community Policing Defined* (Washington, DC: US Department of Justice, 2014 [2012]).

housing for allowing loved ones with drug convictions to live with them.[10]

After eviscerating communal bonds, the police insert themselves into the vacuum of uncertaintly around the idea of community to generate a community in their own image (and in their own likeness), granting legitimacy only to community groups who conform to state conceptions of law, order, and propriety. These new police-centered "communities" revolve around events hosted by the police, public forums moderated by the police, and mental health, social services, and key aspects of daily life mediated through contact with the police. Coincidentally, an enlarged social role for the police requires larger budgets and the expansion of benefits for, you guessed it, the police.

What happens when those who chat with the police over tea have a disagreement with their hosts? Police decide to whom they will listen, which is likely to be those with whom they get along and share similar views, not those with whom they have a historically antagonistic relationship. Studies have shown that police will solicit the opinions of business owners and church leaders and disproportionately seek out whites, later presenting the opinions of this narrow slice of the population as the community voice.[11] A true community policing effort would lend an ear to at-risk youth of color, low-income single mothers, and former prisoners—those with the most consistent contact with police and who are painted by the police as permanent suspects. These groups are the subaltern; they understand more than anyone how race and policing works because their lives and their bodies depend on that knowledge. The omission of their perspective not only impoverishes the discourse, it also invalidates any institutional claims of law enforcement to being authentically democratic or community based.[12] The risk, of course, is that these narratives would complicate the police's moral universe. Police tend to think in the blunt terms of good guys and bad guys,

10   Phillip Smith, "Feature: The Conviction That Keeps on Hurting—Drug Offenders and Federal Benefits," *Drug War Chronicle* 471 (February 4, 2007).

11   Wesley G. Skogan, "The Community's Role in Community Policing," *National Institute of Justice Journal*, August 1996.

12   Mari J. Matsuda, "Looking to the Bottom: Critical Legal Studies and Reparations," *Harvard Civil Rights-Civil Liberties Law Review* 323 (1987).

allowing for the most degenerate brutality against those grouped in the latter category. Truly hearing the voices of these people, and acknowledging their humanity, risks inverting the politics of respectability used to justify the bullying of the most vulnerable.

The other half of the question is, what is meant by policing? Nineteenth- and twentieth-century models present a possible alternative to modern-day policing in the figure of "Officer Friendly." Unfortunately, the officer walking the beat was never very friendly to low-income people or people of color, especially not Black people, who were victimized and terrorized by "Officer Friendly" during the eras of apartheid, Jim Crow, and enslavement. In fact, many historians trace modern American policing practices back to "slave patrols" in the American South in the early 1700s.[13] As opposed to enforcing the law against rapists or murderers, these patrols focused on the elimination of public disorder, which meant whipping and terrorizing slaves who congregated in groups, searching slave quarters, and interrogating any slave who traveled without a pass—all in an effort to create complete submission through fear.[14] In the postbellum context, this paved the way for legal fictions, such as anti-vagrancy laws, and Kafkaesque ordinances, such as Ferguson's "manner of walking" law. Here we find the historical precursors for broken windows policing and quality-of-life policing— supposed innovations that historically formed the substructure of enslavement and in contemporary times forms the substructure of the mass incarceration industry and the community policing approach.

When police use these principles to enforce "law and order," they rely not just on "law" as it exists in statutes and as it is voted on by elected officials, but on the vague "order" that exists only in the heads of the officers—invoked by police granting themselves the power to use deadly force against anyone that they feel is not orderly (i.e., not in accordance with white middle-class and bourgeois sensibilities). All young Black and Brown men with saggy pants and in groups, all LGBT people of color,

---

13   Dominique Wilser and Ihekwoaba D. Onwudiwe, eds., *Community Policing: International Patterns and Comparative Perspectives* (Boca Raton, FL: CRC Press, 2009), 172.

14   Callie Rennison and Mary Dodge, *Introduction to Criminal Justice: Systems, Diversity, and Change* (Thousand Oaks, CA: Sage Publishing, 2015), 99.

all protesters without permits fit the police description of "disorder." "Order" is enforced with violence under the logic of policing; thus all of these populations may be beaten, terrorized, searched, and interrogated, like the enslaved Africans of the not-so-distant nineteenth-century.

Along with three-strikes laws, the school-to-prison pipeline, and prison expansion, many scholars look to broken windows policing and stop and frisk as being among the driving forces behind mass incarceration in the United States.[15] Community policing integrates broken windows and stop-and-frisk tactics through its emphasis on "proactively" promoting public order, involving "hot spot policing," often a code phrase for targeting lower-income areas where people of color reside, and "zero tolerance," which results in the criminalization of minor violations and nuisances. Confrontations that are manufactured by these tactics escalate when minor offenders are Black people, like Sandra Bland (failure to use a turning signal), Eric Garner (selling loose cigarettes), or Mike Brown (jaywalking).

Domestic violence, the violence most often visited upon women, is de-emphasized in this calculus. Hence we see an example of the intersectionality of patriarchy, racism, and classism in modern US law enforcement. These crimes often happen behind closed doors and receive limited community policing resources. In the aftermath of mass incarceration and its decimation of the young Black male population, women make up substantially more than half of the Black community. Instead of centering their interests in supposedly community-driven initiatives that rely on collaborative problem solving, however, community policing paints certain populations as the problems to be solved, with the concerns of those populations considered secondary.

Given law enforcement's military siege mentality of racial conquest, it is difficult to imagine a community policing activity that could not become a tool of racial violence or mass incarceration. Door-to-door surveys become excuses for warrantless searches into the homes of unsuspecting community members. Child registration programs, like one that took place in Mike Brown's apartment complex a few days after

---

15   See James Kilgore, *Understanding Mass Incarceration: A People's Guide to the Key Civil Rights Struggle of Our Time* (New York: New Press, 2015); Alexander, *The New Jim Crow*.

his murder, become tools for intimidation. Meetings with handpicked civic and religious leaders become, at best, opportunities to gain additional community buy-in to already entrenched conservative ideals and, at worst, sites for law enforcement propagandizing. Police are rewarded for making more arrests; prosecutors are rewarded for gaining more convictions with longer sentences. Why would these actors not use the tool of community policing for their own professional self interests?

Community members, unaware of these dynamics or in a Carlton-like state of denial, support law enforcement and even participate in the project of policing one other, helping the state to co-opt community assets and resources that would otherwise be useful for resistance. Churches, nonprofit organizations, community centers—these become conduits to spread law enforcement's ideology of social order. Penetration of community life is a more effective means of civilian control for the state. In the face of mass resistance to mass incarceration, mass re-education of the populace may be simply a smarter repressive approach than brute force alone. As Kristian Williams has noted, the traditional police rebuttal to accusations of violent transgressions of their roles as enforcers of law is to claim, "I'm a policeman, not a social worker"—or, in the words of Mike Brown's killer, Darren Wilson, "I'm a cop, not a psychiatrist."[16] Community members could well respond to community policing efforts in kind: "I'm a teacher, not a cop—stop trying to use me to promote mass incarceration." Public safety issues are best addressed through poverty and inequality reduction, approaches that have been proven to lessen crime, addiction, and a number of social ills.[17] Why not cut law enforcement budgets and use those funds to engage the public in such an approach?

Although the resultant decrease in violent crime could ease the fear of police and citizenry, financial self-interest driven by police unions makes the adoption of this type of approach unlikely. Also, hope for humanity itself often dims when contemplating the degenerate, sadistic joy many police appear to take in perpetrating violence upon members

---

16   Williams, *Our Enemies in Blue*, 208; Wilson quoted in Jake Halpern, "The Cop," *New Yorker*, August 10, 2015.

17   Kate Pickett and Richard Wilkinson, *The Spirit Level: Why Greater Equality Makes Societies Stronger* (New York: Bloomsbury Press, 2009).

of the Black community, as has been evident in cell phone videos taken by Black witnesses that crop up every few months.[18] Can we really hope that these officers want to increase well-being in the Black community, or, as Darren Wilson explained, do they often seek to work in the Black community because they have "more fun" there?[19]

Blacks have good reason to see themselves still as subjects of colonialism, beholden to the power dynamics of the apartheid, slavery, and Jim Crow eras. Community policing notwithstanding, the endurance of these structures can best be understood by resisting the denial of Carlton in *Fresh Prince* and instead reading the current phenomena through the lens of colonialism.[20] Twenty-first-century gentrification, for example, recalls eighteenth-century colonialism, with inner cities our current "unclaimed" frontiers of the past—holding the promise of great wealth as long as the hordes of uncivilized natives are first tamed. A great deal of ink has been spilled on how to pass off violent military rule as stable and legitimate order maintenance, obtain intelligence from behind enemy lines, and present the aggressor as a benevolent problem solver, all so that invaders can more efficiently avoid and suppress resistance.[21] It is tragic to use this colonial, military framework to theorize modern Black community and police interactions, but as James Baldwin noted in his legendary essay "A Report from Occupied Territory" so many decades ago, evidence has accumulated over the years that "the police are simply the hired enemy of this population."[22] As such, anti-colonial struggles for liberation become a more apt lens for understanding the intentions of racial profiling, police violence, and community policing in twenty-first-century America.

---

18   Jen Hayden, "Police Withheld Video of Officers Laughing, Mocking, Re-Enacting Brutal Beating of Floyd Dent," *Daily Kos*, April 27, 2015.

19   Jake Halpern, "The Cop," *New Yorker*, August 10, 2015.

20   See Anibal Quijano, "Coloniality of Power, Eurocentrism and Latin America," *Nepantla: Views from the South* 1, no. 3 (2000): 533.

21   Williams, *Our Enemies in Blue*, 219.

22   James Baldwin, "A Report from Occupied Territory," *The Nation*, July 11, 1966.

A Reason for Hope

This movement is fast becoming my life, causing me to work many late nights in my office, doing double-duty as professor and activist. Security officers in my building, some of whom are police officers or former police officers, know of my involvement in the movement. Some are more hostile than others. A few months ago, one security officer hovered near my door in the minutes leading up to closing time and threatened to eject me forcefully in an attempt to intimidate me. By living among and working with Ferguson activists, I have become much more courageous. I now count myself as one of the tribe who would part with my life before parting with my dignity. This disposition is in explosive contradiction to policing approaches that use humiliation as a tactic. I told that security officer that I was working and that he could shoot me right there if he chose, but I would leave when I was ready. He could do what he wanted to with my body, but he had to come to grips with the loss of his power over my spirit.

I will never forget one particular moment last spring, during the Baltimore uprising. It was on the Monday that middle and high school students were trapped at Mondawmin Mall and chased by police. When kids threw rocks and bricks from a nearby abandoned building at the police who had trapped and were teargassing them, the police picked up the bricks and threw them back at the kids. After the action had died down, I and the other legal observers tried to record statements from the kids. Some had gashes on their legs from the bricks the police had thrown. Some were still coughing from the tear gas. They were afraid to give us their names, to tell us where they lived, fearing that the police would retaliate against them. I will never forget looking into the eyes of one of the kids. He had the most hardened eyes I'd ever seen in a ten-year-old. I tried to wrap my mind around what he had experienced, how he had steeled himself emotionally to survive the trauma he had experienced at the hands of the police.

I think about him often. What do we owe him? The abuse of power by the Baltimore police may have psychologically affected him for the rest of his life, and I ache for that ten-year-old's life chances in a racialized colonial society that will force him to walk with eternal vigilance.

The racism and police violence require, as they did of Carlton, self-splitting self-denial. What story will he have to tell himself about what happened that day in Baltimore in order for him to feel safe under under the watchful eyes of police for the rest of his life? What are our hopes for that ten-year-old, for his emotional life, for his ability to raise a happy healthy family and live well? How do racial profiling, police violence, and the system of mass incarceration threaten those hopes, cloud his spirit? How much time and energy will he have to spend on this, time and energy that he could have otherwise used to live a happy and healthy life? I think we owe it to him to think hard about these questions.

How we treat our children is the litmus test for our humanity. Marian Wright Edelman of the Children's Defense Fund has artfully stated that God did not make two classes of children, and he will hold us accountable for every one of them.[23] If we accept community policing programs as the solution while allowing mass incarceration and police violence to continue, the only values we will be transmitting to the next generation are a lazy willingness to clothe a wolf in sheep's clothing and a moral vacuity to keep punting the key racial justice issue of our time. We owe that ten-year-old more than that. Mass incarceration must be undone. Racial profiling must end. They must stop killing us. The wolf must be defanged and declawed. Nothing less.

~

Justin Hansford is an activist, lawyer, professor, and Fulbright scholar. After his arrest during a protest in Ferguson, he accompanied the Mike Brown family to the United Nations, and he has continued to work as an advocate in support of the movement both locally and globally.

---

23   Marian Wright Edelman, "Standing Up for Our Children," in *The Impossible Will Take a Little While: Perseverance and Hope in Troubled Times* ed. Paul Rogat Loeb (New York: Basic, 2004), 51.

17. HOW LIBERALS LEGITIMATE BROKEN WINDOWS: AN INTERVIEW WITH NAOMI MURAKAWA

Jordan T. Camp and Christina Heatherton

Naomi Murakawa is an associate professor of African American studies at Princeton University. Her research focuses on racial inequality, crime policy, and the carceral state. She is the author of The First Civil Right: How Liberals Built Prison America *(Oxford University Press, 2014), which won the Michael Harrington Award from the American Political Science Association. Her articles have appeared in* Law & Society Review, Du Bois Review, *and* Theoretical Criminology, *among other publications.*

Camp: In response to mass mobilizations, federal agencies have proposed a series of reforms, such as the President's Task Force on 21st Century Policing, that encourage police departments to behave in more "procedurally just" ways. What is your prognosis about such measures?

Murakawa: The Obama administration has, in its own way, done a fair amount to address issues of policing, such as launching the commission that you mentioned and also by starting the National Initiative for Building Community Trust and Justice housed in the Department of Justice. It has given money to city police departments so that they can work on what the administration is calling "enhanced procedural justice," with the aim of producing "racial reconciliation" between police and communities of color. Obama has also supported funding for police body cameras. This battery of reforms falls squarely within a long ideological tradition of liberal law and order. Liberal law and order, with regard to policing in particular, operates with a specific grammar of racism. It starts from the belief that racism is an idea, a misconception, an emotional misfire that is seemingly lodged in individual police officers who are afflicted by stereotypes and irrationalities. These "racist bad apple" officers are seen as elements that contaminate policing—which is otherwise believed to be acceptable. The project of liberal reform then becomes one of sealing off or minimizing those contaminants. This "decontamination" is pursued through administrative tinkering: more monitoring through body cameras (as if we need more evidence of gendered, transphobic, and racist police violence), more training (as if a two-day police seminar could train the racism out of someone), or hiring more police officers of color (with the presumption that they're going to behave very differently from white officers).

Heatherton: President Obama and other state officials concede that there is a problem with racist police, but they ultimately depict the problem as one of mistrust, the inability of Black communities to properly reconcile their anger against police. What do you make of this and other federal officials calling for improving trust between police and communities?

Murakawa: References to mistrust are interesting because they contain two competing parts. First, there is an admission that there are *actual* police practices that generate mistrust. Second, there is a subtext suggesting that Black people are *mistaken* in their assessment of the police, that they have atavistic views of police racism, misguided racial resentment that they unfairly project onto police. These two parts work together to propel reforms that attempt to engender trust in the police, to "help" Black people "accurately" perceive reality. This is why so many reforms are essentially public relations projects.

There are some really telling analogies between this moment, when protesters are compelling Obama to act, and the 1960s, when the Black freedom struggle compelled response from the Kennedy and Johnson administrations. For example, the US Civil Rights Commission Report of 1961 acknowledged and rigorously documented police misconduct in Black neighborhoods. It also argued, however, that policing practices had improved over recent years, but Black attitudes had not kept up with those improvements. Hence, the problem of ineffectively policed "Black criminality" was a problem Black people put on themselves. Because of their own misperceptions Black people refused to call the police, refused to testify, refused to report on suspicious activity—all of which hurts police clearance rates. Furthermore, it explained, if Black people don't trust the police there will be a greater likelihood of spontaneous uprisings after police misconduct.

Let's imagine for a minute that the subtext (of Black misconception of police violence) were gone. Then reforms would begin on this premise: Black people don't trust the police, and they are correct not to. If we were to actually embrace that logic, the interventions would necessarily go deeper. The solutions then would not be about healing mistrust. The interventions would not be about encouraging the police to behave more courteously (addressing people as "sir" or "ma'am"). They would have to be about addressing the project of policing, which I believe is the core of real critique in this case. What is it that the police are doing? What is the scope of their power? What is the scale on which they operate? Not just the courtesy and respect with which they are performing each arrest, but why are there so many arrests? For so many little things? That is precisely the issue that is, for the most part, not being taken on by the Obama administration.

Camp: The rise of the carceral state is often depicted as an outcome of conservative racial politics of the Republican Party and the so-called backlash against civil rights in the late 1960s. Your book, *The First Civil Right*, illuminates the role of postwar Democratic racial liberals in the construction of the carceral state. Why is this history relevant to today's carceral crisis?

Murakawa: It is correct to blame conservatives and Nixon's "Southern Strategy" for the fortification of the carceral state, absolutely correct. My worry is that in concentrating only on that particular constellation of actors, mostly Republicans and Southern Democrats, we actually reinforce the innocence of racial liberalism and miss the ways in which liberal law and order fortified the carceral state. Postwar crime policy

was not only about race conservatives pushing for more aggressive policing, more prisons, and longer sentences. It was also about race liberals
who aimed to build the bias out of the criminal justice system with more
procedural rights, more guidelines, more formal protocols in everything
from arrest to sentencing calculations. These political "sides" appeared
to be in opposition to each other, as they were divided on partisan lines,
but they actually worked together to build a criminal justice system that
is larger, more punitive, more rule-based, more procedurally grounded,
and more "procedurally just." These two forces tend to work together in
mutual escalation, authorizing an even grander scale of racial brutality.
This history is important because we keep cycling back to the same set of
proposals even though they have done nothing to curtail racial brutality;
indeed, they have helped legitimate it.

**Camp: Broken windows theory has been driven by right-wing
politicians, pundits, and the neoliberal think tank the Manhattan
Institute. At the same time, some of the most dedicated adherents
have been liberal mayors like LA's Antonio Villaraigosa, Baltimore's
Martin O'Malley, and New York's Bill de Blasio. How can we understand this seeming contradiction?**

Murakawa: Community policing, order-maintenance policing, broken
windows policing—all of these key phrases are attempts to describe
what the ethos of policing is supposed to be. But these categories
don't hold a lot of meaning when, for example, we talk about funding
structures. Whether under the moniker of community policing or order-
maintenance policing, if you are dropping more personnel into police
departments then you are simply making police departments bigger and
stronger. You are expanding their capacity. There is a hope that community policing will have an ethos that reflects the community—that police
officers will get out of their patrol cars, walk the streets, and befriend
people. But police departments will still do what police departments do,
which is arrest people and give summonses and citations. As Alex Vitale
and others have pointed out, police departments have only certain tools:
handcuffs, guns, citations, and the power to arrest.

In spring of 2015, Bratton defended broken windows policing as "probably the most vivid example of community policing there is."[1] That is, you have to be in close contact with the community to see all of those people littering or spitting or selling loosies. The squishiness of these terms is further evidenced by the fact that when the Clinton administration created the Office of Community Oriented Policing Services in 1994, the legislation did not specify what the money would be spent on. There were no provisions requiring departments receiving the funds to hold community meetings. There were no expectations that officers minimize their arrests or increase positive contact with communities. There was nothing like that. A couple of years after Clinton's legislation, the Department of Justice conducted a study about the funding. What they found was that the police officers hired and the police departments receiving money for community policing were using it for order-maintenance policing.

Heatherton: Why was the turn to broken windows policing important for the consolidation of the carceral state?

Murakawa: In a sense, police officers have difficult, ill-defined jobs. They are meant to enforce penal codes that are so enlarged they cannot possibly know how to prioritize everything that they're supposed to be doing. As Samuel Walker has documented, debates over police discretion intensified with the American Bar Foundation's Survey of the Administration of Criminal Justice in the 1950s. As scholars "discovered" the magnitude of police discretion, many suggested that discretion is inevitable. Police officers must have discretion, especially the discretion *not* to arrest. If police officers had no discretion and were just bureaucrats enforcing the law, they would be arresting people constantly. The generous argument some scholars advanced was that police must have broad discretion because *we*, the polity, have saddled them with so much criminal law that they have to create priorities. But then broken windows policing emerges. It announces that everything is a priority, because, as it argues, even tiny infractions produce a climate of rampant rule breaking that then leads to murder.

---

1   Quoted in Petra Bartosiewicz, "Beyond the Broken Window: William Bratton and the New Police State," *Harper's Magazine*, May 2015.

Camp: For those nostalgic about Bill Clinton's two terms in office in the 1990s, could you describe the legacy of the Clinton administration's carceral policies?

Murakawa: Clinton, and even before him the Democratic Leadership Council and Joe Biden (a key figure on the Senate Judiciary Committee), decided that Democrats would neutralize accusations of being "soft on crime" by outbidding Republican punitiveness. Clinton and the majority of congressional Democrats jacked up money for police, money for state prison construction, money for the death penalty, and so on. They killed Pell Grants for incarcerated people. Under the auspices of fighting violence against women, they gave more resources to prosecutors. In this punitive race to the top, Democrats neutralized the crime issue and forged a bipartisan consensus: we are all tough on crime, we all underwrite the destruction of Black communities.

Heatherton: The current crisis of policing is often described as a problem with police brutality or racial profiling. Could you comment on the limitations of these frameworks?

Murakawa: The terminology we use betrays the notion that policing at its core is acceptable, that it only becomes a problem when things go awry. But let's be clear: there is no such thing as racial profiling. To say the police are profiling suggests the possibility that there could be color-blind policing. There never has been, and the social order in which we live means there never could be.

"Police brutality" is also a hollow term, in the sense that all police interactions, by definition, occur under the threat of brutality. They unfold under the threat of violence. If you are being questioned by someone who has a gun strapped to his or her hip and is authorized to use it, and you know that this person uses it in particular against people of your race in your neighborhood, you may agree to the transaction. The transaction happens because there is the threat of brutality. The gun might not be used against you, but the act is still brutal.

What we need to challenge is routine policing, not the "exceptional abuses" of policing. We need to challenge the core functions of policing, and the core function of policing is to enforce a bloated criminal code and to do so primarily in poor neighborhoods and against people of color.

Camp: What do the recent killings and recent protests against them reveal about the social functions of policing and prisons?

Murakawa: It makes sense that people organize around police murders, because they are so horrifying. But when people mobilize around them it doesn't mean that they are *only* protesting police murders. What worries me about Obama's interventions is that they are oriented towards stopping only these outer extremes. Activists do not see these murders as the outer extreme. Rather, they see these murders as representations of the core logic of policing—the logics of regulating the poor, of segregating, containing, and disciplining poor people of color, and quite often using them as a revenue source. We can look at the Walter Scott case, for example, which got a lot of attention in part because the attempt by police to cover it up was caught on camera. In fact, we should protest the way Walter Scott was policed throughout his entire life, not just at the end. That is, he should not have been entangled in the criminal justice system to begin with for something like the inability to pay child support.

There is a lot to be gained from challenging typical cases rather than the most violent outcome cases. The modal case in the criminal justice system is an arrest for a misdemeanor, which then goes through a low-level court, and then requires having to pay fees and fines. This is the modal case. By focusing on the modal we have to start recalibrating our own sensibilities about what constitutes unacceptable violence. In the typical misdemeanor arrest, the violence levied against people is deep, frightening, and costly. The cost of being arrested, even, in many places, just once, even if charges are dropped, means that you will still have an official rap sheet. A potential employer could just search for your name online and find you. Even if the charges have been dropped and you are cleared, in some places you will still have a record. This is destructive to people's lives. I want us to focus on that violence and say that is a form of violence.

The violence of policing is not only the racial terror that we see in these murder cases, it's also the daily racial tax. The thinking that I admire so much in #BlackLivesMatter is the way it looks intersectionally at every case. When you are really honed intersectionally your project for change always gets bigger, rather than smaller. People have this conception of intersectionality as decreasing demographics, making the pool smaller and smaller. But if we were, for example, to change policing by looking at teenagers who are runaways who are very likely to be trans and gender-nonconforming, and very likely to be people of color, what are all of the issues we would have to think about? We would certainly look at all the pettiness of quality-of-life offenses but also at what Dean Spade talks about as "administrative violence," the fact that people are required to have IDs to get any kind of medical care.[2] We would also be required to ask, what does it mean to be safe in schools? The kind of safety trans and gender-nonconforming people need in schools is not the safety that is supposed to be achieved with metal detectors. It is a deeper kind of safety in a structurally healthy way to go to school. I feel like staying modal and staying intersectional are the best ways to protect ourselves from reformist improvements and move towards transformative change.

Heatherton: Organizers illustrate how high-profile police killings are routine and systemic, while pundits describe them as tragic but exceptional. How are officials reconciling this contradiction?

Murakawa: In Obama's recent speech to the NAACP, he said a lot of things that he has never said before. There were still a ton of problems. He still focused on nonviolent drug offenders. He still focused on police procedure. But he went further than I have ever heard him go. That is a credit to the activist work that has been sustained these many months. That said, it is hard to be hopeful when so much of the reform language is proceduralist and neoliberal. The proceduralist reforms aim just to get superficial or small bureaucratic checks for policing, like bringing in independent prosecutors. That is going to matter for a handful of cases, but really that doesn't do anything to get at the core of polic- ing. Obama's language and the language of a lot of reformers is really geared towards cost cutting. A lot of it emphasizes how expensive it is to

---

2   Dean Spade, *Normal Life: Administrative Violence, Critical Trans Politics and the Limits of Law* (Durham: Duke University Press, 2015).

incarcerate people. That is a dangerous argument because, once again, it simply obfuscates Black Lives Matter. It says instead, "Budget Cuts Matter." When budget deficits are what matter, you might be able to cut the incarcerated population a little bit, but you're also going to end up cutting everything that people need to live.

Heatherton: You often refer to Angela Y. Davis's injunction to more deeply theorize the social functions of policing and prisons in order to imagine something different. What makes this insight so critical for the present moment?

Murakawa: We have to build. What is so frightening about the cost-cutting interventions around mass incarceration is that they repose on the logic that justifies continual destruction of the already diminished social safety net. They also justify pay-as-you-go punishment. If our goal is just to cut costs, then it is perfectly valid to charge people for the use of the Tasers deployed against them. In Missouri you have to pay $26 for a Taser used against you. Marie Gottschalk's book *Caught* demonstrates this point brilliantly.[3]

What I admire so much about the way Angela Y. Davis and Ruth Wilson Gilmore have spoken about the prison industrial complex is that they clearly emphasize that the destruction of the carceral state will happen interactively as we build other things. As we imagine a social landscape that cannot use police and prisons to absorb people with mental illness, people with drug addiction, or, for that matter, people who are simply poor and jobless, we're going to have to build a lot. We're going to have to spend more. We have to build.

---

3   Marie Gottschalk, *Caught: The Prison State and the Lockdown of American Politics* (Princeton: Princeton University Press, 2014), 36.

18. "BROKEN WINDOWS IS NOT THE PANACEA": COMMON SENSE, GOOD SENSE, AND POLICE ACCOUNTABILITY IN AMERICAN CITIES

Don Mitchell, Kafui Attoh, and Lynn A. Staeheli

In the midst of the 2014 nationwide protests against police killings of African Americans, New York City police chief William J. Bratton and criminologist George F. Kelling penned a vigorous defense of broken windows policing. Kelling and criminologist James Q. Wilson had laid out its key tenets in a famous 1982 *Atlantic Monthly* article and developed it in a influential 1996 book *Fixing Broken Windows*.[1] Bratton has served as the theory's main police proponent, agitating for and implementing it across a long career, particularly under conservative-populist mayor Rudolph Giuliani in the 1990s as part of zero-tolerance policing and again under progressive-populist mayor Bill de Blasio. That broken windows theory seems to appeal equally to officials as politically different as Giuliani and de Blasio, we will suggest, indicates that it is now taken by many as common sense.

But like any common sense, it must be developed and defended, secured against its own unmasking. Bratton and Kelling's 2014 defense appeared in *City Journal* in December in the immediate aftermath of the murder of two police officers by a man claiming to be seeking retribution for the choking death of Eric Garner at the hands of the New York City Police Department. *City Journal* is the mouthpiece of the conservative

---

1   James Q. Wilson and George F. Kelling, "Broken Windows: The Police and Neighborhood Safety," *Atlantic Monthly*, March 1982, 29–38; George F. Kelling and Catherine Coles, *Fixing Broken Windows: Restoring Order and Reducing Crime in Our Communities* (New York: Free Press, 1996).

Manhattan Institute, which has long promoted quality-of-life initiatives while insisting on the need for "order" in US cities. In line with much of what appears in *City Journal*, Bratton and Kelling's defense of broken windows policing was presented as a reasoned dismantling of four myths or "misconceptions" about order-maintenance policing (the very policing techniques that had led to Eric Garner's death): that "broken windows is synonymous with the controversial police tactic known as 'stop, question, and frisk,'" that broken windows is discriminatory, that it disproportionately targets minorities, that it has no effect on serious crime, and that it leads to over-incarceration.[2]

Setting aside the rather fanciful construction of critical positions on broken windows, perhaps the most interesting defense Bratton and Kelling make is that civilians are supportive of broken windows polic-ing.[3] "Our experience suggests," they write, "that, whatever the critics might say, the majority of New Yorkers, including minorities, approve of such police order-maintenance activities." Immediately after the death of Eric Garner, who was killed while being arrested for selling untaxed cigarettes (a typical target for broken windows policing), a Quinnipiac University poll saw support for the NYPD rapidly eroding. Bratton and Kelling report, however, that while 90 percent of African American and 71 percent of Hispanic respondents "agreed there was 'no excuse' for how police had acted in the Garner incident," nevertheless "support for Broken Windows remained high," with 56 percent of African Americans approving (37 percent disapproving), 64 percent of Hispanics approv-ing (34 percent disapproving), and 61 percent of whites approving (33 percent disapproving). Here, Bratton and Kelling write, is proof of "underlying support from all races for this kind of enforcement. The

---

2   William J. Bratton and George L. Kelling, "Why We Need Broken Windows Policing: It Has Saved Countless New York Lives—Most of Them Minority—Cut the Jail Population, and Reknit the Social Fabric," *City Journal*, Winter 2015, available at city-journal.org.

3   In reality, few think broken windows policing is *synonymous* with stop and frisk but rather understand the latter to be a tactic closely related to the former. Bratton and Kelling do not acknowledge the large body of work that critiques broken windows on its *own* terms, showing that it is largely ineffective. See, for example, Bernard Harcourt, *Illusion of Order: The False Promise of Broken Windows Policing* (Cambridge: Harvard University Press, 2001).

advocates who say otherwise have never been to a police/community meeting in a poorer, mostly minority neighborhood."[4]

This is not mere propaganda. There *is* plenty of support for broken windows policing in neighborhoods and among the public as a whole, even as it is leavened with a deeper animosity towards the policy than Bratton and Kelling acknowledge. The question then is not so much whether broken windows or other quality-of-life strategies work (though that is important), but what they mean. For Bratton and Kelling, as for many of the theory's advocates (as we discuss below), broken windows policing is community policing. Policing theorists like Bratton and Kelling clearly believe that it is the job of the police to *define, create,* and *maintain* order so that people may live in reasonably contented *subordination* to that order. Police profiling and order-maintenance work, of which police killings seem to be an inevitable consequence, create this order.

At the moment, however, the protests against police killings that rocked the United States in 2014 and 2015 seem to have thrown this police-led project into crisis, perhaps policing's greatest crisis of legitimacy since the 1960s. How else can we explain why Bratton and Kelling thought it was vital to offer a vigorous defense of broken windows *in the midst* of the roiling crisis even if, as they argue, broken windows is *unrelated* to the current unrest?

We seek to address this question in the pages that follow. Through interviews with activists and others in Denver, Colorado, and Oakland, California, we assess the ways in which broken windows is entangled with ideas of community policing—and how it therefore operates as a kind of common sense currently in crisis.[5]

---

4   Bratton and Kelling, "Why We Need Broken Windows Policing."

5   Interviews were undertaken as part of a larger project examining public space and public life in two American and two British cities (Manchester and Glasgow). In addition to analysis of a wide range of documentary evidence, we conducted interviews with community activists, police officials, and residents in all four cities. Much of the research was conducted in 2010 and 2011. Results of the British portion of the research are reported in Don Mitchell, Kafui Attoh, and Lynn A. Staeheli, "Policing-Centered Community Cohesion in Two British Cities," in *Policing Cities: Urban Securitization and Regulation in a Twenty-First Century World*, eds. Randy K. Lippert and Kevin Walby (New York: Routledge, 2013), 58–75.

As Antonio Gramsci made clear, common sense is not the same as good sense. The former is largely a product of induced *un*thinking, while the latter requires hard, critical thought. "Common sense" suggests a relatively unquestioned legitimacy—"a conception of the world that is uncritically absorbed"—that helps cement consent to the ruling ideology of the moment.[6] Broken windows theory, as we will see, has been "uncritically absorbed" into the worldviews of many neighborhood activists, including some who are otherwise critical of the police, though (as we will also see) not by everyone.

The basic precepts of broken windows theory at first appear logical—typically summarized as the inevitable escalation of unpoliced minor crimes (like graffiti or broken windows in abandoned buildings) into bigger crimes, with criminals assuming that police tolerance for small infractions will apply to more serious ones as well. But in their original argument, Wilson and Kelling actually put the matter slightly differently: "Serious crime," they argue, "flourishes in areas where *disorderly behavior* goes unchecked." It is not crime but rather behavior considered disorderly that needs to be controlled ("The unchecked panhandler," they write, "is, in effect, the first broken window").[7] Disorderly behavior, Kelling and Coles later wrote, poses "a grave threat ... to our society."[8] Kelling's repetition of this argument in his *City Journal* article with Bratton confirms that broken windows policing is directed not towards crime but towards social control. Wilson and Kelling said as much back in 1982: "Arresting a single drunk or a single vagrant who has harmed no identifiable person seems unjust ... [but] failing to do anything about a score of drunks or a hundred vagrants may destroy an entire community."[9] Broken windows policing, Bratton, Kelling, and Wilson argue, serves the interests of the community by instilling and upholding order. Fixing small disorders improves quality of life.

There is something quite attractive in this vision. It suggests a world

---

6   Antonio Gramsci, *Selections from the Prison Notebooks*, translated and edited by Q. Hoare and G. Nowell Smith (New York: International Publishers, 1971), esp. 323–6.

7   Wilson and Kelling, "Broken Windows," 29, emphasis added.

8   Kelling and Coles, *Fixing Broken Windows*, 7.

9   Wilson and Kelling, "Broken Windows," 35.

in which police are less an occupying force, as they seemed in the midst of the urban uprisings of the 1960s, and more agents of the community. Indeed, since the end of the 1960s and the seeming erosion of the "professional" (paramilitary) model of policing common in mid-twentieth-century Keynesian-industrial societies (especially the United States), the idea that policing should be tightly bound with "the community" seems obvious to many activists, citizens, police theorists, and the police themselves. As police theorists have shown, community policing is now the dominant ideology of policing across the globe (though its practical implementation is much less consistent).[10] The police *themselves* have, in many instances, become primary advocates for community policing as a means of reinforcing their own legitimacy. Even more, police in many jurisdictions now place themselves at the heart of community formation, central to defining who—and what sorts of behaviors—count as "community," and who and what count as "disorderly."[11]

The legitimacy of community policing itself, as the geographer Steve Herbert argues, "rests in significant part upon the long-treasured ideal of localized democracy."[12] This ideal is *communitarian* in the sense that it assumes the community itself to be already cohesive. But the rise of broken windows policing as practice and common sense suggests something else: namely that communities are perpetually under threat, perhaps even in a state of siege, by bad guys ranging from panhandlers to hardened criminals, which new policing strategies are needed to root out.

Moreover, broken windows policing continues, rather than supercedes, the mid-century paramilitary-style policing that marked the "professional model" of the era. Broken windows does not need for its operation a model in which "citizenry and police are co-equal."[13] To

10   The spread and variations of community policing are examined in Dominique Wissler and Ihekwoaba Onwudiwe, eds., *Community Policing: Comparative Perspectives* (Boca Raton, FL: CRC Press, 2009).

11   Mitchell et al., "Policing-Centered Community Cohesion."

12   Steve Herbert, *Citizens, Cops, and Power: Recognizing the Limits of Community* (Chicago: University of Chicago Press, 2006), 64.

13   Steve Herbert, "Policing the Contemporary City: Fixing Broken Windows or Shoring Up Neo-Liberalism?" *Theoretical Criminology* 5 (2001): 445–56, quotations from 451, 456.

the degree that broken windows theory is accepted as common sense, then, the interests of the police are served. Yet as an arm of the state, the "interests of the police" are not entirely their own.

As police theorists David and Melissa Barlow write, "the criminal justice system is part of the social structure of accumulation in the capitalist political economy."[14] Broken windows policing is in fact quite brazen on this front (which accounts for part of its appeal among some of the neighborhood activists we'll discuss below). Advocates for broken windows policing often attribute the decline of neighborhoods and cities—disinvestment of capital in the urban built environment—to the presence of disorderly people, especially the homeless. Eliminating "disorder"—eliminating the homeless, unemployed "loiterers," or informal market activities—will not just keep "great cities" from being "killed" (as Seattle's city attorney once put it in the midst of a vigorous campign to enforce antihomeless laws), but create the conditions through which capital accumulation in the built environment may once again proceed.[15] This dynamic is particularly clear in the Los Angeles Police's Safer Cities Initiative, developed under Bratton's chiefship and aimed at that city's Skid Row (the largest concentration of homeless people and services in the world), which has made the elimination of homeless people—not homelessness—its central goal in an effort to spur the district's gentrification. Without broken windows, the reasoning goes, "property values" will not "escalate."[16]

Of course, capitalist accumulation—metaphorized in Bratton and Kelling's telling as escalating property values—necessarily entails its opposite, immiseration. Growing urban (and global) inequality is no

---

14   D. Barlow and M. H. Barlow, "Community Policing in the United States: Social Control through Image Management," in *Community Policing*, ed. Wisler and Onwudiwe, 167–88, quotation from 168.

15   Quoted in Don Mitchell, *The Right to the City: Social Justice and the Fight for Public Space* (New York: Guilford, 2003), 168.

16   Alex Vitale, "The Safer Cities Initiative and the Removal of the Homeless: Reducing Crime or Promoting Gentrification on Los Angeles's Skid Row?" *Criminology and Public Policy* 9: 867–73. As the March 1, 2015, police shooting on Skid Row of Charly Keunang, known as "Africa," exemplifies, "the removal of the homeless" can sometimes be quite literal.

accident. Rather, it is a problem that must be continually managed.[17] Paramilitary policing was, and is becoming once again, one means of management.[18] Broken windows policing is another. To the degree that the logic of broken windows is accepted—taken as common sense—and to the degree it is conflated with community policing, police management of police-defined disorderly behavior is accepted as a necessary part of urban life, at least by many. But it is not accepted by everyone. The contradictions that sit at the heart of broken windows policing are not infrequently countered by the good sense of those who are subject to it (or whose lives are otherwise shaped by it), especially when, as is almost always the case, broken windows policing in practice does not live up to the promise of broken windows theory.

Broken Windows: Views from the Neighborhoods

For many of the people we spoke with in Oakland and Denver, broken windows is not only a police practice, it is also a community development strategy. For example, a Latino neighborhood activist in Oakland (who was also a city council member) told us that broken windows was central to the work of his neighborhood council (of which he was president). The council used to be called the Neighborhood Crime Prevention Council, but "we changed the name deliberately … to get away from 'crime prevention'" which, members thought, was too negative. Now they understand "that crime prevention is cleaning blighted property." Cleaning and maintaining public spaces, especially "one of the main entrances to the neighborhood," is essential: "It's the old 'broken windows' theory." Property maintenance practices are a piece of order maintenance activities:

> One of the things we hammer on … is document, document, document. If you see something suspicious call it in [to the police]. If

---

17 See Rowland Atkinson and Gesa Helms, eds., *Securing an Urban Renaissance* (Bristol: Policy Press, 2007).

18 See Stephen Graham, *Cities under Siege: The New Military Urbanism* (London: Verso, 2010), 96–9.

something is happening, people hanging out on the street, get a license number, get a description … Nine o'clock at night, the music is blaring, there's four guys on X corner, document it.

Vital to his neighborhood, the activist told us, was the presence of a community-based "public-service officer" charged with knowing the neighborhood and neighbors and being proactive in addressing "broken windows" in whatever form. Broken windows logic was, for this activist, crucial to neighborhood vitality.[19]

In Denver, a white community activist in a west-side working-class neighborhood told us that she strongly advocated for the importation of broken windows policing after reading about it in the *Wall Street Journal*. For her, broken windows policing was synonymous with community policing: "To me, community policing is, you go out and look for signs of things that could lead to more criminal behavior, or it's already a violation of a zoning code, or it's a violation of a law that says you have to keep your property secure." Of broken windows policing, she said: "Everybody loves it … Everybody wants it in their neighborhood." When we interviewed her, she was advocating for the citywide expansion of broken windows policing. She was thrilled by the effects of a broken windows experiment in her own neighborhood. "What happened is, some of the bad guys, they just got pushed out of the neighborhood." But when the program ended, "some of these characters actually read the newspaper, so they knew" and came back to the neighborhood. If broken windows enforcement went citywide, she argued, then it would be known everywhere that "you're not going to get away with gangster behavior, with intimidating people, with trashing people's houses, breaking into abandoned houses, putting up graffiti." Such vigilant policing, she told us, needed also to extend to the homeless and panhandlers. Her organization was thus lobbying actively to have the "sit-lie" and anti–aggressive panhandling laws that covered downtown extended to her neighborhood. Without the proactive policing of minor problems, she told us, the community wouldn't feel safe and the neighborhood would decline. With broken windows policing, there would be

---

19 Authors' interview with Oakland neighborhood activist 1, September 21, 2010.

a chance for real community development. There is no doubt that this activist believed in the efficacy of broken-windows-as-community policing. She could have been reading from Bratton and Kelling's script.[20]

Yet contrary to Bratton and Kelling's arguments, our research also revealed a great deal of opposition to broken windows policing. As an Afro-Latina Denver activist told us, she had already been involved in a range of issues confronting communities of color when she and others learned that the Denver police were conferring with policing consultants—including, it seems, George Kelling—to begin implementing broken windows policing.[21] Because the national organization she was working with was not focusing on the issue, her group had to "do our own researching of it." Her organization "looked at the Giuliani administration's application of broken windows and looked at how it was being presented in Denver by the mayor" and the city council as a solution to problems of public safety. In particular, the city insisted that people of color and especially young Latina women were the chief beneficiaries of broken windows policing—and young men of color the primary threat to it. "So, the problem with that is, you know, when have public officials ever created policy based upon young Latina input?" she asked rhetorically. "So this was clearly a ruse to say that this was grassroots," after police had been planning the introduction of broken windows policing for some time. The activist continued:

> We know that there's a lot of money [for] bringing in more police. There's a lot of justice system funding for more police and building up their resources and more of their weapons. And so, you know, we try to educate the public, starting with our own neighborhoods—this is not good news; don't believe the hype.

Our interviewee conceded that broken windows policing had intuitive appeal for many—its logic made common sense—despite what she saw as a cynical campaign to build up its popularity in Denver. With others, therefore, this activist founded an organization called Fixing Broken

20 Authors' interview with Denver neighborhood activist 1, June 21, 2010.
21 Authors' interview with police consultant, Denver, June 28, 2010.

Policing to drive home the message that broken windows policing was more likely to exacerbate than alleviate problems for people of color in Denver.[22]

In fact, neighborhoods in Denver were split over the worth of the broken windows policing model. Another west-side activist, a student intern at an organization helping to implement "creative policing strategies," explained that while broken windows policing was politically encouraged in Denver, some neighborhoods balked. While these neighborhoods "also had issues with high crime and quality-of-life issues like graffiti and illegal dumping, which fit some of the broken windows thinking about how to handle disorder," they "want to go completely in the other direction." Our interviewee took it upon herself to read the academic literature on broken windows theory and found "there was a lack of empirical support for broken windows, that some people considered it aggressive policing, police harassment, racial profiling, those sorts of things. So we did our own evaluation" in the neighborhood where it was being implemented. "We kept a critical lens." Her organization canvassed residents and held community meetings in the neighborhood where broken windows policing was being implemented, and it heard serious concerns about racial profiling. "We had teenage African American residents ... who would be stopped by the gang unit when they were pushing the lawnmower back to the office having mowed the lawn. They would assume they were a gang member and harass them."

Residents in this first neighborhood "were afraid that broken windows was the wrong strategy, since they already had profiling issues"; they therefore rejected broken windows policing and sought other forms based less on ticketing and order maintenance and more on cooperative community–police interactions. In particular they advocated for more police foot patrols that emphasized "positive contacts with individual residents" and for the police and other agencies to address environmental concerns, like the preponderance of "dark and unsafe places" in the neighborhood. They wanted positive investment rather than prohibitionary practices. Residents said, "We want to focus on positive

---

22   Authors' interview with Fixing Broken Policing activist, Denver, June 18, 2010.

contacts, decrease chances for people just loitering and hanging out and causing problems by making it uncomfortable [for others] because they're [hanging out under the only streetlight] in the dark." They saw this as a "totally different approach" from broken windows policing, necessary because neighborhood problems resulted not from disorderly behavior by "bad guys" external to the community but rather from deprivation within the community.[23]

Broken Windows and Community Policing

The desire for cooperative and deep community–police interactions is a desire for the *ideal* of community policing as Herbert defined it. That some Denver residents see such an ideal as a "totally different approach" to policing than broken windows is interesting, given how hard broken windows advocates like Bratton and Kelling seek to conflate the two. The differences lie mainly in emphasis: residents in Denver neighborhoods both in favor of and against broken windows policing were equally concerned with questions of quality of life and public order. Similarly, in our Oakland interviews, broken windows common sense was almost always invoked within the context of community development and neighborhood vitality. In both Denver and Oakland, the key question was always the nature of the community–police relation; those who opposed broken windows tended to understand the police as, institutionally, an outside force with its own needs, agenda, and (often) racist assumptions about the policed.[24] Opponents of broken windows policing desired greater control over policing and a deeper, positive integration of the police into the community. Those who supported it wanted the same thing but also to drive the "unwanted" out of the neighborhood.[25]

---

23 Authors' interview with Denver neighborhood activist 2, June 25, 2010.

24 Authors' interview with policing activist, Oakland, September 21, 2010; authors' interview with civil rights activist, Denver, June 16, 2010; authors' interview with Fixing Broken Policing activist, Denver, June 18, 2010.

25 Authors' interview with Oakland neighborhood activist 2, September 23, 2010.

The differences in emphasis between community and broken windows policing is perhaps best understood through a brief foray into the former's meaning and history. Community policing is, as Herbert notes, "a remarkably amorphous term" and highly varied in practice,[26] though it seems to consist of these main practices: a focus on problem-oriented policing (paying attention to the context of crimes as well as the crimes themselves); the (re)creation of neighborhood beats, often walked on foot; the use of neighborhood-based "problem-solving officers" or "police community support officers" (who are often allowed fewer police actions than other officers); the encouragement of community involvement in setting neighborhood policing priorities and crime prevention strategies (as with Oakland's Neighborhood Crime Prevention Councils); an emphasis on the prevention of disorder; a similar concern with enhancing "quality of life" and preventing its undoing (the total ambit of broken windows theory); and efforts to reduce people's fear of crime and to provide reassurance.[27] By contrast, broken windows policing is a quite narrow, much more tactical mode of policing that is also police-driven.

There are two origin stories for community policing. The first, which has yet to be fully told, begins with "the community," particularly African American and Latino communities during the uprisings of the 1960s, as residents demanded the removal of the police as an occupying force, and its return under the auspices of community control. The "professional" paramilitary-style of policing was losing legitimacy in many cities, increasingly viewed as a racist form of oppression and control. What the geographer Bill Bunge would call "sympathetic authority" over the police (and other institutions, such as schools) was necessary both to restore legitimacy and to transform the institutions of the state from oppressive into liberatory.[28] The second story, told by

---

26   Herbert, "Policing the Contemporary City."

27   Mitchell et al., "Policing-Centered Community Cohesion," 60; Martin Innis, "Reinventing Tradition? Reassurance, Neighbourhood Security and Policing," *Criminal Justice* 4 (2004): 151–71; Anna Barker and Adam Crawford, "Policing Urban Insecurities: Managing Public Expectations in Times of Fiscal Restraints," in *Policing Cities*, ed. Randy K. Lippert and Kevin Walby, 1–28.

28   William Bunge, *Fitzgerald: Geography of a Revolution* (New York: Schenkman, 1971); Willam Bunge et al., "A Report to the Parents of Detroit on School Decentralization," in *Man, Space, and Environment*, ed. P.W. English and R. C. Mayfield

police-friendly criminologists, recognizes the slipping legitimacy of the police in the 1960s but attributes it to contradictions within the professional model itself, granting full responsibility for police reform to actors within the police force itself rather than any external movements. With the professional model showing cracks, farsighted police reformers like George Kelling quickly recognized an opportunity and a need for reform and instigated a set of experiments (in Flint, Newark, and Houston, among other cities) that got police out of their cars, walking beats, and paying attention to community concerns about disorder. These experiments produced evidence of a significant reduction in fear of crime (if not crime itself) and led Kelling, Wilson, and others towards a stronger focus on urban disorder as a significant criminogenic factor.[29] In the process of this experimentation and reform, and "given the ambiguities that surround both the definition of disorder and the authority of the police to do something about it," Kelling summarized, "police learned they had to seek authorization from local citizens to intervene in disorderly situations."[30]

Policing now required what Herman Goldstein defined as a problem orientation, in which instead of merely responding to service calls (a common tactic under the professional model), police had to engage in continuous problem definition, research, and exploration of alternative solutions.[31] The aloof model of professional-era policing needed to give way to a model in which a police officer, especially the beat-walking officer, had to be a cross between a traditional cop, a social worker, and an urban sociologist.[32]

Some of our informants in Oakland and Denver dream of such a role for the police. They desire their central presence. During our time conducting interviews in Oakland in the fall of 2010, debate was raging

(New York: Oxford University Press, 1972), 499–533.

29   The now classic account is Kelling's own: George Kelling and Mark Moore, "The Evolving Strategy of Policing," *Perspectives on Policing* 4 (1988): 1–15.

30   Ibid., 10.

31   Herman Goldstein, "Improving Policing: A Problem-Oriented Approach," *Crime and Deliquency* 25 (1979): 236–58; Goldstein, *Problem-Oriented Policing* (New York: McGraw-Hill, 1990); Gary Cordner and Elizabeth Perkins Biebel, "Problem Oriented Policing in Practice," *Criminology and Public Policy* 4 (2005): 155–80.

32   Mitchell et al., "Policing-Centered Community Cohesion."

on the value of—and funding for—that city's problem-solving officers. In 2004, Oakland voters had overwhelmingly passed Measure Y, which created a new tax to support enhanced fire and police services. In particular it provided for the hiring of 63 neighborhood-based problem-solving officers to supplement the 739-officer regular police force. A provision of the measure banned the city from using Measure Y funds on police services if the regular force fell below 739. Several rounds of budget cuts in the ensuing years had reduced the Oakland police force to below that number, so in 2010 voters considered whether to suspend the staffing-level provision of Measure Y and keep their problem-solving officers. An earlier RAND Corporation report had shown that neighborhood experience with the problem-oriented, community policing part of Measure Y was "not altogether positive" due to poor training, frequent transfers of officers out of their beats, infringement on problem-solving officers' time, and "lack of community participation."[33] Nonetheless, voters passed the amendment, again with an overwhelming majority. The idea of community policing had wide appeal.

But few thought it worked very well. In Oakland, neighborhood activists complained that their own problem-solving officers often did not do "very much here in the area," in one case "because her captain, her superior, used to take her off duty here ... because that was his right," in the words of a white, middle-class activist in a rapidly changing neighborhood near the Berkeley border.[34] The Latino neighborhood activist quoted earlier served as the chair of the Measure Y oversight committee. He concurred that redeployment was often a problem and went a step further: "The problem-solving officers were specifically to work on the problems identified by the Neighborhood Crime Prevention Council specific to that beat that they were assigned to ... What better way to deal with crime problems than to have somebody that's really focused on the problems that are identified by the people that live in that specific beat or have a business or are a part of an institution ... taking it through a process by which the problems get resolved?"

33   J. Wilson et al., *Community Policing and Violence Prevention: Measure Y in Action* (Santa Monica: RAND Corporation, 2007), xiv.

34   Authors' interview with neighborhood activist 2, Oakland, September 23, 2010.

But in his neighborhood, "I didn't see that happen." The police never took "one of our priorities that we established and [made] it a project of the problem-solving officer that they take … through what is known as the SARA process: scan, analyze, respond, and assess. They've written libraries on this technique. It's been around for decades. I've never seen it applied once. That's my pet peeve about community policing. It's not being applied in Oakland." To be effective, PSOs need to be "not social workers, but let's call them community workers. I think you really have to have a specific skill set in order to relate to the neighborhoods and all the different aspects, as opposed to some guy who was just gung-ho and just looking to drive down the street ninety miles an hour going after the bad guys." There has to be a "partnership" between community and police, one that has continued to "come up short" in Oakland's implementation of community policing.[35] In part this may be because the Oakland Police Department "really, really fought community polic-ing," according to a city employee who works closely with the police in implementing various community policing projects. "They thought it was really a waste of time, that they needed to be out there arresting people." As mayoral administrations changed, so too did official support for community policing.[36]

Community policing was seen to be a "waste" in contexts like these because police and some community members conflated it with broken windows policing, according to some of our sources. In the words of a Denver activist seeking to distinguish between the two: "Community policing is about getting to know who lives in the neighborhood; is about getting out of your car; is about walking through the neighbor-hood; is about knowing my son … when he's coming home at night, he's coming from college or from work. He is not a gang member. You know this because you know him, because you are familiar with our neighborhood." Community policing is also when the police are held accountable. By contrast, "Broken windows is simply more police targeted on hot-spot areas based on data … It's to target areas, find sus-picious individuals, question them until they consent to [a] search, and

---

35 Authors' interview with neighborhood activist 1, Oakland, September 21, 2010.

36 Authors' interview with city employee, Oakland, October 13, 2010.

get lucky by finding something on them." In Denver, community policing "never really got fully rooted, and then funding was discontinued"
and foot patrols were eliminated from many neighborhoods.[37]

"Broken Windows Is Not the Panacea"

"We cannot arrest our way out" of the "many challenges to public order
confronting cities and communities," Bratton and Kelling write. "Police
need partners to help solve or manage complex social issues."[38] If such a
vision does not exactly accord with the ideology and practices of broken
windows policing, it is nonetheless shared by many. An Oakland city
employee who works on police oversight matters told us a story that
encapsulated many residents' dreams of what their neighborhood could
be. People in Oakland, he said, want "a community where people know
their neighbors, they have a relationship so you don't even need to call
a cop. 'Johnny, what are you doing trying to break into my house? Are
you hungry?' We had that happen. The kids were trying to break into
this lady's house because they were hungry. She said, 'I'll buy you some
food. Stop trying to break into my house.' To me, that's community
policing. If you can get to that level you are really making progress."
Using the same words as Bratton and Kelling, but to a quite different
end, he continued: "We cannot arrest our way out of the problem of
crime in Oakland. We have to work on root causes, which include huge
economic disparity, education gap, technology gap, lack of jobs, lack of
social services, poor health, health inequality."[39]

Such work, an Oakland activist told us, would require not only the
building of a new kind of community (and the institutional and state
support to do so), but also a significant change in police "culture," a
real "systemic change." Such systemic change was urgent, she argued:
current local and state laws "have given the police the kind of power
that they have and the kind of immunity to scrutiny and accountability

---

37   Authors' interview with Fixing Broken Policing activist, Denver, June 18,
2010.
38   Bratton and Kelling, "Why We Need Broken Windows Policing."
39   Authors' interview with city employee, Oakland, October 13, 2010.

[that] is really shocking." This activist had been working on police brutality and accountability issues for nearly twenty years since her African
American husband was shot and killed by police during an altercation
with their son at the front door to their house. "People of color," she
argues, "are disproportionately negatively impacted by the Oakland
Police Department." Her organization sponsored a study that concluded, "We basically have two different systems of policing in Oakland,
one for the more affluent and typically lighter-complected residents,
and another system of policing for folks in what we call 'the flats,' the
lower elevations, predominantly people of color."[40] For her, the institu-
tionalization of problem solving officers through Measure Y had been a
"mixed bag": while the Neighborhood Crime Prevention Councils have
in some instances helped improve police–community communication,
in other instances, they have promoted "a kind of official vigilantism"
and reinforced owner-versus-renter tensions. "This is not in our view the
way community policing is supposed to work. It's not supposed to essentially demonize those people who are perceived to be problematic by the
more well-heeled and more vocal members of the neighborhood." Her
organization was "involved in the liftoff" of community policing "in the
early 90s … Our understanding is that community policing is meant to
establish the community's role in how policing is conducted." But "we
have a very clearly polarized community here. Community policing has
not been successful in establishing any kind of clear communication
or receptivity from the part of this community that does not trust the
police."[41] When the police are not accountable to the people, trust is
impossible.

At the time of our interviews in 2010, the Oakland Police Department
had been under a federal consent decree for seven years. That decree,
resulting from years of police misconduct and abuse (including false
arrests, planting evidence, and physical abuse, largely in the poor Black
and Latino neighborhoods of West Oakland), was designed to force the

40   Oakland stretches from the San Francisco Bay in the west to the peaks of the
Oakland Hills in the northeast; in general terms, socioeconomics follow elevation,
with poorer people in the lowlands to the west and wealthier people in the hills to the
east.

41   Authors' interview with policing activist, Oakland, September 21, 2010.

police department to undertake fifty-one significant reforms. In 2012, a federal judge placed the department in receivership because of its failure to comply with the decree.[42] In Denver, the city government paid out more than $13 million between 2004 and 2014 to settle police misconduct cases.[43] Broken windows policing has significant police support because it promotes community policing while hinting at but allowing for very little involvement in community problems. For this reason, as the Fixing Broken Policing activist told us, "broken windows is actually not the panacea," no matter how vigorously Bratton and Kelling may defend it or how popular they may claim it to be.[44]

Broken Windows and Good Sense

Broken windows may indeed retain a good deal of popularity, as Bratton and Kelling argue. And as Bratton's reappointment as New York's police chief under progressive mayor Bill de Blasio indicates, that popularity extends across the political spectrum. Many of those we interviewed who favor broken windows policing position themselves as politically progressive: a testament to the success of broken windows advocates in conflating broken windows with community policing and with the notion of a holistic approach to neighborhood vitality, even if it comes up far short in practice. The timing of Bratton and Kelling's defense in *City Journal* therefore becomes all the more interesting, given that activists against broken windows policing, racial profiling, police brutality, and police killings want not a tactical shift but police *accountability* to

---

42   In late 2009, Anthony Batts was named the new chief of police in Oakland, and our interviewees were cautiously optimistic about the prospects for reform under a Black police leader. Batts left when the OPD was placed in receivership in 2012 (saying he was fed up with Oakland city politics) and assumed the chiefship in Baltimore, where he recently became famous in the wake of the police killing of Freddie Gray. See Shoshana Walter, "Oakland Police Caught between Reform and Crime Surge," *New York Times*, April 20, 2012.

43   Jon Murray, "Denver Pays Millions to Settle Abuse Claims Against Police and Sheriff," *Denver Post*, August 3, 2014.

44   Authors' interview with Fixing Broken Policing activist, Denver, June 18, 2010.

those who benefit less, if at all, from what Barrow and Barrow identified as the central role of police in capitalist society: "to preserve the status quo in relation to power."[45]

For this reason, activists in Denver have been working to change how complaints against the police are handled. Charges of police misconduct by the Denver Police Department, which are frequent and often contain allegations of racial bias, are handled primarily by an Internal Affairs Bureau, which is now required to offer mediation between police and citizens when a complaint is filed.[46] Officers who agree to mediation will not be investigated by Internal Affairs (cases that might result in serious disciplinary action against an officer are excluded from mediation). The goal is not only to provide satisfaction to many complainants, but also to heal the highly antagonistic relationship that exists between many citizens of Denver and the police force.

In the view of many, however, such mediation merely perpetuates police power and minimizes community oversight. The Fixing Broken Policing activist explains why: one day, she told us, her sixteen year-old son was pulled away from his bus stop by two white police officers who "jumped out [of their police car] and basically roughed him up, took him into the alley ... handcuffed, humiliated, essentially ... They made fun of him for wanting to call his mother ... And these are white cops. I mean, so it's like can you imagine the—the seed of infuriation you have now planted in that Black kid for white police." When he was finally allowed to call his mother she could hear "the terror and the humiliation in his voice ... So, you know, we of course decide[d] to fight it." After filing a complaint, the office assigned to handle complaints called and asked her to take the complaint into mediation. "And I was livid. And I said you would not ask a batterer to—a victim and a batterer to sit down and for them to share their perspective and they can see each other and 'This is why I hurt you; can't you understand why and see my side of things?' I said when there is a power imbalance like this, when there is violence used, and that interaction with my son was a violent

45   Barrow and Barrow, "Community Policing in the United States," 168.

46   Community activist Patsy Hathaway has compiled a timeline of forty-two charges of serious brutality from 2002 to 2011: "Denver Police Brutality Scandal: A Timeline," November 27, 2011, available at patsyhathaway.wordpress.com.

interaction, you don't sit down and mediate that; you want someone to be accountable for that. I want better training for police. That's not something we're going to get when my son sits down and talks with them." As this activist notes, "most Internal Affairs complaints regarding racial profiling" in Denver "are not sustained." Even so, "it's in the police's best interest to mediate it, and they'll tell you they want to mediate," especially since "if you [mediate], your complaint gets dropped … It ends the internal investigation. They do nothing else; they don't look at their procedures, nothing." This is especially problematic because the goal "has to be changing the police department culture."[47]

Oakland activists make a similar argument. As one argued, the only way that trust will be built is if those subject to police brutality, aggressive policing practices, "pretext stops," and racial profiling begin to file complaints: to assert their rights and authority vis-à-vis the police. The problem in Oakland, she contends, is that such complaining is usually ineffectual in Oakland, powerful as it potentially may be ("the power of complaining … will drive reform more powerfully than any other single thing … because [it] will impact an officer's chances of promotion and might even get an officer demoted").[48] Lauded by criminal justice scholars as one of the best in the country, Oakland's Internal Affairs Division is mistrusted by many community members and activists.[49] They do not find the internal review process to be accountable, especially since California law protects police personnel records from public scrutiny. A number of Oakland organizations are therefore fighting to "close Internal Affairs completely to citizens' complaints" and to redirect them instead to the Citizens Police Review Board, a recommendation formally made by an Oakland City Council committee in 2000, though never put into practice.[50]

---

47   Authors' interview with Fixing Broken Policing activist, Denver, June 18, 2010.

48   Authors' interview with policing activist, Oakland, September 21, 2010.

49   Such a perception has persisted despite the fact that the OPD has operated under a federally administered negotiated settlement since 2003 that "requires the Oakland Police Department to conduct an in-depth review of its entire operation with the aim of becoming more responsive, effective and accountable." "The Negotiated Settlement Agreement," available at 2.oaklandnet.com.

50   Authors' interview with policing activist, Oakland, September 21, 2010.

Civilians' experiences in Denver and Oakland suggest that *there is no panacea* for police–community tensions. Rather, "good sense" requires making police accountable to those they police (not just to powerful neighborhood interests or those who profit from gentrification and urban development). By contrast, common sense or not, broken windows policing is part of a larger suite of unaccountable policing tactics (e.g., stop and frisk) that target particular populations (the homeless, youth hanging out on the street, the poor and people of color) and exacerbate tensions between police and some communities. Bratton and Kelling, and those they speak for, defend broken windows policing in the midst of this new crisis of police legitimacy because it creates the appearance of being actual community involvement and a solution to community ills while *not* being community policing. Instead, it perpetrates, under a different guise, the aggressive paramilitary "professional model" of policing. With broken windows, authority remains with the police, not the people. Police remain unaccountable.

~

Don Mitchell teaches geography at Syracuse University, where he conducts research on social struggles in urban space and capital-labor struggles in the agribusiness landscape. He is the author, with Lynn Staeheli, of *The People's Property? Power, Politics, and the Public* (Routledge, 2008) and most recently *They Saved the Crops: Labor, Landscape and the Struggle over Industrial Farming in Bracero-Era California* (University of Georgia Press, 2012).

Kafui Attoh is an assistant professor of urban studies at the Joseph P. Murphy Institute of Labor Studies and Worker Education, City University of New York. His work focuses on the relationships between social justice, urban transportation, and the right to the city.

Lynn Staeheli is the director of the School of Geography and Development at the University of Arizona. Among much else, she conducts research on the paradoxical nature of citizenship in a wide range of settings from South Africa, Lebanon, and Bosnia to the United States. She is the author, with Don Mitchell, of *The People's Property: Power, Politics, and the Public* (Routledge, 2008).

19. WE CHARGE GENOCIDE: AN INTERVIEW WITH BREANNA CHAMPION, PAGE MAY, AND ASHA ROSA RANSBY-SPORN

Jordan T. Camp and Christina Heatherton

In response to the systemic police violence around the country, particularly in Chicago, eight members of the group We Charge Genocide traveled to Geneva, Switzerland, in November 2014 to submit a report before the United Nations Committee Against Torture documenting systemic racialized violence by the Chicago Police Department. Drawing on oral testimony and statistical evidence, the report shows that police repression has served to silence and criminalize communities of color in Chicago, an argument that resounds both nationally and globally. This interview was conducted with three of the members of We Charge Genocide: Breanna Champion, Page May, and Asha Rosa Ransby-Sporn.

Camp: Could you talk about how you came to the project?

May: Back in June 2014, Mariame Kaba, who's been organizing around police violence in Chicago for decades and who's doing work around abolishing police and the police state, sent out an email calling for people to come together to create some collective effort in response to the murder of Dominique Franklin. She proposed a group rooted in the original We Charge Genocide petition of 1951 that was submitted to the UN. She had the idea for the name We Charge Genocide, but that was just the start. We started meeting in June and very quickly everything started falling into place. We've been at work ever since.

Champion: Dominique, or "Damo," was a friend of a bunch of our friends, and was Tasered by Chicago police twice, causing him to go into a coma that he never woke up from. He died a few days later. Mariame Kaba called us all together to do something about it.

Camp: You named your organization after the We Charge Genocide petition submitted by the Civil Rights Congress to the United Nations in 1951. The petition documented widespread, state-sanctioned, and extralegal violence against Black people in the postwar period. What is the significance of the petition in your work today?

May: As an organizer, Mariame sees history as something to study as well as something that provides context for the current moment. We learn what tactics our ancestors have used to struggle against violence. We learn to understand police violence not as something new but as historic and systemic—something built into the infrastructure of policing. By choosing the name We Charge Genocide, we can immediately demonstrate that this is not a new problem. It's not limited to just Dominique Franklin or Mike Brown. It is a feature of the current carceral state. With the name, we don't have many conversations about whether police violence is a problem. We say right off the bat, "We Charge Genocide. If you're with us, you're with us, and if you're not, we've got plenty of other work to do."

Ransby-Sporn: Going to the UN in the spirit of this history was particularly important and strategic. This new movement looks different but is addressing old problems. Right now, 150 years after the "abolition of slavery," we're seeing new iterations of violence against Black bodies that persist under capitalism in this country. The strength of calling this out as genocide is declaring that this violence has persisted and has come back again and again in new forms. With the name We Charge Genocide, we're not saying that this violence is "disproportionate," we're not saying it's "unintentional," we're saying it's built into the system and is part of a legacy that has been built up over hundreds and hundred of years.

Heatherton: You describe the need to "draw international attention to the struggle for police accountability." What compelled you to seek a global forum?

Ransby-Sporn: Who else are we going to go to? It's not that we respect a lot of the things that the United Nations does, but we wanted to address these issues from as many different angles as possible. The United Nations was one angle. You don't often see global superpowers like the United States condemn state violence against their own people. We wanted to call out the United States for the violence it enacts around the world. We also wanted to call out the ways that it covers up that violence with the democratic rhetoric of equality and human rights both here in the US and around the world.

May: We knew the UN wasn't going to "save us" in any shape or form. At the same time young people like us never thought growing up that we would ever get to go to the UN, let alone be listened to and have our message recognized, acknowledged, and affirmed. It was huge for eight young people of color to go to the UN, with the support of a big community, demanding that the US be called out for its violence against Black and Brown young people. That just doesn't happen. Dominique's friends were there. When Dominique died they thought no one was going to know or care about him. For them to go and be a part of this effort was incredibly transformative. I think it was a revolutionary act in and of itself that has helped build power. We need more spaces like that.

Heatherton: You also staged a protest at the UN. Can you talk about that?

May: One of the most significant moments for me was when Asha read this statement at the Civil Society Consultation. She said, "Our delegation of eight Black and Brown young people who have traveled here are not asking for any favors and are not accepting any apologies. We are calling on you to admit the endemic and structural violence that exists within the system of policing and criminalization. We charge torture. We charge genocide." Asha insisted on finishing, even though they were telling her to stop.

After we listened to two and a half hours of soul-crushing stories, the US finally responded to the charges of police violence. They started out by saying something like, "We know that there's a problem, but look, we're doing really great because in the past five years we've prosecuted 300 people." We laughed, looked at each other, stood up, and walked out. That was actually the first protest we did there.

Camp: Could you talk about some of the silences you've encountered, such as silences based on the fear of police violence or fear of state violence?

May: There are a lot of silences we're speaking to. Primarily, we're naming anti-Blackness. We're saying that this is not just about police violence, it's not just that the police are racist; we're saying that they are an anti-Black institution. Also, people often talk about police violence as something that can be reformed, so there's a silence around ideas of abolition. This is either because people can't imagine a world without police or because it's seen as too radical. The cops are too embedded in our heads and our hearts. It's too scary. For us to claim not just that abolition is possible but that it is necessary and that the state can't be reformed is exceptional. When people show up for us, they are with us. We're able to do so much more and more quickly because we're starting far on the left.

Heatherton: The question of abolition has been critical to your political vision. Can you describe how?

Ransby-Sporn: I think I believed in prison abolition before I ever had the words to explain why. I believe now in the abolition of prisons and the abolition of police. I think the actual function of these institutions is to contain and control people. I don't believe they are going to keep people safe, especially my people. We need to think about community safety and how to sustain healthy communities. I think a prison abolitionist and a police abolitionist lens allows us to think more rigorously about the work that we're actually doing and what we're moving towards.

Oftentimes organizers get caught up in reforms that are going to make things better right now but fail to ask the big questions, like, "How is this actually transforming institutions?" and "What is this going to look like in the future?" Prison abolition forces us to ask those questions. What do we want instead? We need to be thinking only about reforms that take power away from police, because we don't trust police and we don't believe in policing as a way to treat other people.

May: Abolition is something that I was really slow to embrace. Even when I started to get down with the ideas, I hated the word. I got used to the idea of abolition by working around prisons. Then I had to go through another process of imagining abolition around the police. It's been a journey, for sure. I now believe in it fiercely. All of this has helped me understand that abolition is not just about expanding our imaginations; it's also about seeing what's happening around us currently and starting to recognize abolition when it is happening.

Camp: Could you talk about how you understand the impact of broken windows policing on poor communities of color in Chicago?

Ransby-Sporn: There was a study done in a poor Black neighborhood in Chicago. It looked at what happens when you put more police on the streets in neighborhoods where there's supposedly a lot of crime and already a lot of police. Nothing really changes. If in that same community you give young people jobs, violent crime actually goes down. I don't really like to use the rhetoric of crime to gauge whether or not communities are healthy, because it's an invented category. Wherever there are police there is going to be crime, because it's their job to find it. But the study showed that if you support people, they do well, but if you assume that they're going to mess up, they get punished. That is really how the system works. You have lines drawn along race and class primarily, and then other identity categories as well.

Camp: Garry McCarthy, the police chief in Chicago, is calling for the implementation of the New York model in Chicago. How have you witnessed those developments?

Ransby-Sporn: We're coming up on a mayoral election [in February 2015]. Every single Democratic and progressive candidate is running on a campaign platform asking for more police. It's so warped. There's no real, coherent politics that supports the idea that people, especially Black people, and especially poor people—the people that these candidates are supposedly running for—are going to be kept safe by putting more police on the streets.

It's also interesting then to look at the political influence of the police unions and the correctional workers' unions. Rahm Emanuel, the current mayor, even gave a retroactive raise to the police force this past year. He, who we see as a conservative candidate, is the only candidate *not* running on a platform of putting more police on the streets, because he's already done that. He's trying to scoop up more liberal votes. When you put more police on the streets, when you give more power to that system, it's so hard to take it back.

What I would love to see in Chicago is a youth jobs bill. I would envision it as a bill that takes the 39 percent of the city government's operating budget that goes towards police and puts it towards schools, mental health clinics, and giving young people jobs. The electoral possibility of making something like that happen is hard to imagine because the police unions are so strong. Proposing something that will put police out of their jobs, which is consistent with my politics, is really hard to do.

Heatherton: Could you talk about how Black queer feminist theory has influenced the analysis of police violence in your organizing and activism?

Ransby-Sporn: In both We Charge Genocide and Black Youth Project (BYP) 100 there has been a really nice integration of direct action, organizing, and theory. The fact that we're trying to take action has never compromised the intellectual or theoretical rigor with which we're thinking about these issues. That, I think, is cool. When we talk about criminalization, obviously we're bringing in an analysis that is a Black analysis. Notions of "criminal" in this country have always been explicitly tied to Blackness. I also think queer and feminist analyses are equally important. Queer, because structures that are seen as deviant—people, families, or relationships, for example—are criminalized. This means not just centering queer people within our organizing, it also means thinking about what Black queer liberation looks like. It means resisting these categories of "criminal," "deviant," or "other," and queering the ways in which our lives and communities can be structured. We use a Black feminist analysis because Black women's voices have historically been, and still are, silenced in this system. Ending violence against Black women is not something that the system of policing and prisons that we have today can even render as possible. For all those reasons, we use that lens to address issues in a way that points towards our liberation.

Champion: We're figuring it out as we go. It's not like there is a book that we have all read and suddenly know things. I'm a Black queer woman, so that informs my understanding of Black queer feminism. A lot of organizing is led by Black queer women, but they're made invisible. I really appreciate the ways that BYP 100 is pushing people to understand that you don't have to be a Black queer woman to have a Black queer feminist analysis. It's something that is completely essential to the work, but it's also something that we have to learn.

Camp: Is there anything that we haven't asked you that you would like to add?

Ransby-Sporn: When we got back, we had to wait about two weeks before the UN released its "Concluding Observations." There was one section of the report on police brutality. The only police department specifically named in that section is the Chicago Police Department for its violence against young Black and Brown people. This was a huge affirmation of our work. It's something we can use to bring international attention to and local shame upon the police department. It will also help us pressure whoever becomes the next mayor to pass the legislation that we're fighting for. The report also specifically talked about Taser usage. That was really notable because the last time this committee met, they were advocating for Tasers as a way to reduce deadly force. They now said that they are concerned about how Tasers were contributing to people's deaths. They named two people in the report, Israel "Reefa" Hernandez from Miami Beach, Florida, and Dominique Franklin. That report is something we can use to start chipping away police power and prevent them from being given new tools, like body cameras.

There was also another big victory in the UN's report. The UN endorsed the work of another group of Chicago advocates who went to Geneva with us. The former Chicago Police Department commander John Burge was recently convicted of torturing and overseeing the torture of many people in police custody between 1972 and 1991. There's been a huge campaign advocating for those torture survivors. We Charge Genocide and other groups have been working with them on this issue. The UN report recognized this campaign and encouraged the city of Chicago to pass an ordinance they produced based on the desires of the survivors.

This proposed ordinance is extraordinary. Advocates asked the survivors, "What does justice look like to you?" The survivors said, "Justice looks like a memorial. Justice looks like making it mandatory that this episode get taught in Chicago public schools. Justice looks like a youth center with mental health services. Justice looks like financial compensation and reparations. Justice looks like free job training for survivors and their family members, and access to the city college system." That is so rad. By the time the bill is passed, we will have made history.

20. THE MAGICAL LIFE OF BROKEN WINDOWS

Rachel Herzing

Broken windows theory is not much of a theory at all. Nine pages of opinions by two social scientists in a magazine of cultural and literary commentary has taken on a magical life. It has become an incantation, a spell used by law enforcement, advocates, and social scientists alike to do everything from designing social service programs to training cops. The very repetition of the phrase is enough to explain away centuries of capitalist and white supremacist legacies.

Magic, we're told, usually by social scientists, is the crutch of backward societies. It is rooted in irrationality and underdeveloped intellect. It is the enemy of science. Yet, when employed in the service of maintaining social control, magic is used to dazzle and amaze—to demonstrate how the systems of our subjugation actually protect us. Magic can have real utility and play an important role in making sense of our surroundings when those surroundings are so frequently confounding and counter-intuitive. But magic is likely not the means to make systemic changes in power structures.

Policing is a set of practices empowered by the state to enforce law and maintain social control and cultural hegemony through the use of force. Policing is actively implemented by people serving the interests of the most powerful elements of the state, regardless of the scale at which it is carried out. The magic of policing rests in its ability to appear as the remedy to the very harm it maintains.

If broken windows policing is magical, William Bratton is a master magician. Bratton is nearly single-handedly responsible for turning commentary from a popular magazine into a set of policing practices that are now pervasive across the globe. Beginning during his first go around as police commissioner in New York City with what he and then New York mayor, Rudy Giuliani, called "the quality of life initiative," Bratton set his sights on stomping out disorder by aggressively enforcing minor quality-of-life infractions such as public drunkenness, littering, subway fare evasion, and begging. No crime, no matter how insignificant, would go unnoticed and unpunished: zero tolerance. Bratton's approach also encouraged police to fish for additional incriminating evidence from violators and surveil people suspected of higher-level offenses such as drug-dealing or gang involvement.

Under these zero-tolerance policies, police sweeps have become standard procedure as cops remove whole portions of communities from the streets—the houseless, queer and gender-nonconforming people, sex workers, day laborers, youths—under the rationalization that their very presence creates disorder. Stop and search, a key tactic of zero-tolerance policing, has entrenched the logic of racial profiling. Its determining who is deemed suspicious and worthy of being stopped is based as much in the future chaos that a "suspicious" person's presence could create as in the observations of specific criminalized activities by cops. Notably, the rise in zero-tolerance policing has also coincided with the continued militarization of all branches of law enforcement, the creation of specialized policing units, longer prison and jail sentences, a tripling of the US prison population, and the increased use of solitary confinement within prisons, jails, and detention centers.

Magic is often performed through the logic of contagion, or the belief that contact with something will transfer its properties to whatever or whomever touches it next. Contagion can transfer new powers to inanimate objects or people. Contagion can also help to enforce prohibitions or maintain power structures by encouraging fear of contact with specific people, objects, or places. The magic of broken windows is dependent on the latter conception of contagion. Engendering a fear of contact connected to James Q. Wilson and George Kelling's "broken windows" indicators of disorder is key to making people compliant with suppression policing tactics. Without being encouraged to fear these indicators, neighbors might otherwise attribute the visible signs of poverty, mental illness, and substance abuse to socioeconomic inequities remediable with care or mutual aid. The picture painted by Kelling and Wilson about what happens when disorder is tolerated and when contact is made with an agent of contagion, however, is one of devastation.

Bratton exploited the fear of contagion during his quality-of-life initiative in New York City. By demonizing panhandlers, window washers known infamously as "squeegie men," and those without consistent housing as pathogenic agents determined to spread their disorder, violence, and harm to everyone around, Bratton gained support for widespread and continuous sweeps in places where the city's poor and transient converged. The sweeps, described as "clean-ups," drew on the long history of classist and racist removals central to preserving capitalism and white supremacy in the United States. Policing sweeps have become increasingly commonplace as the popularity of zero-tolerance policing has grown, displacing entire segments of communities deemed to be nuisances and rendering them invisible either by locking them away in jails and prisons or by making the swept environments physically and psychologically intolerable places to live.

Bratton's quality-of-life initiative brought not only a hyper-aggressive style of policing to the city but 7,000 more cops to the NYPD as well. Bratton also decentralized the police administration structure, putting substantially more power in the hands of local precinct commanders in what one of Bratton's subordinates referred to as "taking the handcuffs off the cops."[1] He initiated regular Compstat (comprehensive computer statistics) meetings during which precinct commanders were made to share statistics on the results of their policing efforts during the previous month. As a result of Bratton's experiment, arrest rates in New York City skyrocketed, whole communities of people were rendered invisible, and a miracle remedy for urban crime was proffered. In his next position as chief of the Los Angeles Police Department (LAPD), Bratton cranked up his New York miracle to the next level, turning the Skid Row neighborhood into one of the most heavily policed places in the world through the initiation of the Safer Cities Initiative. Bratton's promotion of zero-tolerance policing turned him into an international

---

1   David C. Anderson, "Crime Stoppers," *New York Times Magazine*, February 9, 1997.

supercop and zero tolerance into the gold standard of policing across the world during the late 1990s and early 2000s.

And while zero tolerance has gained followers, there is no reliable evidence of the glowing results that Bratton claims. Bernard E. Harcourt has demonstrated repeatedly that the New York "miracle" upon which so much of Bratton's prestige is based is likely a result of what he and his colleague Jens Ludwig have called Newton's Law of Crime, suggesting that "what goes up, must come down (and what goes up the most, tends to come down the most)."[2] Examining other US cities in the same period during which Bratton's miracle is claimed to have occurred, Harcourt and Ludwig point out that cities that employed different approaches other than suppression policing had even higher drops in their crime rates. They further note that isolating zero-tolerance policing as a factor without situating it within a context of rates of imprisonment, trends in drug use, and societal and ideational changes reveals only a sliver of the picture.

Analyses of zero-tolerance policing consistently suggest that other factors, such as trust between neighbors and poverty rates, are much stronger indicators of whether or not harm will occur within a community than the factors identified by Wilson and Kelling as disorder. As recently as 2004, James Q. Wilson himself maintained that broken windows theory was speculative and that he had no idea if improving order reduced crime rates.[3]

In cities where Bratton-style policing is the primary approach (and especially where Bratton has been the head of the police force), police departments tend to see a spike in complaints of illegal searches, police harassment, brutality, and misconduct as well as an increase in lawsuits brought against departments concerning abuse, harassment, and death at the hands of cops.[4] Those same cities also suffer the social and

---

2   Bernard E. Harcourt and Jens Ludwig, "Broken Windows: New Evidence from New York and a Five-City Social Experiment," *University of Chicago Law Review* 73 (2006): 271–320.

3   Dan Hurley, "Scientist at Work—Felton Earls: On Crime as Science (a Neighbor at a Time)," *New York Times*, January 6, 2004.

4   Justin Peters, "They Couldn't Breathe Either," *Slate*, January 19, 2015, available at slate.com.

economic costs that come with those complaints and suits. The only result that seems to be reliably attached to zero-tolerance policing is the entrenchment of racial profiling.

Exacerbating the long-standing demonization of Blacks and Latinos, and the poor, zero-tolerance policing unleashes its potent magic like a laser beam against the menacing hordes. Upon his return for a second round as police commissioner in New York City, Bratton redoubled quality-of-life policing by the NYPD. In his first few months back on the job, arrests on the subway for panhandling increased 271 percent and those for illegal peddling by 55 percent compared to the previous year. During the same period fifty subway performers were charged with reckless endangerment for dancing on trains and another fifty subway dancers were charged with disorderly conduct. In response to questions regarding the clampdown, Bratton responded: "Those activities just create a sense of fear, or that we're not paying attention to disorder. We are paying a lot of attention to disorder."[5]

Part of what is most magical about zero-tolerance policing is its durability despite the lack of clear evidence that it makes communities safer.[6] For example, a 2008 ACLU study of the LAPD yielded startling information on police stops under Bratton. Although Black people stopped by the LAPD were 127 percent more likely to be frisked than whites who were stopped, the report revealed that Black people were 42.3 percent less likely to have a weapon found on them when frisked, 25 percent less likely to be found with drugs, and 33 percent less likely to be found with anything that would provide a legitimate reason for frisking. The author's reports also found that stop, frisk, search, and arrest rates for Black and Latino people could not be explained by claiming that they lived in higher-crime areas or that they carried weapons more often.[7]

The Compstat crime tracking program is also one of Bratton's most

---

5   "NYPD Cracks Down on Subway Dancers, Arrests Spike," NBC New York, April 29, 2014, available at nbcnewyork.com.

6   Khaled Taqi-Eddin and Dan Macallair, "Shattering Broken Windows: An Analysis of San Francisco's Alternative Crime Policies," Justice Policy Institute, October 1999.

7   Ian Ayres and Jonathan Borowsky, "A Study of Racially Disparate Outcomes in the Los Angeles Police Department," prepared for the ACLU of Southern California, October 2008.

fundamental tools. The system is touted as crucial for tracking what kinds of harms are occurring and where. The reliability of Compstat data is questionable, however. In 2010 researchers Eli B. Silverman and John A. Eterno, a retired NYPD police captain, conducted a survey of retired high-ranking police officials about Compstat. Their survey found that precinct commanders and supervisors felt so much pressure to reduce crime rates that they entered distorted crime statistics into the Compstat system.

According to Silverman and Eterno, who have continued to monitor the use of Compstat, "when crime control becomes the be all and end all, then the ends justifies the means ... It also means almost 700,000 stop and frisks in predominantly minority neighborhoods [in 2011] alone." They continue, "Compstat has morphed into a centralized top down numbers dominated system which places unrelenting pressure on commanders to produce favorable crime statistics, summonses, arrests, stop and frisks and other activity." The manipulation of Compstat results not only falsely bolsters the success of suppression policing, but also further entrenches policing practices based on racial and economic profiling and similar biases—frequently with deadly consequences.[8] According to a report by Amnesty International on excessive police violence by the NYPD between 1993 and 1994, there was a 34 percent increase in people fatally shot by the NYPD in Bratton's first year as police commissioner alone, despite a significant decrease in violent crime during the early 1990s.[9]

On August 9, 2014, Michael Brown was shot at least six times by cop Darren Wilson in Ferguson, Missouri. Wilson's first contact with Brown was to tell him to move from walking in the street to the sidewalk. Witnesses state that Brown's hands were in the air when Wilson started shooting. Brown's bleeding body was left on public display in the street for more than four hours in the midday sun. As in the case of Eric Garner, Brown's resistance to instructions from a cop unleashed

8   Eli B. Silverman and John A. Eterno, "Eterno and Silverman, Criminologists, Say NYPD's Crime Stat Manipulation a Factor in Recent Corruption Scandals," *Village Voice*, November 29, 2011.

9   Amnesty International, *Police Brutality and Excessive Force in the New York City Police Department*, June 1, 1996, available at amnesty.org.

maximum force—the suppression of disorder in favor of the chaos sure to follow if not put down decisively.

Michael Brown's murder sparked protests in the Ferguson community as well as across the United States and the globe. The shock at Wilson's exaggerated reaction to Brown, the callousness of Brown's body being left in the street, the quick work the St. Louis police made of casting aspersions on Brown's character all stoked the fires that ignited Ferguson and the world. While excruciating and exceptional for Brown's loved ones and neighbors, his death was also the logical conclusion of zero-tolerance policing, a fact that was not lost on the protesters.

Brown's image became a charm, drawing power and recognition among those primed to act against repressive policing. Incantations were repeated: "Hands up, don't shoot," "I can't breathe," "Black lives matter." These incantations were potent means of calling relations together, recognizing each other and signaling a shared purpose—to raise the spirits of the departed and put a call for action into the air. Articulating intentions and fears will likely not be enough to shift the terms of policing, however.

In the months following Eric Garner's and Brown's deaths, grand juries found neither assaulting officer Daniel Pantaleo nor Darren Wilson guilty of wrongdoing. Their deaths, as well as those of Dontre Hamilton, months before them, or Tamir Rice, Roshad McIntosh, Akai Gurley, Ezell Ford, Michelle Cusseaux, Alex Nieto, and the dozens of others whose names we do not even know, sparked discussion about how to remedy the police assault on Black communities. Law enforcement agents from the attorney general of the United States to beat cops in cities and towns across the country offered suggestions about magic solutions and quick fixes—body cameras, racial profiling legislation, more cops on the streets, more Black cops on the streets, and so forth. Bratton himself repeated his most magical word over and over: "training."

People also took action. Protesters sustained acts of civil disobedience and large-scale mobilizations, disrupting business as usual in order to draw attention to the crisis. After two cops were killed by Ismaaiyl Abdullah Brinsley during this same period, NYPD cops staged a work slowdown, failing to enforce zero-tolerance policing practices and demonstrating the clear lack of correlation between suppression policing and increases in incidents of harm in the process.

A mist of magical thinking clings to much of the thought and action associated with this period. Magical thinking attributes causal relationships between actions and events that can't be explained by observation or reason. People may engage in magical thinking when they imagine that a thought itself will bring about a desired effect or that the thinking itself is the same as actually doing the thing they are thinking. Others might use magical thinking to relieve anxiety or to bolster their courage in the face of danger or to feel that they are able to exercise control in situations largely beyond their control. And while the reasons for engaging in magical thinking make perfect sense, it will not be sufficient to shift our material conditions.

As demonstrated above, zero-tolerance policing relies heavily on magic. Contagion, redirection, sleight of hand, spells, and similar elements of magical practice are fundamental tools in this type of policing and in most policing practices. Increasing the number of cops on forces, reviewing training protocols, encouraging neighbors to police each other through community policing programs, and recruiting Black and Latino cops are some of the magical thoughts law enforcement officials have connected to an end to the violence of policing. They also advocate, however, that the standard tricks of the trade, including stop and search, sweeps, and predictive policing remain at the ready.

Advocates and organizers have magically connected data collection, video documentation of police interactions, archives of incidents of the violence of policing that result directly in death, civilian review boards, and anti-profiling legislation with an end to the violence of policing, as if knowing the breadth and depth of the issue will be its demise. While part of the smoke and mirrors that law enforcement uses to hide its nefarious dealings is to withhold information, there is surely enough data to demonstrate that things must change. There is no rational connection between simply documenting the violence of policing and that violence stopping.

Even if magic is real, there is nothing magical about policing. The structures that policing protects and that empower them are real. They are not phantoms, nor are they natural features of the environment. The actions leading to deaths at the hands of cops must be understood with an acknowledgment that policing is actively empowered and legitimated by real people and institutions and implemented through real policies and practices. And as terrible and heart-stopping as the deaths of our loved ones by agents of the state are, they are also not the mainstay of policing. Equally terrible are the slow, grinding social and literal deaths that so many people experience as a result of policing, especially zero-tolerance policing. This type of law enforcement destabilizes our social networks, increases our suspicion and erodes our empathy for each other, creates fear of dissent, and encourages us to capitulate to social control in the guise of protection and care. It suggests that the structural inequities maintained by capitalism, white supremacy, and hetero-patriarchy are simply our individual pathologies and lack of self-control. It paints those most vulnerable to the ravages of these inequities as nuisances to be swept away.

Policing is also not a broken system in need of repair. It is a highly accurate and efficient means of protecting state interests and maintaining social control. The goal must not be to help policing become more efficient, but rather to erode the power policing has over our lives. The clearest way to eliminate the harms so many of us suffer from the violence of policing is to eliminate our contact with it. Understanding the function of policing then requires recognizing that when cops persistently harass members of a local community for loitering, when they follow young Black people because they deem them suspicious, when they use maximum force to resolve routine matters even when that force results in death, these are not the acts of bad apples, cops taking matters into their own hands, or exceptional incidences of policing. This is what policing *is*.

Policing is not magical; we can fight it. Just as incantations are raised into the air to draw each other closer, bring people together, and ignite their spirits, so can policy and practice recommendations help illuminate the terrain on which the fight must occur. The variety of carefully crafted, painstakingly negotiated platforms, briefs, and policy proposals circulating in the wake of events in Ferguson and New York have already resulted in conversations among lawmakers previously silent on the issues, in new task forces and committees, and in proposals for new pieces of legislation. These are significant changes.

Yet we must study movement history. The history of anti-policing organizing and activism is long and rich. In the United States, poor people of color, especially Black people, have often been the leaders in those struggles. We must study that history not only to reject it as outmoded or to seize on its failures, but to engage with the threads of struggle that have persisted through the centuries and to acknowledge that we are joining a movement already in progress. Our study should inform how we enter the movement, who we credit and acknowledge, and what aspects of the movement we must evolve and grow.

We must build power. Using our organizational forms and collaborative efforts, we need to take steps together to shift the conditions in which we live and the terms on which we engage. We do not need to be controlled. We need the resources, tools, and structures to live full, beautiful, healthy lives. We need to create the conditions in which we can recognize and affirm each other. We need terms of engagement that don't root our own survival in the suppression or denial of another's humanity. Los Angeles Community Action Network's consistent protests against "Skid Row Walks" hosted by a business association to entice developers to the area reaffirmed Skid Row as a residential neighborhood with long-standing residents, amplifying the voices of those intended to have been swept away by Bratton's Safer Cities Initiative. Critical Resistance's Oakland Power Projects incubate models for building local capacity and confidence to increase the likelihood that neighbors will call on each other rather than the cops to address their immediate concerns.

In efforts to build power we must also exercise caution about what we advocate. As we take the incremental steps necessary to meet our goals, we need to be mindful to avoid increments that ultimately will block our long-term vision in the next stage of the fight. Further, we must be cautious of incremental changes that are primarily stalling tactics, such as gathering additional data and issuing reports, when we are fully aware of the nature of the problem, or offering relief to some at the expense of others and similar delays.

We must work collaboratively. Coalitions, networks, and partnerships make us stronger than we can be alone. Strong organizations are made even more powerful when each plays an appropriate role and joins effectively with other organizations in a shared purpose.

National hubs, such as the one supported by Ferguson Action, have helped groups and individuals, those interested in contributing to coordinated direct actions in response to the grand jury verdicts mentioned above, talk to each other, share information about the results of their actions, and focus their tactics, targets, and messages. The Malcolm X Grassroots Movement's (MXGM) nationally circulated "Report on the Extrajudicial Killings of Black People by Police, Security Guards or Self-Appointed Law Enforcers" put the statistic that a Black person is killed every twenty-eight hours on the lips of people across the country (though MXGM is rarely credited). Regional efforts such as the Homeless Bill of Rights Campaign, initiated by the Western Regional Advocacy Project and spanning California, Oregon, and Colorado, coordinate legislative advocacy work to overturn local laws aimed at removing people from public space. Through the Oakland-based Stop the Injunctions Coalition, organizers from a wide variety of neighborhoods, racial identities, and issue areas were able to eliminate the use of civil gang injunctions (nuisance ordinances targeting alleged gang members) by employing a mix of grassroots organizing, cultural work, legal strategies, and policy advocacy. Collaborations of this sort challenge us to elevate our shared work to the ceiling of what we think is possible rather than the lowest common denominator.

In periods during which increased attention is paid to the elements of policing that are always present, organizers, activists, and advocates have the opportunity to activate new groups of people and push their agendas forward. The increased attention creates openings in which to make bigger, bolder demands and suggest more expansive creative remedies—such as a stop to excessive ticketing and sweeps, an end to responses of maximum force to small infractions, and access to safe, quality housing and employment for all.

The increased focus on anti-Black racism and the genocidal implications of policing for Black communities creates opportunities to take the decimation of these communities seriously. The question is how to make the most of this opportunity. The current trend is towards demands for recognition of Black humanity and claims to a legitimate place in US society. Will such demands generate responses that increase the power of Black communities, however? Demands for reductions in the size and role of police forces in Black communities and for increased participation and control over community resources have the potential to not only stem the tide of state violence unleashed on Black people, but also to shore up our ability to extend and expand community defenses against such onslaughts while augmenting possibilities for self-determination.

With so many more people ready to talk, think, and act, how can organizers go beyond disrupting business as usual to pull people into the long-term campaigns and projects necessary to do more than temporarily draw attention to the violence of policing? Groups and organizations must prepare themselves for these periodic openings and offer invitations and concrete means through which to highlight how direct action is best used in the service of campaigns rather than as an end in itself. We need to keep dreaming, and we need to dream big. Even if policing is not magical, it casts a spell that prevents us from thinking that it's possible to imagine a world without it. We need to begin by asking for what we want, not simply what we think we can get or what we're told we're entitled to. Distinct from the magical thinking that relies on an intention to make change, our dreams should be our guides for taking action. Each moment of crisis in the history of policing presents new challenges and new opportunities for us to act on our dreams. No magic needed.

~

Rachel Herzing lives and works in Oakland, where she fights the violence of policing and imprisonment. She is a co-founder of Critical Resistance and the co-director of the StoryTelling & Organizing Project. She is a 2015–2016 Soros Justice Fellow.

21. POETRY AND THE POLITICAL IMAGINATION: AN INTERVIEW WITH MARTÍN ESPADA

Jordan T. Camp and Christina Heatherton

Martín Espada is a poet, essayist, critic, translator, former tenant lawyer, professor of English at the University of Massachusetts Amherst, and the author of a number of books, including Vivas to Those Who Have Failed, The Republic of Poetry, The Trouble Ball, *and* Zapata's Disciple. *He is the recipient of numerous awards and fellowships, including the Shelley Memorial Award and a Guggenheim Fellowship. Through his poetry and activism Espada has sought to fulfill what Pablo Neruda called "the poet's obligation" to represent the political imagination.*

Camp: You've been called the "Pablo Neruda of North American authors." The most robust critiques of capitalism and US imperialism have come from Left poets of the Americas, including Neruda, Julia de Burgos, and Langston Hughes—many of whom you reference in your own poems. How can this poetic tradition inform contemporary social movements?

Espada: Contemporary social movements have to recognize the poetic tradition. If we look at the great social movements of the twentieth century in this country, we can see an embrace of literature as part and parcel of those social movements. I believe that poets can inform social movements by doing what poets do: invoking the power of language, the musicality of language, the vividness of language, to move people, to win the proverbial hearts and minds, because that, indeed, is what social movements must do in order to effect social change.

Heatherton: Your new poem "How We Could Have Lived or Died This Way" [that opens this volume] moves through time and space across a *changing same* of racist state violence. It is written as a powerful act of witnessing. How do you make sense of the act of witnessing at this moment? What is the message you hope might reach those "generations unborn" that you describe in the poem?

Espada: One of the responsibilities of a poet, as far as I'm concerned, is to dissent from the official story. If people want to know what really happened, they can always consult with the poets. We spoke against it. I'm speaking against it. That is part of the time capsule that we preserve for "generations unborn."

The poem in question refers to eight different documented cases of lethal police violence against men and boys of color. They were mostly African Americans, but I also refer to the case, in the first stanza, of John T. Williams, a Native American, who was shot and killed by a police officer in Seattle. In the second stanza, I go back forty years, returning to the case of Martín "Tito" Pérez, a Puerto Rican musician and visual artist who was arrested for drumming on the subway, taken to the 25th Precinct in East Harlem, and later wheeled out on a stretcher, dead, with his hands still cuffed behind him. There was an inquest and a grand jury convened. There was pressure from the December First Committee, named for the day in 1974 that Pérez was arrested and apparently murdered. The grand jury concluded that it was possible for a man to hang himself with his hands cuffed behind him. We're talking about a case that goes back forty years, that involved a Puerto Rican male. This case was my awakening to lethal police violence because my father knew this man. He brought home something about Pérez for me to read. I read it, and here's the poem.

Camp: In your presentation at the 2015 Left Forum in New York, you talked about the impact of McCarthyism and of the Cold War in silencing radical critiques articulated in the poetry of the political imagination. Could you say more about that?

Espada: There is a commonly held belief in the poetry world that political poetry is an oxymoron—that, in essence, you cannot write a good political poem. It is impossible because, somehow, by definition, you're subordinating the needs of art to the needs of politics. Where did this daffy idea come from? What happened? McCarthyism happened. The Cold War happened. These were not only political but cultural reactions in the middle of the twentieth century that changed the way we think and feel. The blacklist and the mentality of the blacklist extended beyond Hollywood. The blacklist was also academic and literary. Whereas, in the 1930s, it was a given that political poetry was part of the spectrum, poetically speaking, this was no longer the case after the Second World War. Many poets who were identified as communist or socialist or radical, or even vaguely leftist were frozen out, obscured, fired, jailed, forgotten.

In 1932, an African American poet by the name of Sterling Brown published a book called *Southern Road*. The book was hailed by critics and readers, and he was well on his way. Then Sterling Brown's poetry disappeared for almost forty years. It wasn't until the publication of his *Collected Poems* in 1980, edited by Michael Harper and published in the National Poetry Series, that the world remembered Sterling Brown as a poet. He'd been teaching at Howard University in relative obscurity. Brown published a poem in the 1930s called "Southern Cop," a poem that could have been written last week. In the poem, he adopts the position of someone who speaks as an apologist for the police officer who shoots an unarmed Black man, a cop by the name of Ty Kendricks. Sterling Brown had a wonderful ear. He could adapt and reproduce almost any voice on the page: "Let us forgive Ty Kendricks." The poem fairly drips with irony. It's also relevant. It was written and published in the 1930s. We can still learn from this poem.

Camp: Your poem "Imagine the Angels of Bread" is a poetic expression of the role of the political imagination. It also represents the struggle against police violence: "This is the year that police revolvers, / stove-hot, blister the fingers / of raging cops, / and nightsticks splinter / in their palms." Could you reflect on the dialectical relationship between struggles in the present, the political imagination, and the poetry of the future?

Espada: I wrote that poem more than twenty years ago. The lines you quote refer to Rodney King. I wish those lines were no longer relevant. Sadly, they are. I wish I had to explain that language to people today. Sadly, I don't. Police violence is, like the poor, always with us.

No change for the good ever happens without it being imagined first, even if that change seems hopeless or impossible in the present. History teaches us otherwise and teaches us too that we are the agents of change. Change does not come from the White House; it comes from our house. Eduardo Galeano gives us a wonderful allegory of utopianism as, essentially, a dot on the horizon. Every time he walks towards the dot, it keeps moving away—but he keeps on walking. Within the lifetimes of people we know or people they knew, changes in this society occurred that were once considered utopian. There was a time when the elimination of chattel slavery was considered utopian. There was a time when the elimination of de jure segregation was considered utopian. There was a time when the eradication of lynching was considered utopian. We no longer have the slave catchers; we no longer have the slave patrols; we no longer have the lynch mobs—all of which used violence and terror to repress the African American population. Some of those elements, however, are reemerging through police violence as a form of social control. Of course, I'm not saying that what this society is going through right now is the equivalent of the antebellum South. I am saying that this system still uses violence to enforce the social order. What happens if you no longer have the slave patrol and no longer have the slave catchers and no longer have the lynch mob? Who performs those functions? And against whom is that violence utilized?

It's important for us to think of the world as a place not only where things could be better, but where visionaries have said, "Things could be better," and they turned out to be right. That's the political imagination. I see poetry as having everything to do with that. The political imagination requires its most eloquent possible expression to move from imagination to reality. We are not going to change anything by boring people. We have to move people, but more than that we have to stir them up. We have to get people past the point of nodding politely. We need not only to move people but to get them moving.

22. THIS ENDS BADLY: RACE AND CAPITALISM

Vijay Prashad

Black Bodies, Brown Worlds

What is this America that we live in? This country where police officers feel emboldened to shoot with impunity Black people, people whose humanity has been cast aside by a culture of intolerance. There are a string of names from Eric Garner in Staten Island (2014) to Thomas Shipp and Abram Smith in Marion, Indiana (1930) and backward through slavery times. Watching the events unfold in Ferguson, Missouri, and New York City, I was reminded of the 1935 Harlem riot—which began when a sixteen-year-old Afro–Puerto Rican boy, Lino Rivera, was threatened with a beating for shoplifting. In the aftermath of the unrest, the mayor of New York City commissioned an inquiry, whose report *The Negro in Harlem* suggested that the riots were "spontaneous" and that the causes of the rioting were "injustices of discrimination in employment, the aggressions of the police and racial segregation." Reading the report in 2014 provokes a sense of frozen time.

Resistance to the everyday atrocities against Black bodies takes me back to 1803, when a shipload of enslaved Igbo peoples, chained together, disembarked from their ships in Georgia and walked into the sea under the protection of their Water Spirit. Over the course of these past few months, chained humanity in the United States has gathered on the frozen plains of Chicago's Lake Shore Drive and beneath the high peaks of New York's Brooklyn Bridge—shutting down these arteries to register dissent. Humanity is outraged against abuse—and humanity is not an American value alone, but a universal one. Humanity is a value that suggests that these killings are despicable and that the lack of justice is intolerable. The people refuse. They will not tolerate this any longer. They say it must end.

But why do these killings happen? They are not to be blamed on the policemen alone. That is too easy. This is a problem of a system. Inequality rates in the United States are at historic highs. The rich not only refuse to pay taxes, they have used their wealth and power to ensure that the idea of taxes is seen as illegitimate: we live in a post-tax society. General Electric, Bristol-Myers Squibb, and Verizon are non-tax firms in a post-tax economy. A man ducking the cigarette excise tax is killed; Fortune 500 firms that duck tax in general are applauded. At 0 percent interest, the government turned over billions of dollars to the banks for their reserves as a protection against the meltdown of the credit system ($1.8 trillion of government money sits in "excess reserves" in private banks). Banks sat on this money, just as the rich sit on their fortunes. We have little investment inside the country to provide jobs for increasingly disposable people; we have no money for services to provide to those who have been cast aside. Global unemployment is at spectacularly high levels, with an "alarming" future for joblessness, according to the International Labour Organization's *World of Work Report*. Young people are nearly three times as likely as adults to be unemployed. An estimated 6.4 million young people have given up hope of finding a job. African American youth unemployment is now at 35 percent. There is no plan to undo this dynamic.

The money that funds interactions between the people and the state goes to police and prisons. Three quarters of those who entered jail in the past two decades stand accused of nonviolent drug offences. The scandal of US jail expansion is this: that prisons have become the holding pens for the chronically unemployed population. Ferguson's depleted municipal budget has come to rely more and more on levies generated by such things as traffic fines (the second highest item in its revenue stream). In 2013, the police issued 32,975 arrest warrants to Ferguson's population of only 21,135. The police write tickets to people for harmless infractions. These tickets come with high fines, which are priced beyond the poverty wages in the city (the official poverty rate is at 20 percent). When these tickets are not paid, the police make arrests and put the population into the prison pipeline. The population is not a part of *society*; it is seen as a threat to law and order.

American society has been broken by these mechanisms—high rates of economic inequality, high rates of poverty, impossible entry into robust educational systems, unattainable opportunity for economic advancement, remarkable warlike conditions put in place to manage populations seen not as the citizenry but as criminals. Such a corrosive set of processes should leave us necessarily despondent. The names Michael Brown, Sandra Bland and Eric Garner are the names of the present. Somewhere in America tonight, another person will be killed— another poor person who the police deem to be a threat. Tomorrow another, and then another. These deaths are not an *outrage* against this system. They are *normal* for this system.

The terrible social consequences of income and wealth inequality multiply the horses of the apocalypse. Four are not enough. Poverty, pestilence, illiteracy, racial supremacy, misogyny, wars and occupations, Mexican drug gangs, the "Islamic State," and so on. When there are no decent jobs and no decent state apparatus, society putrefies. It leads inevitably to frustration and disorder, to civil war that manifests itself in different places in accordance with their different histories. Here it is the ghastly military and prison industrial complexes, the antidote to chronic joblessness; there it is the narcotics and terrorist industrial complexes. If the present is allowed to continue, it will end badly. The task is to identify the limitations of the present and to produce an actual future. We need to outgrow our madness.

1. Theory

> *Thou shalt not sit with statisticians, nor*
> *commit a social science.*
>
> —W. H. Auden, Harvard
> University, 1946

We know about inequality. It takes little to digest the facts and be horrified by their consequences. But we don't have an adequate theory for it. Some of the responsibility for this goes to the desiccation of thought, notably in fields such as economics. In 2001, a group of Cambridge University doctoral students issued a letter complaining about the narrow focus of their training, and how irrelevant it was to the world's problems. In France, students created a movement called the Post-Autistic Economics Group—with the argument that social sciences had become, supposedly, "autistic," meaning less capable of relations with the external world. The year before this student-led challenge to economics, an anonymous professor who went by the name Mr. Perestroika wrote a letter to the American Political Science Association, condemning game theory and an overemphasis on statistics. "Why are simple, baby-stuff models of political science being propagated in our discipline?" he asked. "Why are these people allowed to throw their weight around based on undergrad maths and stats—an Econ 101. We are in the business of Political Science and not failed Economics." In 2009, Harvard professor Joseph Nye said of his field, "The danger is that political science is moving in the direction of saying more and more about less and less." Put more pointedly by the Cambridge economist Ha-Joon Chang, "Mainstream economics today is an almost religious belief. Never mind if it works or not in the real world, as long as it works for the powers that be, it is fine."

Trickle Down

Mainstream economics, followed loyally by mainstream political science, has barricaded the avenues for public policy. Fiscal policy, namely budgetary allocations, is not so easy to utilize because of balanced budget amendments and penalties from ratings agencies and the IMF for running high debt-to-GDP ratios. What is left is monetary policy—the preferred instrument of monetarism, the theory of trickle-down economics. The lever here is interest rate manipulation, which is left out of democratic decision making (by governments) and turned over to the technocrats of central banks. Central bankers toy with interest rates to increase or decrease the money supply—that is, the credit provided to banks. With lower interest rates, there is the hope that money will slosh around the system, encouraging investment and creating growth. If there is too much economic activity and therefore a danger of inflation, the central bankers can swoop in and raise interest rates. This is the theory. It relies on the assumption that the presence of capital will encourage economic activity.

There are some problems with this assumption. After the onset of the 2007–2008 Great Recession, governments in the West flooded the market with capital, which did not, however, increase productive economic activity. This is known as the global savings glut. A 2012 report from Standard & Poor's pointed to a "fragile equilibrium" in the "global corporate credit landscape," with firms hoarding a "record amount of cash." If they do lend, it is not necessarily for job-creating productive investments, but to inflate asset bubbles such as the housing debt market, the credit card debt market, and the college tuition debt market. Andrew Ross suggests, in his book *Creditocracy*, that the growth rates in the United States since the Great Recession of 2008 have been substantially debt-driven. This is why the US democracy is built on its citizens living on credit. The United States, for Ross, is a *creditocracy*. "Indebtedness," Ross writes, "becomes the precondition not just for material improvements in the quality of life, but for the basic require-ments of life." The increase in money handed over to banks through interest rate manipulation has led, therefore, not to an enhancement of the productive sector but to debt-fueled growth. Governments no longer go into debt against future earnings to produce opportunities in the present. Instead, they transfer the burdens of debt from the public sector to private hands. Individuals are now free to go into grotesque levels of debt.

In the middle of the housing boom, the government delivery of liquidity to banks was called the Greenspan Put—the chair of the Federal Reserve was famous for flooding the markets with capital, which was used to inflate asset bubbles such as housing prices. Without real social security and retirement, Americans had come to rely upon increased home prices as their main asset. This is what Greenspan's Put enabled—the American Dream now cemented in the foundations of rising property prices. When the housing market—an overinflated bubble—burst, Greenspan, one of America's leading monetarist practi-tioners, said he was "shocked." When Greenspan came before Congress in 2008, he faced sharp questions from Representative Henry Waxman:

GREENSPAN: "I made a mistake in presuming that the self-interest of organizations, specifically banks and others, were such that they were capable of protecting their own shareholders and their equity in the firms."

WAXMAN: "In other words, you found that your view of the world, your ideology, was not right, it was not working."

GREENSPAN: "Absolutely, precisely. You know that's precisely the reason I was shocked, because I have been going for forty years or more with very considerable evidence that it was working exceptionally well."

Greenspan's ideology, his theory, was flawed, and he was shocked—yet it had no impact on the professions or on the public policy frameworks. Monetarism comes out of this crisis unscathed. Worse, it comes out of this crisis fully confident of its ability to produce an escape from it. No wonder that the Greek finance minister Yanis Varoufakis said in March 2015, "The danger of a coup these days comes not from a tank but from a bank."

Stimulus

Few students these days know the history of economic thought or ever read any John Maynard Keynes or even Adam Smith. Keynes was the hegemonic voice from the aftermath of the 1929 crash until the rise of neoliberalism in the 1970s. Keynesian economists had to be removed from international institutions in the 1970s in a manner that resembled the McCarthyite expulsion of Marxists from the US academy. Keynes disappeared from syllabi, replaced by Friedman and the Chicago school.

What was it about Keynesianism that threatened neoliberal policy? Keynes looked back at long-term economic cycles, with the assumption that as more and more firms competed with each other to produce for a relatively finite number of consumers, these firms would produce too much and experience a decline in profits. Overproduction from firms would be met by underconsumption from the public. Joseph Schumpeter, a distinguished economist in the line of Keynes, argued that in the heat of competition to outdo each other, some firms would have to go out of business. They would not be able to find consumers for their products. The runt of the sector would not survive. Others, however, would either innovate or use their size to muscle out these weak firms, and, through a process he called Creative Destruction, triumph. The problem was that when the decline set in, with too much being produced and too little demand existing for products, how deep would the economic recession run before Creative Destruction kicked in? To counter the downturn, Keynes had promoted a raft of tools, including fiscal policy. In other words, the government would come in and spend money to stave off the depression, stimulating the economy through creative spending (even on a jobs program, such as the New Deal). Where would this government money come from? From taxation on the higher income and wealth brackets, and from borrowing against the future.

The stimulus program of the US government after the Great Recession began was not a classical Keynesian stimulus funded by budgetary allocations. For one, the rich around the planet had gone on tax strike. They refused to pay taxes, and their intellectuals defended this low tax situation. Second, governments avoided borrowing against the future out of fear of the penalty from credit ratings agencies for having too much debt. The government used its funds to maintain liquidity in the banks and in the financial markets—that is, to help the financial sector stay afloat. JP Morgan Chase's boss Jamie Dimon claimed that the government's intervention had bailed out not just the banks but the American way of life as well: "Damaging the whole bank system also damaged the country. It damaged the belief in the system. In hindsight, if you look back, what really saved the system wasn't TARP [Troubled Asset Relief Program to purchase "troubled" assets and equity related to the mortgage crisis] and it wasn't the stress test. What really saved the system was the wall of liquidity that the Fed put up … Businesses had liquidity and the market started to come back and the confidence returned." In other words, this was Keynesianism of finance, not Keynesianism of the economy at large; it was government liquidity that enabled a new Wall Street expansion through wash trades, layering, spoofing, high-speed trading, and other innovative deceptions the finance industry has likely used against Americans.

Finance Keynesianism—disbursements of public money to rescue banks—and military Keynesianism—disbursement of public money to war making—do not solve the problems of chronic joblessness and underemployment. A glance at recent International Labour Organization reports confirms that since the start of the Great Recession, the world has lost 61 million recorded jobs. Hundreds of millions of people are without jobs. On the one side, Keynesianism is not up to the task of job creation; on the other side, the theory itself does not recognize the tendency of capital to prefer machines to humans, to displace human labor in favor of mechanization. This tendency deepens the trough of unemployment, robbing more and more people of the possibility of decent work. One of the great achievements of Karl Marx's *Capital* is its acknowledgment of capital's preference for machines and of its tendency to move to finance and debt-fueled growth once it becomes clear that reduced demand because of systematic unemployment will delay the realization of profit. But who reads Marx these days?

II. Social Consequences of Joblessness

The ILO report with the new data on joblessness offers a sense of its social consequences. "Social unrest has gradually increased as joblessness persists. It tended to decline before the global crisis and has increased since then. Countries facing high or rapidly rising youth unemployment are especially vulnerable to social unrest."

Given the social consequences of neoliberalism, it is far more effective and logical to build a security apparatus, to cage people in devastated cities, or to hold them in congested high-security prisons. It is far more rational to go to war than to sue for peace. There is nothing irrational about the prison industrial complex or the military industrial complex. From a neoliberal perspective, they are perfectly reasonable. Neoliberalism was always purchased with the iron fist, rarely with the velvet glove.

In the United States, the social consequences always fall along the axes of race. But even here there are mechanisms, driven by the humanities now, that defend racism through the discourse of multiculturalism. How does that work? By making racial backwardness a cultural matter rather than an attachment to the tumult of capitalism.

Why Don't Blacks Work?

In 1988, the National Urban League reported, "More blacks have lost jobs through industrial decline than through job discrimination." Deindustrialization crippled the economy, and whatever gains African Americans made in the industrial sector (against enormous odds) were quickly revoked when the plant closures that swept the nation turned the region from Gary, Indiana, to Syracuse, New York, into a rust belt. Manufacturing jobs, which would have provided some measured upward mobility to a section of the population, disappeared in large measure from US shores. In its place was left a newly enfranchised population with few opportunities.

When the Civil Rights Movement won juridical equality for all citizens, Martin Luther King, Jr., recognized that much needed to be done beyond what had already been accomplished by the movement. Legal equality was only a first step; economic and social equality seemed out of reach. On January 15, 1968, King reflected on the problems of the disposable class, "an underclass that is not a working class," among whom numbered "thousands and thousands of Negroes working on full-time jobs with part-time income," who "work on two and three jobs to make ends meet." A few years earlier, King had pointedly remarked that the Civil Rights Movement's changes "were at best surface changes, they were not really substantive changes." Since they "did not penetrate the lower depths of Negro deprivation" and since their gains were "limited mainly to the Negro middle class," King called for a deepening of the struggle. This was to be the Poor People's Campaign that would start only after his assassination. In 1966 King told his staff that the new movement would be powerful because it would ask for a radical reconstruction of the republic: "We are now making demands that will cost the nation something. You can't talk about solving the economic problem of the Negro without talking about billions of dollars. You can't talk about ending slums without first saying profit must be taken out of slums. You're really tampering and getting on dangerous ground because you are messing with folk then. You are messing with Wall Street. You are messing with captains of industry ... In other words, we are dealing with class issues, that is the problem." As King made this speech, the ground shifted: the state altered and deindustrialization shuttered the dreams of upward class mobility for workers. Wage arbitrage took manufacturing jobs elsewhere, as lower transport costs, satellite technology, and the newly available workers of an indebted Third World acted as sirens for Western capital. Decent jobs anchoring working-class life vanished from the United States. That population now had to work at unpleasant jobs and off the books, or else it would find itself increasingly in and out of the criminal justice system. It was structural unemployment that set in motion the major social crisis among the American working class.

Why Is My Doctor an Indian?

Meanwhile, the US government, which had blocked migration from Asia until 1965, now opened its doors to highly skilled Asian migrants. It was state selection and not natural selection that created a population of Asians with high skills and successful careers. To compare these Asians—the model minority—to African Americans was disingenuous. But the ideology of the model minority pushed the view that African Americans had only themselves to blame for social failure. This was an ideology that many Asians benefited from and therefore found salutary. It was the death knell for activist hopes of solidarity among people of color in the United States.

Convulsed by the fierce struggles from below for recognition and redistribution, the powers that be settled on a far more palatable social theory than full equality: multiculturalism. Rather than annul the social basis of discrimination, these powers cracked open the doors to privilege: people of color entered the upper reaches of the military and the corporate boardroom, the college campus and the Supreme Court, and eventually the Oval Office. Order recognized that apartheid was anachronistic. It was now going to be necessary to incorporate the most talented of the populations of color into the hallways of money and power. Those anointed might then stand in for their fellows left out in the cold. Even those who entered would know that some "races" were models of success while others were models of failure, and their representatives mere exceptions.

The same politicians who favored multicultural advancement for the few strengthened the social polices to throttle the multitudinous lives of color: the end of welfare, the increase in police and prisons, and the free pass given to Wall Street shackled large sections of our cities with the chains of starvation, incarceration, and indebtedness. Meanwhile, in ones and twos, people of color gained the mantle of success. Their success was both a false beacon and a standing rebuke to populations that could not hope to achieve it. There is a cruelty in the posture of multiculturalism. When Barack Obama ascended the podium at Grant Park in Chicago on November 4, 2010, to declare himself the victor in the presidential election, multiculturalism's promise was fulfilled. For decades, people of color had moved to the highest reaches of corporate and military life, of the state and of society. The only post unoccupied until November 4 was the presidency. No wonder that even Jesse Jackson, Sr., wept when Obama accepted victory. That night, multiculturalism ended. It has now exhausted itself as a progressive force.

Obama has completed his historical mission, to slay the bugbear of social distinction: in the higher offices, all colors can come. Obama's minor mission, also completed, has been to give the hard-core racists a daily dose of acid reflux when he appears on television. What did not end, of course, was racism. When the economy tanked in 2007 and 2008, the victims of the harshest asset stripping were African Americans and Latinos. They lost more than half their assets—loss of a generation's savings. Even Obama knew that it was silly to speak of post-racism. Before he won the presidential election, Obama had told journalist Gwen Ifill for her 2009 book *The Breakthrough*, "Race is a factor in this society. The legacy of Jim Crow and slavery has not gone away. It is not an accident that the African Americans experience high crime rates, are poor, and have less wealth. It is a direct result of our racial history. We have never fully come to grips with that history."

The jubilation of Obama's victory meant that we are in a post-multicultural era. Racism is alive and well. It is rooted in the political economy. Racism enabled primitive capitalism to steal wealth and make capital; racism provides the ammunition for the prison and military industrial complexes that secure capitalism against its social outcomes.

III. Future

> *You are not defeated as long as you are*
> *resisting.*
> —Mahdi Amel [Hassan Hamdan],
> 1936–87

The political class has failed us. No longer do we see the unapologetic standard-bearers for the good side of history—those who call for public education and public health care, public this and public that, financed by higher, progressive taxes on income and inheritance. Why do we cower from publicly protesting against so few families so obscenely enjoying the fruits of social wealth? It is not enough to think of justice as the procedure that kicks into motion when someone has been killed; what about justice at the heart of social lives? Where is the justice in denying children the right to decent schools, to decent work? What would Michael Brown have majored in if he were allowed to go to a liberal arts college? What would Eric Garner have named his small shop?

Better ideas do not change the world by themselves. The suffocation of the dominant social forces precludes alternate ideas from being taken seriously. There are hundreds of designs in engineering labs for smokeless chimneys and waterless toilets, but their existence has not meant that they have been adopted for mass usage. It will require a shift in social power to allow new ideas and new technologies to become acceptable in our time. In the absence of such a change, an "alternative" will simply mean a solution of a practical nature that is not capable of being fully embraced.

What is possible within the current dispensation is social welfare. Though this is not a systematic alternative, it should not be dismissed. When the social crisis is acute, as it is now, any form of relief is to be welcomed. Measures to bring down the price of foodstuffs, provide unemployment benefits, and generate government employment schemes are necessary, but they should not be confused with an alternative path. Does this mean that alternatives are impossible? Far from it. Popular struggles and innovative social incubators have given rise to several policy ideas. These ideas often emerge from the energy of mass social movements, but they are given short shrift by media that do not or choose not to understand their language.

Below are three broad principles to conceive of a future out of the present:

1. Universal Access: The idea of basic needs came out of the UN and then was impounded by the neoliberal framework of the Millennium Development Goals (MDG). What was lost in the MDG's accountancy was the principle of universal access to certain basic needs—food, health care, employment, social security, and so on. The core demand of the basic needs campaign, comprehensible to the majority of the world, is that access must be institutionalized. Those in authority cannot discount these demands, though they tend to accept them in principle and then hollow them out in implementation, claiming that universal access is too expensive. It is certainly expensive, but it is not beyond our means. Given how social surplus is appropriated by the very few and spent on wars and security, such demands are certainly impractical. But that is a political problem, not an economic one, and therefore two elements must be considered: the growth of political movements to champion and defend universal access, and the role of international agencies in monitoring such access.

2. Economic Power: When economics became a technical science, it abjured considerations of economic power. It seems embarrassing to talk about land reforms and trade unions. Control over land is crucial in Africa and Asia, where farmers continue to battle against all odds to maintain their sovereignty over their livelihood. Alongside this lingering and urgent demand for control over land is that for control over industrial processes. The global commodity chain has annulled the policy of nationalization—rendering mute the ability of a state to take hold of its industrial plants. This means that those whose tentacles stretch across continents exercise power over industry. These multinational corporations were studied by the UN at the Centre on Transnational Corporations, set up in 1974, but Northern power closed down that office in 1993. It is hard for workers to build their own power to combat these firms, and it is hard for the UN even to study the way in which

corporate power operates outside the purview of democratic account-ability. If the UN cannot assert itself over multinational companies, it certainly has no regulatory authority over money. Mysterious social forces, hidden behind ratings agencies and ideas such as the "confidence of the markets," seem to dampen the ability of states to widen their policy framework—if novel policy decisions are taken, money goes on strike. The price of borrowing is a form of power that is rarely under-stood in public, and the idea that economics is a kind of undecipherable hieroglyphic simply reinforces the undemocratic way in which money commands economic activity.

3. Social Wage: Any investigation of an alternative, in an age of eco-logical crisis and structural unemployment, has to take seriously the forgotten idea of the social wage. Better public goods, forged with the best of today's science, would not only reduce the burden on individuals and families, but also would enable societies to create socio-ecological solutions to problems. Rather than using private cars with high insur-ance premiums, people will use more public transport, such as light rail. The focus should be on high-quality public health care rather than private health care. These are elementary policies burdened by the calcu-lated failures of the public sector in an earlier era and overshadowed by the highly subsidized and malignant private sector of our times. Absent a discussion about the creation of public goods, it is doubtful whether any solution to the climate catastrophe can be envisaged.

This is the framework of an alternative. This is a formulation that should be taken seriously by those of us who are interested in ideas of develop-ment and social justice. In the Middle Ages, Theodor Adorno reflected, "fools tell their masters the truth. The dialectician's duty is thus to help this fool's truth to attain its own reasons, without which it will certainly succumb to the abyss of the sickness implacably dictated by the healthy common sense of the rest." The common sense of our times will lead us to a bad end. Foolishness is needed as an antidote. Consider this the fool's science.

~

Vijay Prashad is the George and Martha Kellner Chair of South Asian History and Professor of International Studies at Trinity College and chief editor of LeftWord Books (New Delhi). He is the author of seventeen books and most recently edited *Letters to Palestine: Writers Respond to War and Occupation* (Verso, 2015).

ACKNOWLEDGMENTS

Policing the Planet is the result of conversations with friends, colleagues, and social movement activists. The project owes much to our collaborations with the Los Angeles Community Action Network, particularly Pete White, Becky Dennison, General Dogon, Eric Ares, Joe Thomas, Deborah Burton, Steve Diaz, Hamid Khan, and many others. Our earlier publications, *Downtown Blues: A Skid Row Reader* (2011) and *Freedom Now! Struggles for the Human Right to Housing in LA and Beyond* (2012), showed us that scholars, organizers, and artists could enter into productive dialogues—ones that could be useful to classrooms, newsrooms, and social movements alike.

Our conversations with Joo-Hyun Kang, Mizue Aizeki, and members of the Communities United for Police Reform in New York City were foundational. Many thanks to Mizue for allowing us to use the photo which graces the cover as well as another of her photos which appears inside the book. We would also like to thank David Correia, Diane Gamboa, Gary Gutiérrez, Anjali Kamat, Nicholas Dahmann, and Todd St. Hill for permission to feature their photos.

We are indebted to Ari Wohlfeiler, Gabe Freiman, and Zuriel Ruth Madison Freiman for their extraordinary generosity. We are also grateful to David Harvey for helping us think through broken windows as a neoliberal urban strategy and for his feedback on the title. Our deepest thanks to Camille Acey, Ujju Aggarwal, Gary Blasi, Eliza Bettinger, Paul Boden, Rachel Buff, Lisa Brock, Chuck D, Thulani Davis, Deshonay Dozier, Sudhanva Deshpande, Treva Ellison, Betsy Esch, Ann Fink, J. R. Fleming, Diane Gamboa, Andrea Gibbons, Avery Gordon, Kai M.

Green, Sarah Haley, Analena Hope, Gaye Theresa Johnson, Cindi Katz, Tammy Bang Luu, Keith Miyake, Zumi Mizokami, S. Ani Muhkerji, Preeti Sampat, Barbara Ransby, David Roediger, Cedric J. Robinson, Elizabeth Robinson, Rob Robinson, Stephen R. Thornton, Bryan Welton, Tiffany Willoughby-Herard, and Craig Wilse for their invaluable insights. We're grateful to Jake Villareal for his superb research assistance. Our deepest thanks always to Linda Inouye for her support.

Policing the Planet is a better volume because of opportunities to present our arguments and engage in discussions across the country and world. Many thanks to John Munro for organizing a roundtable at the Social Science History Association meeting in Vancouver; to our co-panelists Jack O'Dell, Ivan Drury, Pete White, and Harsha Walia for the opportunity to discuss transnational struggles against racism, capitalism, and settler colonialism; and to Glen Coulthard and Jane Power for their exceptional feedback. Thanks to Daniel Widener and to Christina Hanhardt for each chairing sessions at separate meetings of the Association of American Geographers in Los Angeles and Chicago, and to our fellow panelists Tammy Bang Luu, Steven Osuna, Marisol Lebrón, and Pete White. Naomi Murakawa kindly invited us to present at the International Conference of Critical Geography in Ramallah alongside Abou Farman and Gillian Harkins. We owe Naomi special thanks for her encouragement and brilliant feedback.

Jordan T. Camp would like to thank the Center for the Study of Race and Ethnicity in America (CSREA) and the Watson Institute for International and Public Affairs at Brown University for offering vital and generative spaces to complete the book. Conversations with Tricia Rose, Anthony Bogues, Paget Henry, Brian Meeks, Catherine Lutz, Geri Augusto, Naoko Shibusawa, Patsy Lewis, Nicole Burrowes, and other friends and colleagues have sustained and nourished the editing process. Jordan owes an enormous debt of gratitude to the Department of African American Studies at Princeton University, and particularly to Naomi Murakawa, Eddie Glaude, Josh Guild, Tera Hunter, Imani Perry, Kinohi Nishikawa, Keeanga Yamahtta-Taylor, Courtney Bryan, Tanisha Ford, and Anand Jahi for lively and inspirational conversations about the stakes of the project.

At Trinity College, Christina Heatherton gratefully acknowledges the support of Anida Yoeu Ali, Zayde Antrim, Scott Gac, Isaac Kamola, Seth Markle, Vijay Prashad, Bishop John Selders, Linda Tabar, Prabhakar Venkateswaran, and Johnny Eric Williams, as well as the Trinity College Faculty Research Committee for a generous research grant. Davarian Baldwin in particular offered guidance and generosity throughout the editing process and made valuable introductions in St. Louis as well. At the Center for Place, Culture, and Politics at CUNY Graduate Center, the project benefited from discussions with Ruth Wilson Gilmore, David Harvey, Sujatha Fernandes, Peter Hitchcock, Don Mitchell, Loïse Bilat, Alf Gunwald Nilsen, and many others. Hector Agredano, Denisse Andrade, Lydia Pelot-Hobbs, Kaitlin Noss, and Nathaniel Sheets also shared insights on race, space, and security. Special thanks to Leela Fernandes for the opportunity to present at the "Understanding the Neoliberal State" symposium at the University of Michigan's Institute for Research on Women and Gender and to Padmini Biswas for a platform through the School for International Training to consider these issues.

Working with our editor Andrew Hsiao has been a delight. His enthusiasm, vision, and kindness have been essential to the book's formulation. Angelica Sgorous graciously guided us through the production process. The questions elaborated here began over a decade ago with many people who have since passed, including Dee Gray, Allan Pred, Neil Smith, and Clyde A. Woods. Clyde was particularly committed to the questions posed here and unfailingly supportive of our efforts to answer them.

We owe our greatest intellectual and political debts to all of the contributors to this volume. We are humbled and inspired by their collective wisdom. As an early reader commented, the book functions like a town hall meeting that cannot yet come into being, composed of voices from different sites and spaces, accompanying one another in a necessary struggle. We hope that by assembling the voices here we have produced a useful resource—one that might aid and abet activists, scholars, and scholar-activists alike across the planet.

Jordan T. Camp and Christina Heatherton
February 2016